A COMPREHENSIVE APPROACH TO TEACHING THINKING

A COMPREHENSIVE APPROACH TO TEACHING THINKING

Shirley W. Schiever
Tucson Unified School District

Allyn and Bacon
Boston London Toronto Sydney Tokyo Singapore

Copyright © 1991 by Allyn and Bacon
A Division of Simon & Schuster, Inc.
160 Gould Street
Needham Heights, Massachusetts 02194

Library of Congress Cataloging-in-Publication Data

Schiever, Shirley W.
    A comprehensive approach to teaching thinking / Shirley W. Schiever.
        p.   cm.
    Includes bibliographical references and index.
    ISBN 0-205-12680-4
    1. Thought and thinking—Study and teaching.   I. Title.
LB1590.3.S35   1991   90–37519
370.15′2—dc20   CIP

Printed in the United States of America

10 9 8 7 6 5 4 3 2 1 94 93 92 91 90

To the late **Hilda Taba,**
and the other giants on whose shoulders I stand.

Contents

Figures

Foreword

With the greatest of pleasure I am writing a foreword to a book I had intended to co-author. This may seem to be a strange statement, and indeed I may have perceived it as strange myself, a few months ago. The greatest of all joys, for a teacher, is to see one of our students go far beyond what we believe we taught, and to produce a work much better than we believe we could have done ourselves. Such is the case with Shirley Schiever and this book. I can hardly contain my pride in her and my joy in what she has accomplished!

This book began as an idea in Shirley's mind. Then I read some chapters and gave her suggestions for improvement. Next we began working together on several projects, including reconceptualizing (several times) the book and team teaching a class on teaching thinking. Working together as colleagues after several years of a teacher–student relationship was truly exciting. Philosophically, our views always have been similar, and practically, our skills and ideas are complementary. Through the process of teaching the Spiral Model to our class of respected graduate students, and with their assistance, we changed, refined, and increased our understanding of how the Spiral Model of Thinking could be explained and taught to others.

Since this work together was so exciting and rewarding, I had intended to participate equally in the design and "idea production" and write as much as possible. Before I had time to write, however, my father, and best friend, became ill with cancer. I immediately went to live with my parents at my childhood home on a farm in Kentucky. After that, I was no help to Shirley at all, since I wanted to give all my time and energy to my friend in his last months and weeks.

As I write this foreword, I am using several chapters of the unpublished manuscript in a class on teaching thinking through questioning strategies. Last semester I used other chapters as the framework for a class on teaching thinking through use of productive thinking models. The book is excellent, and it makes a unique contribution to the teaching process. No other resource is available that does what this book does.

In the past I have needed to rely on lectures, faded copies of outdated materials, and the patience of students to put all the elements together into a comprehensive view of thinking processes and how they can be taught, especially through teacher questions. Now all the old resources are together in one place, new ideas and references have been integrated with the older classics, and literally thousands of practical ideas for applying the principles have been supplied for us. For me and my students, one of the major strengths of the book is that many examples are connected clearly to underlying principles. In short, we like the book's comprehensiveness, its practicality, its readability, its organization, and its *connectedness*. Teaching and learning are easier and happier with this book as our support.

The Spiral Model is presented and explained in Part 1. Using this model and thinking about it have increased my belief in its value, not only as a framework for viewing the development of thinking, but also as a structure for understanding many, if not all, areas of human development. Constantly we return to themes in our lives that once we thought we had "learned," and relearn them at a higher level based on our current knowledge, skills, and maturation. Sometimes we feel we are spiraling downward rather than upward, but after the needed learning occurs, we usually see it as progress and realize that the new way of looking at things is infinitely better than the old. What we perceived as a downward spiral was instead a "blessing in disguise," and new vistas have opened at higher levels!

Sometimes I wonder if the phrase *problem solving*, which Shirley and I use frequently (as do many educators and psychologists), should perhaps be changed to *meeting challenges*. The continuum of problems presented in Chapter 3 would become a continuum of challenges, and our perception of the real-life processes would change from partially positive (e.g., problems often are viewed as negative, but as having a positive aspect) to wholly positive. Who can see meeting challenges as being anything other than wholly positive?

Part 2 is one of the most practical guides I have ever read to help teachers integrate the teaching of thinking into their curriculum, regardless of their teaching style and the other conditions around them. If no other part of the book is used except the chapter on questioning, teaching will be improved significantly, learning will be infinitely more enjoyable for students, and the book will have been worth its purchase price and more. Research, practical techniques, and underlying principles useful for guiding the teaching/learning process are integrated in this one chapter. Following the processes outlined in Part 2, teachers and administrators will be able to make thinking a fundamental part of the curriculum *without* sacrificing the teaching of important content.

The last section of the book, Part 3, contains valuable information previously unavailable to most teachers. The Hilda Taba Teaching Strategies were developed through federal grants and described in technical reports that were difficult if not impossible to access. Materials for use in training teachers to use the strategies were developed but were available only to individuals who received training by the institute that published them. When this training was discontinued, the materials were no longer available except through individuals like myself, who had learned the strategies and participated in a second level of leadership training. At one time the strategies were described in a social studies curriculum authored by Hilda Taba, but this series also is out of print.

Of all the teaching models, questioning strategies have had the greatest impact. Not only did they change my teaching style, but they also changed my way of interacting with people in all kinds of situations. Using the Taba strategies the way they were designed and found to be effective means that one is (a) sincerely interested in what another human being thinks, (b) able to communicate that interest by asking questions that can be answered easily and thoughtfully, (c) more interested in the other person's answer than in one's own ideas about how it should be answered, (d) willing to listen and question further without imposing one's own beliefs or values, (e) able to ask further questions without threatening the person, and (f) willing to wait for the other individual to ask before giving one's own opinion or answer.

If all of us could incorporate these principles into all our interactions with our spouses, parents, children, supervisors, students, friends, and (above all) enemies, the world would be a much better place to live in and communication would be joyful and peaceful much more often than it is.

Each of the chapters in this section contains a wealth of practical ideas for implementing the teaching strategies, integrated with the rationale and research supporting the use of these questioning sequences. I find them to be well organized, easy to read, and thorough. Very few questions about the strategies are not answered in a direct way by the text.

Now that you've read this far, you perhaps can understand my first statement; but if you read and use the book, you'll understand and appreciate it even more. I am very happy to be writing a foreword to this excellent book because one of my students now knows she has the ability to write a book by herself—and has the self-confidence needed to write the next one. I shall look forward to reading it also.

C. June Maker

Introduction

As the blind men ventured forth haltingly to experience and describe the elephant, so do earnest academicians read, investigate, observe, and bravely or foolishly attempt to understand and describe thinking. The human mind remains the most fascinating and uncharted wilderness, one of the last frontiers. Knowing how feeble her efforts may be in relation to actuality or even to what will be known in twenty years, the author nevertheless sets out to reduce the infinitely complex to understandable and usable terms and examples. Future generations may see this work as primitive and comparable to the blind men's descriptions of the elephant. Nevertheless, with stout heart the author attempts to describe thought processes and offer practical ways to present thinking to teachers and their students.

The purpose of this book is to provide a practical, comprehensive text for educators and others who may be interested in thinking processes and how people learn to be better thinkers. Examples have been provided to clarify meaning and to make the concepts "real." The author has attempted to make the approach comprehensive through offering a model of thinking, curriculum applications, teaching suggestions, procedures to improve teaching skills, and discussion strategies complete with sample lesson plans.

The book is divided into three major sections, devoted to a fundamental model of thinking, the application of the model to teaching, and specific strategies for making the application effective.

Part 1—Thinking: The Most Basic Skill The Spiral Model of Thinking is introduced and explained in this section. An overview of the processes and strategies within the model is provided as a foundation for later chapters.

Part 2—Teaching and Thinking The focus of the second section is the application of the Spiral Model within schools. The application of the model to curriculum as well as techniques and models teachers can use to improve their teaching skills are discussed. Questioning and classroom discussions are considered very important to developing thinking processes and strategies, and a chapter is devoted to each of these topics. The use of self-evaluation to improve skills is suggested for both students and teachers, and four models for staff development are examined.

Part 3—The Hilda Taba Teaching Strategies   The third section is devoted to the Hilda Taba Teaching Strategies. The research base that underlies the development of the strategies is discussed, as well as research on their effectiveness. Additionally, one chapter is devoted to each strategy, providing step-by-step suggestions and samples for planning, implementing, and applying each task.

More than anything else, the author hopes this book will be useful to teachers and that ultimately it will make learning more exciting for students. Certainly no more significant goal exists than to spark the mental powers of youth; our future and theirs will benefit if we succeed. Through this volume may teachers and students be empowered to use their cognitive abilities as fully as possible. Then surely I shall have touched the future and made a positive contribution.

Acknowledgments

Many people influence, enhance, and make possible the production of a book. Friends, family, and colleagues listen, critique, contribute ideas, and provide support to the author during the creation of such a work. Space prohibits the mention of all who have assisted or contributed, but special thanks go to the people named here.

Graduate students were a great help, applying their knowledge, expertise, and impressive intellectual abilities to assist me in conceptualizing, refining, and expanding the Spiral Model. I especially appreciate the interactions and insights that students in the Fall 1988 teaching methods class provided. Their reactions to ideas, their discussions, and their experiences as they used the model were invaluable.

Miri Fleming, who was a member of the Fall class, also drew the first and third versions of the model, visualizing and conceptualizing the essence of the spiral and its components. Miri is a colleague, an artist, an intellectual, and a delightful person; I am fortunate to be able to count her as a friend as well.

Colleagues who read drafts of the manuscript and gave suggestions include Gail Hanninen, Jennine Jackson, Sandi Sherman, and Anne Udall. They spent significant amounts of time reading and thinking about the manuscript, and their effort is no small part of the end result.

Roseanne Lopez helped in a unique way by using early drafts of the Hilda Taba Teaching Strategies chapters for inservice training classes. She required participants in her workshops to evaluate the clarity and helpfulness of the manuscript, providing invaluable feedback.

Recognition must be given to Ann Ferraro's contribution. Ann typed the sample lesson plans, a task that would have reduced a lesser person or less skilled typist to tears.

Bill Lamperes, who critiqued the initial manuscript as well as the final version, proved himself to be knowledgeable and diligent, spending untold hours reading and making suggestions for improvement. The book is far better for his scholarly examination of the manuscripts, and I appreciate his expertise and investment of time.

Robert Kanellas, who reviewed the final manuscript, also invested significant time in reading, thinking, and making suggestions for improvement. I appreciate his perspective, as well as his effort.

The organization of the book, many ideas it contains, and parts of the Spiral Model came about during, or as a result of, my interactions with C. June Maker. The birth of the Spiral Model occurred at her kitchen table, and I doubt that either of us could say which was "mother" of the model and which the midwife. As with many of our endeavors, the origin of ideas is difficult or impossible to identify; the intellectual sparks we generate meld into ideas that are "ours" rather than "hers" or "mine." Thank you, June, for being a catalyst and my intellectual mentor and facilitator.

Finally, I acknowledge the silent but monumental contributions made by my husband, Larry. He is a proofreader par excellence, best friend, loyal supporter, and possessor of an unparalleled ability to smile and be cheerful, even when existing on fast food. His faith in me and his love provide the foundation from which all of my endeavors spring. Thank you, Larry, for always being there.

PART ONE

THINKING: THE MOST BASIC SKILL

1

The Spiral Model of Thinking

The age-old question "What is thinking?" has become increasingly pertinent for educators as the call for a move "back to basics" has come to include thinking as a basic skill that should be taught in school. Human thought is wondrous and complex; explanations and diagrams of the thinking process or thinking skills cannot capture the richness or the essence of cognition. The human mind is capable of more than we dare dream, yet we must attempt to analyze, label, categorize, visualize, and conceptualize the mind's intricate behaviors if we are to discuss or attempt to teach them.

The author of this text, drawing on the work of others (Bruner, Goodnow, and Austin 1956; Costa 1985b; Getzels and Csikszentmihalyi 1967; Piaget 1977; Presseisen 1985b; Taba 1966; Taba, Levine, and Elzey 1964; Winocur 1985), has developed the Spiral Model of Thinking. In the Spiral Model, basic cognitive processes such as determining relevance or discerning meaning are considered enabling skills. These enabling skills make possible the five developmental processes: classification, concept development, deriving principles, drawing conclusions, and making generalizations. The developmental processes move in a spiral, as depicted in Figure 1-1, from simple operations at a concrete level though maturation and experience toward complex operations at an abstract level. The spiral symbolizes the developmental nature of thinking and represents the "revisitation" of the thinker to prior knowledge, or concepts and cognitive processes, at increasing levels of abstractness. Developmentally, young children learn the concept of *cold* by feeling objects that are cold. Through repeated experiences in which the word *cold* is used in a variety of ways, an understanding of cold as an abstraction develops, and terms such as *cold war* or *cold personality* are understood.

The developmental processes do not develop simultaneously, but from simplest (classification) to more intricate (making generalizations). These processes are necessary for the cognitive tasks of

FIGURE 1–1 The Spiral Model of Thinking

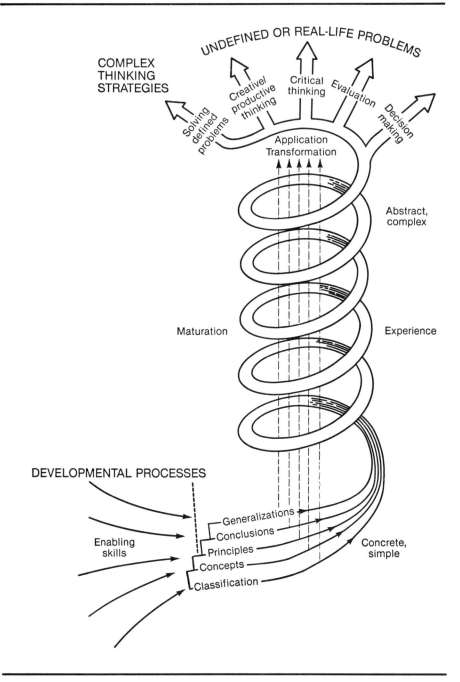

the complex thinking strategies: solving defined problems, creative/ productive thinking, critical thinking, evaluation, and decision making. The appropriate developmental processes are transformed (modified to fit the task) and applied to the complex thinking strategies.

The most sophisticated cognition is required for the solving of undefined or real-life problems. For this reason, this type of thinking forms an "umbrella" over the rest of the model, as shown in Figure 1-1. The end-state or goal of cognition is seen as the ability to solve real problems.

Any of the developmental processes can be transformed and applied to complex thinking tasks and problem solving *at the level of the thinker's maturity and experience*. Transformation and application appear at the top of the spiral, below the complex thinking strategies and the real-life problems umbrella, to indicate that these processes are necessary before the developmental processes can be applied to complex thinking strategies. However, very young children classify building blocks and use the classifications or groups to help them in making decisions and solving problems. Adolescents might use classification to organize information and develop paragraphs, essays, or reports. Adults classify abstract concepts such as patriotism and loyalty and retrieve the clusters or individual concepts as needed for reasoning. All these applications, from the concrete (blocks) to the abstract (patriotism), require transformation of requisite processes at the appropriate level.

Each new maturational level brings more sophistication to cognition, and the ability to process increasingly abstract content. Simple conclusions based on common experiences may be made by first-grade students and applied to a complex strategy such as creative/ productive thinking. Based on prior knowledge and experiences, students might conclude that playground problems are related to a lack of equipment. This conclusion might motivate them to devise unique ways to improve playground conditions. High school students might gather data regarding study habits, hours of TV watched, and student grades. Conclusions based on such data might lead to peer counseling or tutoring programs, an awareness campaign, or other, innovative ideas. When three-year-old children push a chair to the counter so they can climb up to the cookie jar, their problem solution is made possible by a generalization. High school students may develop generalizations about human commonalities and examine the validity of specific stereotypic statements, using critical thinking.

Solving undefined or real-life problems is the most demanding cognitive task. Some, most, or all of the developmental processes and complex strategies may be required to define and solve "real" problems. These are the problems adults face every day in their personal and professional lives; the requisite skills for solving them need to be recognized and addressed in school curricula.

The first of the developmental processes, *classification*, is putting together items or phenomena on the basis of some perceived similarity. The classification strand of the spiral moves from categorizing concrete objects to categorizing abstract ideas. The second of the developmental processes is *concept development*. A concept, which is a cognitive construct, is formed by organizing (classifying) information so an entity can be identified as a member or nonmember of the class. Concept development begins with concrete objects and personal experiences and moves toward abstract ideas and information. The third strand of cognitive development is *deriving principles*. Principles are composed of two or more concepts that have an ordered relationship to each other. Early development of principles is based on concrete concepts related in simple ways, such as the understanding that a lit match is hot, will burn the skin if touched, and can be used to light a candle or a fire. At a higher level of development, principles are abstract, such as the probability of getting heads on one toss of a coin. The fourth strand, *drawing conclusions*, is reaching a summary judgment based on information available. Conclusions may be drawn based on personal experiences and about concrete objects or with a much broader, more abstract base. The fifth process, *making generalizations*, is projecting experience with a few phenomena to a broad category or whole group. Early generalizations may extend from one person to the small group; later development allows for making generalizations that apply to a broad range of groups and situations.

The movement of the developmental processes in an upward spiral through maturation and life experience (or curriculum content) brings people to a level at which they can process abstract ideas and information from a variety of sources and viewpoints. The processes may be executed at a variety of levels, depending on the task at hand and the knowledge level and skill of the thinker. Very young children develop a concept of ownership; the average two-year-old child uses the word *mine* appropriately and frequently. As children mature physiologically and experientially, neural connections and their base of knowledge and experience enable them to understand not only personal ownership, but also property rights and legal, moral, and ethical issues related to property.

As the developmental spiral moves through life experiences, concepts may be presented or encountered repeatedly, with each revisitation of the concept not only building on, but expanding and modifying, the existing conceptualization. The developmental processes are continually refined and expanded through maturation, experience, and transformation and application to complex cognitive tasks. This is not to imply that the processes must be developed fully before they can be transformed and applied to complex thinking strategies. A young child may classify attribute blocks by shape, color, and size and then select the necessary blocks to replicate a specific design (solving a defined problem). At a more sophisticated level, a person might classify human behaviors by assumed cause (hereditary or environmental factors) and then plan intervention to change selected behaviors (solving real-life problems). This type of problem solving requires the most complex and sophisticated thinking, drawing on skills, processes, and strategies for its execution.

The Spiral Model incorporates elements of Bloom's Taxonomy of Cognitive Objectives (Bloom 1956); the Taxonomy of Affective Objectives (Krathwohl, Bloom, and Masia 1964); Winocur's (1985) Universe of Critical Thinking Skills; the extensive list of thinking skills collected and defined by Costa and Presseisen (Costa 1985b); Beyer's (1987) thinking strategies, critical thinking skills, and micro thinking skills; Getzels and Csikszentmihalyi's (1967) problem types; Marzano and colleagues' (Marzano et al. 1988) dimensions of thinking; and Presseisen's (1986) complex thinking processes, as well as Piaget's (1977) belief that cognition develops as a result of maturation and experience. The spiraling continuum is based on Bruner's (1960) and Taba, Durkin, and Fraenkel's (1971) conceptualizations and illustrates the developmental nature of thinking and the levels (concrete to abstract, simple to complex) at which it may occur. (The Spiral Model includes an affective dimension, the development of feelings, attitudes, and values. This dimension will be developed in a later work.)

When cognitive development is nurtured and the content as well as the process becomes increasingly challenging, students are empowered to function effectively and efficiently. The goal of this text is to present a model of thinking that lends itself to the development of teaching skills and to curriculum development. No model alone can promise better teaching; however, the existence of an understandable and usable model may help teachers as well as those who train teachers to work toward this goal.

A brief discussion of the enabling skills, the developmental processes, the transformation and application of these processes, the complex thinking strategies, and undefined or real-life problems follows. This discussion is designed as an introduction to the components of the Spiral Model. Chapters 2 and 3 build on and expand this introductory information.

ENABLING SKILLS

As used in this text, the term *enabling skills* means the basic skills required for a specific task. Enabling skills are necessary for the developmental processes, and they vary according to the task at hand, both in type and level. For example, scientific investigations require observation, which can be considered an enabling skill. When first-grade students observe seeds sprout and grow, their observations are simple and stated in broad terms. Scientists observing the effect of acid rain on the environment must make observations that are detailed and comprehensive. In addition to observation, the enabling skills of remembering, understanding, determining relevance, and perhaps comparing and contrasting would be required by the scientists. For a list of enabling skills, see Figure 1-2. As illustrated by their position at the beginning of the spiral in Figure 1-1, the enabling skills drive or make possible the developmental processes; without them, higher and more complex levels of cognition are not possible.

The premise of the Spiral Model is different from that underlying hierarchical models of thinking. Hierarchical models, such as Bloom's Taxonomy of Educational Objectives (1956), set an invariant structure or order of thinking (e.g., evaluation requires the highest level of thinking and includes knowledge, comprehension, appli-

FIGURE 1–2 Enabling Skills

Compare	Contrast
Determine relevance	Discern meaning
Elaborate	Encode
Establish priorities	Formulate questions
Identify attributes	Identify components
Identify errors	Identify main idea
Identify problem situation	Identify relationships
Infer	Interpret
Observe	Order
Pattern	Remember
Predict	Restructure
Sequence	Seriate
Set goals	Summarize
Translate	Understand
Verify	

cation, analysis, and synthesis). The premise of the Spiral Model is that the nature of the task determines the level of thinking required. Evaluation, for example, does not always require the highest level of thinking. The evaluation of a concrete object, such as determining the usefulness of a screwdriver for a specific task, requires a rather low level of cognitive functioning, while the analysis of environmental problems requires high levels of cognition.

DEVELOPMENTAL PROCESSES

Developmental processes (a) consist of sequential steps of cognitive operations, (b) use several or many enabling skills, and (c) are components of and prerequisites for complex thinking strategies. All the developmental processes except classification require one or more of the other developmental processes. Each of the five processes is explained briefly in the following section.

Classification

Costa and Presseisen (1985) define *classification* as sorting objects, events, or people into clusters according to their common elements, factors, or characteristics and giving the cluster a label that communicates its essential characteristics. This definition describes classification as used in this text.

The ability to classify objects, events, living things, and phenomena is necessary for the development of concepts and generalizations. For example, if students were not able to process information regarding their experiences with mathematics through grouping, categorizing, and labeling integers as odd or even, whole or fractional, rational or irrational, prime or not prime, conceptualizing and performing higher mathematical operations would not be possible. The mark of an efficient thinker is proficiency and flexibility of classification.

Concept Development

A *concept* is a mental construct commonly symbolized by a word; it is organized information that enables an individual to discriminate a specific entity or class of entities and relate them to other entities and classes of entities (Klausmeier 1985). Classification skills are necessary to concept development, since the development of a concept requires the organization of information into a meaningful whole.

Concepts allow people to make sense of their world, to organize their experiences and observations. Incoming sensory input can be organized according to existing concepts, which may require reorganization in light of the new input, or new concepts may need to be formed. Concepts may be simple and concrete, such as the concept of triangle, or complex and abstract, such as the concept of patriotism. In the Spiral Model of Thinking, concepts are seen as being expanded and modified and moving toward a higher level of abstraction through developmental and experiential factors.

Principles

A *principle* is a type of generalization that describes the ordered relationship between or among concepts (Gagné 1966; Klausmeier 1980; Marzano et al. 1988). While the derivation of principles is a generalizing process, in the Spiral Model principles and generalizations are treated as two separate but related entities. Generalizations may include two or more principles, but principles are more narrowly defined than generalizations. A principle rules or governs relationships, such as additive principles of mathematics.

Conclusions

Costa and Presseisen (Costa 1985) define a *conclusion* as an inferential belief derived from premises. Drawing sound conclusions requires the gathering, examination, evaluation, and synthesis of information before making the conclusive inference. Determining the probable cause of high school dropout rates, for example, requires careful collection and review of data, as well as insightful consideration of the information before drawing a conclusion. Conclusions also can be made at a relatively low cognitive level; a recommendation from kindergarten students regarding the best way to reduce the waste of supplies is an example of a low-level conclusion.

Students of varying ages, developmental levels, experiential bases, and intellectual abilities can be taught to make conclusions based on available data. Sound conclusions are necessary for more complex thinking. For example, decision making should be based on conclusions regarding the viability of the various options available.

Generalizations

A *generalization* is a statement that applies universally or to many situations. Good generalizations are formed on the basis of many related experiences. Learning to generalize is part of becoming an efficient thinker, as it allows one to deal with groups of similar information or ideas rather than with each piece of information individually.

Very young children can make generalizations about animals, such as "Dogs have four legs and bark." The more sophisticated generalizations of older students might deal with types of government, human behavior in specific but varying situations, or human conflict, such as "Similarities exist among conflict situations, whether the situations arise between individuals, groups, or nations."

TRANSFORMATION AND APPLICATION

Transformation is the process of manipulating knowledge to make it fit new tasks (Bruner 1960) and situations. Transformation involves changes of known information—changes in meaning, significance, use, interpretation, mood, or sensory qualities (Guilford 1967), or selective use or change of a known process. The elements of transformation include (a) viewing from a different perspective, (b) reinterpreting, (c) elaborating, (d) extending or going beyond, and (e) combining (Maker 1982a).

Transformation of the developmental processes entails the selection and manipulation of those processes or parts of processes required for a task, so they fit the situation and the personal style of the thinker. In creating a poem, for example, an individual might classify phenomena or events from an unusual perspective, combine, expand or elaborate on concepts, and develop unique conclusions and generalizations. These conclusions and generalizations become the basis for creative/productive thinking about the images or ideas to be expressed, and, ultimately, the poetic form. Transformation can occur at all levels of development, from the activity of a child who combines two nursery rhymes into a new one to the task of a novelist who transforms historic facts and creates compelling prose.

In the Spiral Model, *application* involves the use of transformed information or processes in a complex thinking task. Evaluation of the Electoral College system, for example, includes the following: (a) the classification of pertinent information; (b) possession, expansion, and clarification of such concepts as criteria, evaluation, the Electoral College, and political parties; (c) drawing conclusions about suitable criteria; (d) understanding the cause-and-effect principles inherent in political processes; (e) generalization about effectiveness, based on specific outcomes; (f) transformation of the criteria and selected components to form a matrix or other workable format; and

(g) application of the pertinent information and necessary skills to accomplish the task.

Bloom (1956) and his colleagues saw application as the third of six hierarchical levels of thinking. In the Spiral Model, application occurs at many different levels of sophistication. The application of math algorithms to defined problems is at a relatively low level of cognitive functioning. Applying analogical reasoning to a scientific investigation, however, requires transformation of information and processes, and is a high-level function. In such a transformation, pertinent information or processes must be selected, modified or expanded as necessary, and applied to new or unique situations.

COMPLEX THINKING STRATEGIES

Figure 1-3 illustrates the relationship of the developmental processes to complex thinking strategies. The processes are listed on the left and the strategies across the top of the table. Entries in the grid provide examples of specific processes used for each complex thinking strategy.

The complex thinking strategies (a) use a number of developmental processes in varying combinations; (b) entail purposeful, goal-related thinking; (c) require one or more of the other complex strategies; and (d) are prerequisite for solving undefined or real-life problems. Each of the five complex strategies is discussed briefly in the following subsections.

Solving Defined Problems

In the Spiral Model a distinction is made between the thinking required to solve known or defined problems and that required for undefined or real-life problems. This distinction is based on Getzels and Csikszentmihalyi's (1967) conceptualization of types of problems. These researchers distinguish problem situations based on (a) how clearly and completely the problem is stated at the beginning, (b) how much of the method for reaching the solution is available to the solver, and (c) how general is the agreement about an acceptable solution. Two ends of a continuum can be identified. At one end is a situation in which the problem, method, and solution are known. The problem solver only needs to employ the appropriate steps to arrive at the correct solution. At the other end of the continuum is a situation in which the problem is not formulated and no known method for solving the problem and no known solution exist.

FIGURE 1–3 The Use of Developmental Processes Within the Complex Thinking Strategies

DEVELOPMENTAL PROCESSES	DEFINED PROBLEM SOLVING	CRITICAL THINKING	CREATIVE/ PRODUCTIVE THINKING	DECISION MAKING	EVALUATION
Classification	Categorizing possible solutions; categorizing enablers and inhibiters	Classifying elements of statements or arguments; developing reasoning patterns	Categorizing creative ideas; classifying aspects of need (e.g., for inventions)	Categorizing options and consequences	Classifying attributes according to criteria
Concepts	Understanding problem	Providing examples	Expanding on known; exploring options	Choosing workable options	Developing criteria
Principles	Choosing and applying method of solution	Determining soundness or validity of statements	Developing product; hypothesizing performance/ acceptance of product	Examining alternatives; determining (e.g., long-term effects)	Choosing criteria
Conclusions	Determining suitability or correctness of solution	Choosing soundest or most valid statement	Choosing usable elements	Choosing better or best option	Selecting better or best choice or offering
Generalizations	Applying method of solution	Developing statements based on examples	Hypothesizing; predicting performance, practicality, or acceptance	Predicting effects or consequences of options	Using past experience as basis for selecting criteria

Maker (1986) and the author of this text found the continuum conceptualization useful but the problem types incomplete. Therefore, they each added one problem type to the original three, resulting in the following five problem types.

- *Type I:* The problem and the method of solution are known to the problem presenter and the problem solver; the problem presenter knows the correct solution. Solving math problems by a known method or algorithm is a Type I problem.
- *Type II:* The problem is known by the presenter and the solver, but the method of solution and solution are known only to the presenter. Story problems or answering questions about factual material are Type II problems.
- *Type III:* The problem is known to the presenter and the solver, more than one method may be used to solve the problem, and the solution or range of solutions is known only to the presenter. Problems that can be solved inductively but that have an accepted answer or range of answers are Type III problems. Solving a geometry problem by using manipulatives is a Type III problem.
- *Type IV:* The problem is known to the presenter and solver, but the method and solution are unknown to both. Open-ended problems that can be solved in a number of ways and that have more than one correct or acceptable solution are Type IV. A question such as "In what ways might you share the results of your survey?" exemplifies this type of problem.
- *Type V:* The problem is unknown or undefined and the method and solution are unknown to both presenter and solver. Problem situations, in which the problem may be defined in more than one way, and real-life problems are Type V. This type of problem includes cafeteria waste, environmental pollution, or student behavior on the playground or campus.

See Figure 1-4 for a chart demonstrating problem types.

The term *defined problems* as used in this text refers to problem types I, II, III and IV—problems that are defined and/or presented to the problem solver. As is evident from the type descriptions and Figure 1-4, traditional curricula contain primarily types I and II problems and few or no problems or situations of types III through V. However, educators can use the concept of problem types to examine and modify existing curricula or to develop new curricula that include problem-solving processes and therefore the higher levels of thinking.

FIGURE 1–4 Types of Problem Situations

	PROBLEM		METHOD		SOLUTION	
TYPE	*Presenter*	*Solver*	*Presenter*	*Solver*	*Presenter*	*Solver*
I	K	K	K	K	K	U
II	K	K	K	U	K	U
III	K	K	R	U	R	U
IV	K	K	U	U	U	U
V	U	U	U	U	U	U

K = Known   U = Unknown   R = Range

Creative/Productive Thinking

Creative/productive thinking results in the development or invention of novel, constructive ideas or products. The emphasis is on using information or material to generate the possible and to elaborate on the thinker's original perspective (Presseisen 1985b). However, the process is not random; an evaluative component is critical, and the developmental processes are essential for creative productivity. The foundation of the creative process is a sound knowledge base. Such a knowledge base is established by expanding and developing related concepts, incorporating principles, making conclusions based on available information, and generalizing. That is, writing poetry requires a linguistic knowledge base—the sound and symmetry of words, as well as word meanings and poetic principles. The poet generalizes emotions and moods based on specific experiences, internalizes the feelings, and creates poetry.

Critical Thinking

Critical thinking uses enabling skills and developmental thinking processes to analyze arguments and generate insight into specific meanings and interpretations; to develop cohesive logical reasoning patterns and understand underlying assumptions and biases; and to attain a credible, concise, and convincing style of presentation (Presseisen 1985b).

Critical thinking requires that statements be analyzed for soundness and logic. This complex process requires raising relevant questions, breaking complex ideas into components, applying prior knowledge, and translating complicated ideas into examples (Heiman and Slomianko 1986). Experience with drawing sound conclusions, deriving and applying principles, and making good generalizations aids the thinker in recognizing elements or arguments that are based on invalid premises or unsupported assumptions. To be critical of ideas, the thinker must have internalized and transformed the developmental processes before applying them to the ideas in question. Analyzing the soundness and logic of a statement such as "American Indians are talented artists and craftspeople" requires not only conceptual knowledge, but also an understanding of how generalizations are formed and what distinguishes a valid from an invalid generalization.

Evaluation

Evaluation is examination or judgment based on a set of internal or external criteria, reaching a conclusion based on predetermined standards. The selection or development of criteria requires concluding which criteria will serve the purpose best. Effective evaluation includes the use of concepts and generalizations; as with the other complex strategies, evaluation cannot be accomplished without the presence of the developmental processes. A group of students might plan an advertising campaign to increase participation in student council elections. The plan should include (a) important concepts to focus on in the campaign, (b) generalizations about what approach and format will be most appealing to their peers, and (c) criteria by which they will judge the effectiveness of the campaign.

Decision Making

Decision making is choosing a best response or option from several possibilities. Advantages and disadvantages of alternative approaches are compared and the most effective response and its justification are decided on (Presseisen 1985b). Sound decisions are related not only to experience, but also to the thinking processes used prior to the decision. Unless the decision is based only on emotions, obvious factors and information usually are considered. However, considering less obvious factors and applying generalizations to determine long-term effects, the reactions of others, and implications results in a sounder decision.

For effective decision making, the appropriate developmental processes must be filtered through the individual's cognitive structure, or *schema*. Middle school students who want to earn money to take a class trip must categorize their skills and the (possible) demand for related services, apply the principle of supply and demand, understand concepts of available time and possible income, and apply generalizations they have made about how to make a maximum amount of money in a minimum amount of time. Based on these processes, a sound decision can be made.

UNDEFINED OR REAL-LIFE PROBLEMS

Undefined or real-life problems are those labeled Type V, those in which the problem is unknown or undefined and the method of solution and solution are unknown both to the problem presenter and the solver. The solution of real-life problems may require all the other cognitive operations in the Spiral Model, which is why undefined problems arc over the top of the model. Most problems, or tasks and projects in people's personal and professional lives, are of this type, which requires sophisticated thinking. If educators want to prepare students adequately for adult life, school curricula should include the requisite skills for, and practice in, solving the type of problems they will be expected to solve as adults. The concept of problem types can be used as a structure to develop students' abilities to solve types III, IV and V problems.

CHAPTER SUMMARY

Thinking defies simple explanation. The author of this text proposes a Spiral Model of Thinking that illustrates the continuous developmental aspects as well as the interrelatedness of the cognitive processes. Five cognitive processes that are considered developmental are transformed and applied to tasks that require complex cognitive strategies. The strategies are solving defined problems, creative/productive thinking, critical thinking, evaluation, and decision making. The most sophisticated and demanding cognitive function is solving undefined or real-life problems. This function overarches the spiral and all other skills, processes, and strategies that are necessary to and contained within the solution of undefined problems.

2

The Developmental Thinking Processes

Textbooks, plans for school curricula, teaching methods, and indeed the concept of education are based on the assumption that thinking is developmental. However, little effort is made within teacher education programs or existing texts to help teachers conceptualize the components of higher-level or complex thinking. This chapter provides information on and examples of what the author believes are the processes and behaviors that students must develop if they are to become proficient thinkers. The developmental processes, introduced in Chapter 1 build on each other and are sequential within a specified topic. Students must learn to classify before they develop concepts, and concepts are building blocks for the principles, conclusions, and generalizations related to the same and related topics. The developmental processes should be experienced repeatedly, using increasingly abstract or intricate ideas, content, and/or phenomena.

In this chapter the processes are discussed in order from simple to complex: classification, concept development, deriving principles, drawing conclusions, and making generalizations. Some of the processes are discussed in greater depth than are others, due to discrepancies in the amount of information available. What follows is a synthesis of information about the five developmental processes and examples of ways in which teachers can facilitate their development in the classroom.

CLASSIFICATION

The importance of categorizing or classifying phenomena becomes apparent if we think what life would be like if we did not categorize and classify events and phenomena. Jerome Bruner says that if we used fully our capacity for registering the difference between objects and responded to each as unique, we would be overwhelmed by the complexity of our environment (Bruner, Goodnow, and Austin 1956).

For example, if we were to note the differences between and details of each automobile on a freeway during rush hour rather than classifying them generally as "heavy traffic," we would not be able to attend to the task of driving.

The use of categories is one of the most elementary and general forms of cognition by which people adjust to their environment. By categorizing discriminably different events, (a) the complexity of the environment is reduced, (b) objects are identified and the necessity for constant learning is reduced, (c) direction is provided and attention allowed for specific activity, and (d) classes of phenomena can be ordered and relationships discovered or established (Bruner, Goodnow, and Austin 1956).

What is true for adults is no less true for children in school. Students need to develop classification skills on a systematic basis; therefore teachers must understand the rationale for and importance of teaching classification behaviors. The purpose of this section is to develop this understanding and to suggest direct applications for the classroom.

Thinking in Terms of Classes*

Students tend to put things in groups for different reasons, and some individuals—and sometimes a whole class—tend to use one particular method more than any other for all their groupings. A student or the class in general may tend to group items according to function; for example, grouping "hammer," "golf club," and "baseball bat" because each item is used to hit something. Having discovered characteristic styles, the teacher will have information that can be used in a number of different ways:

- As a means of knowing when to encourage various ways of grouping. (Flexibility is an important characteristic of effective thinking.)
- As a means of determining the level at which a student or a group typically classifies ideas, events, or objects. This information is useful in the assessment and evaluation of thinking skills.
- As a means of measuring changes and development in grouping styles. If students typically group by function but after practice begin to use descriptive groups ("baseball bat," "oar," and "beam" because they are all made of wood), the teacher knows that growth has occurred in classification behavior.

*Unless otherwise noted, the information in this section is drawn from and based on materials developed by the Institute for Staff Development (1971a, b, and c).

According to Piaget (1977), one of the cornerstones of logical thought is the ability to think in class terms. For example, furniture is a class that includes chairs, tables, sofas, beds, lamps, and many other items. During the elementary school years, children acquire the competency to add classes together, multiply classes, divide classes into smaller units, expand classes, and think in terms of classes of items that are progressively more abstract or more inclusive.

Class labels are commonly thought of as terms such as *animals, vehicles, men,* or *women.* However, items can be classified according to many other criteria, such as size, shape, color, texture, function, locale, or material. Every object, event, or person is multidimensional and therefore has many characteristics that can be considered attributes. *Instances,* which is the term used to refer to items, persons, or events, can be classified on the basis of one or more of their attributes. That is, a dog can be classified on the basis of color, gender, size, breed, or a variety of other attributes. Instances are not fixed members of a single class but can be included within various classes, depending on the attribute selected as a criterion for class membership. The dog might be included in a class of black, female, shepherds, or working animals, according to the criterion named.

The realization that items have many dimensions is necessary for the development of the concept that class membership is relative. Kindergarten students have difficulty with a task such as making groups of small, blue, square attribute blocks. They can easily sort out the blue blocks, the squares, or the smaller blocks, but seeing several attributes simultaneously is beyond their developmental level.

Classes are formed and reformed on the basis of single attributes until the person learns to build classes on the basis of two or more attributes. This is known as *multiple classification,* whereby objects can be classified on the basis of size and texture, size and function, function and locale, or any other combination of two or more attributes. In other words, a dog may be put into a specific group or category because it is black *and* female, or black *and* a shepherd. The ability to *subsume*—that is, to identify more inclusive categories and labels—is a high level of multiple classification. Using the previous example, black female dogs and black shepherds can be subsumed under the more inclusive label "dogs," and "dogs" can be subsumed under "mammals."

The ability to use two discrete attributes simultaneously as the basis for classification is difficult to develop; children usually are not able to master this until about the fourth grade. Classification behavior is developmental, but guided experience enhances its appearance and development. Learning experiences in the lower grades should include frequent classification practice, using concrete objects and shared events to assist the development of multiple classification skills.

The Sequence of Cognitive Growth

Piagetian theory holds that intellect develops in invariant sequential order and that children must proceed through each step to achieve the type of logical thinking usually practiced by adults. The ability of the child to handle particular kinds of tasks depends on prerequisite experiences and competencies. Performance at each level is related to past experiences and previous competencies integrated with current abilities, and sets the stage for subsequent experiences. Adult thinking is ascribed to the person who is capable of hypothesis formation, manipulation of symbolic material, and the ability to deal with representations.

Central to Piaget's theory of intellectual development is the premise that the ability to think in logical terms has as one of its crucial prerequisites the ability to deal in multiple classifications and multiple relations and to add, subtract, and divide classes. For example, when a young adult is choosing a career or a job, these skills are important to making an informed choice. Any job can be classified according to the type of work required, training needed, location, salary, and mobility, as well as other attributes. A young adult who has the necessary education, for example, and likes teaching but not the salary might investigate teaching salaries in different locations. Teaching in Alaska pays relatively well, but perhaps the location is not desirable. Teaching overseas might offer a desirable location, mobility, and an acceptable salary. By being aware of the multiple classifications of various jobs as well as able to add, subtract, multiply and divide classes, an acceptable solution (position) may be found.

Class Labeling

An awareness of the range of attributes or aspects of any instance is necessary for the development of complex classification behaviors. If we are able to specify many labels, we can classify instances in many categories. For example, we can classify an apple under the following classes: "edible," "red," "having a curved surface," and "fruit." The American Revolution could be categorized by the classes "revolution," "independence," "anti-British," and "war."

The number and kind of instances brought under a particular heading depend on the criterial attribute selected. For the class "fruit," such objects as pears and oranges could be included, but if the criterial attribute "red" were added, other instances such as apples, cherries, and strawberries, which possess both attributes, would be selected.

Being aware that objects have many attributes is an important step in recognizing the complexity of the environment. Having access to a broader range of information about people, objects, and events reduces stereotypical thinking. Thinking of Russians only in terms of their politics, or Catholics only in terms of their religion, is thinking in terms of only one attribute, when many other attributes of each of these social instances exist. Stereotypical thinking occurs when classifications are based on a limited number of attributes. However, when children see that every object, event, and person has many attributes, they see that no one member is fixed in any particular class, but can be in any number of classes, depending on the attribute selected as a criterion. Thus, if students were asked to list things in the classroom that are black, they might include a black person, a chalkboard eraser, a shoe, and a belt. If the next task were to list things having legs, they might mention black, Hispanic, and Anglo people; the piano; chairs; desks; and a table. Through experiences such as these, children learn about the relativity of class membership.

Types of Categorization

Types and levels of categorization are determined not by the items in a group but by the reason given for putting them together. That is, a group consisting of "fish," "crabs," and "octopus" might be categorized functionally (they all can be eaten by human beings) or by location (they all are found in bodies of salt water).

Styles of categorization, described in order from least to most abstract, include:

1. *Relational-contextual:* Classifying items because they are related by context such as time, place, or function. Subcategories of this type of grouping include the following:

   • *Locational:* Items are grouped because they are found in the same place in the student's experience. "Sheet, pillow, bedspread, and bed, because they all are in my bedroom" is an example of locational grouping.

   • *Temporal:* Items are grouped because of a time relationship, such as "Orange juice, cereal, and toast, because I eat those in the morning."

- *Functional:* Items are grouped because they operate together, are used together, or happen in concert or as a result of the action of each other. For example, "Match, wood, and fire, because striking the match makes the fire start, which makes the wood burn."

2. *Descriptive:* The use of size, shape, color, or other physical features as the criterial attribute. An example of descriptive criteria for grouping is "Rain, cloud, and fog, because they are all water and white or grey."

3. *Categorical-inferential:* Groups are formed on the basis of inferred attributes. Items are grouped because they belong to a class of things, the name of which is abstract in that it does not refer to any tangible quality such as color, shape, or material, but rather to an abstracted quality of the whole group. In this case, every instance in an array is an instance of the class. For example, "Rain, cloud, and fog, because they all have to do with weather."

In terms of the objectives for examining types of groupings, noticing the characteristic style of grouping used by a student or group of students is important. This style should be noted to determine what steps should be taken to provide greater opportunity to learn to group items for a variety of reasons or on a more abstract level.

Other things to look for in students' groupings include:

- Number of items that are used spontaneously in more than one group. Noticing that items can fit in several groups is evidence of mental flexibility, a desirable quality in thinking about the ways things go together.
- Number of different ways items can be grouped. This also can be used as a measure of flexibility.

Flexibility is basic to good thinking. Cognitive flexibility should be developed in students inductively by having them respond to questions such as "What are some other ways to group these items?", "Which ones can be put together for a different reason?", and "What would be another good name/label for this group?"

As children become older they make less use of relational-contextual criteria for classification and more use of descriptive and categorical-inferential criteria. For example, the child who grouped "orange juice, cereal, and toast, because I eat those in the morning" may begin to group them because of their inclusion in the basic food groups. These changes reflect the child's increased awareness of the complexity of items, as well as the ability to deal with materials on the basis of their objective features. In other words, as children mature they rely less on personal, unique, subjective experiences as bases for classifying instances and more on collective experiences and abstract reasoning. Additionally, as the students become more familiar with a content area or discipline, they tend to see beyond the functional or descriptive relationships and to develop more abstract relationships.

Teachers can expand students' knowledge of and options for using a variety of categorization styles through asking reasoning questions such as "Why do you think pen, pencil, and eraser go together?" and encouraging students to interact (compare or contrast groups or reasons for grouping) with each other's ideas. When students share with the group the basis for their classification, and when they interact in a guided discussion, the entire group benefits from being exposed to a variety of types and higher levels of categorization.

Complex Classification Behavior

When children understand the logic of single classification they are ready to learn multiple classification. The essential logical processes of multiple classification are addition and multiplication. Addition of classes is the use of two or more attributes for classification rather than one, but the *combination* of the attributes is *not* used. Grouping pythons, bears, whales, and Gila monsters because they are all either mammals *or* reptiles is an example of addition of classes.

Multiplication of classes occurs when two or more attributes are combined to form the grouping. A group of bears, cats, dogs, and mink formed because they are all mammals *and* they have fur exemplifies the multiplication of classes.

Even very young children can learn how to add or multiply classes through the use of concrete objects or sets of pictures. Pictures of a variety of clowns could be used for this purpose. Addition of classes can be illustrated by forming the following groups (classes): (a) clowns who either are wearing flowers or carrying something; (b) clowns who either are not wearing flowers or are carrying something; (c) clowns who either are wearing flowers or not carrying anything; (d) clowns who either are or are not wearing flowers; (e) clowns who either are or are not carrying something; and (f) clowns who are not wearing flowers or are not carrying anything. Notice the use of the either-or condition in each of the six classes.

Multiplication of classes can be taught using the same pictures. The following classes can be formed by multiplication: (a) all clowns who are wearing flowers and carrying something; (b) all clowns who are wearing flowers and not carrying anything; and (c) all clowns not wearing flowers and carrying something. Notice the presence of two attributes in each of the classes.

The ability to combine two or more attributes is significant in the logical development of thought; it is a prototype of complex thinking, in which classes are combined and recombined as the needs of the problem dictate. For example, if students need to discern what the basic elements of government are and generalize to the universal characteristics of governing bodies, they need to examine attributes of tribal, community, state, and national governing bodies and be able to combine these attributes if they are to develop a plausible generalization. In the process of combining and recombining, students have to shift their criteria; flexibility is required in the manipulation of multiple criteria.

Children who are able to multiply classes also are able to conserve; that is, to hold a characteristic of an item invariant in the face of transformation. Classic examples of conservation tasks include pouring liquid from a tall, narrow container into a short, wide one, or rolling a ball of clay into a long thin "rope." When children understand that the amount of liquid or clay has not changed just because the shape has, they are able to conserve. This ability is relevant to many kinds of logical thought problems in the physical and social sciences. If the ability to multiply classes aids the development of conservation, the obvious implication is that teachers of young children should incorporate appropriate tasks into the curriculum.

Reversibility and Reciprocity

To deal with problems of multiple classification and interdependence of attributes, a child must be capable of reversibility and reciprocity.

Reversibility is a mental operation in which materials or ideas are reorganized to reconstruct the original state or class. When a lump of clay is formed into a ball and then into a "rope," children understand reversibility when they are aware that the rope can be transformed back into a ball. In arithmetic, reversibility is manifest in the proof of subtraction. In classification, reversibility is manifest when classes are reorganized and then brought back to the original state. If students create a group of domestic animals, or pets, consisting of "cat," "dog," "hamster," and "guppies" and a group of wild animals consisting of "deer," "ostrich," "buffalo," and "piranha," they could reorganize the animals into classes of "mammals," "birds," and "fish." Reversibility is exemplified by again classifying the animals as domestic or wild. Comprehension of reversibility reflects the awareness that instances conserve their identity even though placed in another class. That is, "cat" is the same animal, whether it is classified as a domestic animal or a mammal.

Reciprocity connotes an interaction between things, as when the United States imposes tariffs on specific manufactured items from Japan. The principle is that tariffs are related to the number of goods bought and sold. An increase in tariffs causes a decrease in trade, while a decrease in tariffs leads to an increase in trade. A reciprocal relationship exists between trade and tariffs. Young children understand reciprocity in interpersonal relationships—they share toys and cooperate with each other to gain good will. They understand that a breach of kindness or cooperation will result in the loss of friends and possible retaliation. Simple science demonstrations also can be used to illustrate reciprocity. When a plant is watered and given nourishment and light, it grows and produces flowers or fruit. A reciprocal relationship exists between the plant and its environment; if its essential needs are not met, it will not produce.

Student Readiness

A wide range in student responses exists at every grade level. With very young children, a teacher can expect functional or egocentric grouping, such as "I put cats and dogs together because I have a cat and a dog." This child may not yet be aware that a cat and dog are not standard to all families. While seven- to twelve-year-olds use primarily a functional or descriptive basis for grouping, many children within this age range are able to use abstract class-type groups. The inclusion of multi-age and multi-level discussion groups provides the opportunity for students to interact with others whose ideas and groupings are at a higher level of abstraction than their own.

Students' grouping behavior may differ according to the data with which they are working. Individuals are more apt to find complex and abstract relationships when working with familiar data, than when working in a new or unfamiliar area. Additionally, students who are intellectually more competent than their peers will be more likely to discover complex and abstract relationships. Many times the superior ability of students is "hidden" when the intellectual requirement is at a low level. Developing tasks and facilitating discussions that entail reasoning at a variety of levels may reveal thinking talent that previously was not apparent.

CONCEPTS

A *concept* is a mental construct symbolized by a word—organized information that enables an individual to discriminate a specific entity or class of entities and relate them to other entities (Klausmeier 1985). Concepts are the basic tools of thought, the building blocks of cognitive learning and development. Concepts not only enable one to understand and relate many otherwise discrete phenomena, but also provide the basis for vertical and horizontal transfer of learning. *Vertical transfer* refers to the development of successively higher levels of the same concept; *horizontal transfer* refers to the ability to use the concept in a problem or different context (Klausmeier 1980). Individuals at all levels of cognitive development constantly are learning new concepts and extending and using old concepts in new situations. Concepts are the fundamental agents of intellectual activity from early childhood through adulthood (Klausmeier, Ghatala, and Frayer 1974); they are essential components of schema, the organization of related information (Norris and Phillips 1987).

The Nature of Concepts

The word *concept* is used to designate both mental constructs of individuals and identifiable public entities that are part of the substance of various disciplines. Klausmeier, Ghatala, and Frayer (1974) define concepts in terms of eight attributes: learnability, usability, validity, generality, power, structure, instance perceptibility, and instance numerousness. Each of these attributes and their implications for teaching will be discussed.

Learnability

Some concepts are learned more readily than others. Generally, the more concrete the concept or the closer to the learner's experiences, the more easily it will be learned. The teaching maxim "Take the students from where they *are*" refers to the learnability of concepts. Students in the primary grades typically learn about families, then neighborhoods, then communities. Most students are part of a family and have many related experiences. The closeness of the concept to their personal experiences increases its learnability. At the high school level, teachers need to assess past experiences and level of knowledge before attempting to teach an abstract concept such as "valence."

Usability

Concepts vary in usability for understanding principles and solving problems. For example, the mathematical concepts of "number" and "set" are used more frequently in solving a variety of problems than are the concepts of "proportion" and "ratio" (Klausmeier, Ghatala, and Frayer 1974).

Concepts become more usable to the individual as they are attained at successively higher levels (Klausmeier, Ghatala, and Frayer 1974). For example, the concept of "individual rights" becomes increasingly usable (applicable to a variety of situations) to students who understand the rights of individuals in families, see the relationship of individual rights to societal values, and thus begin to develop the concept of universal human rights.

Validity

A concept is valid to the extent that experts agree on its definition. An individual's concept increases in validity as it is expanded and developed and as it comes closer to the definition of experts (Klausmeier, Ghatala, and Frayer 1974). The teacher's role is to provide sequential experiences that will bring the students' conceptualizations closer to the experts' definitions. Concept attainment is related to the amount of informal experience with examples of the concept and to formal instruction (Rampaul 1976). For example, students need a variety of experiences and information, in addition to time for incubation and maturation, before they can articulate accurately the concept of the water cycle. Science investigations, informal observations, life experiences, and factual information from printed materials, experts, and audiovisual materials provide the basis for the development of valid concepts; the teacher also needs to provide guided development of cognitive processes so that valid concepts are developed.

Generality

Higher-level concepts are more general (in terms of the number of subclasses or subordinate concepts included) than are lower-level concepts. "Living things" is a highly general concept; "vertebrate," "mammal," and "man" are successively less general (Klausmeier, Ghatala, and Frayer 1974). Teachers should see to the development of general concepts and the differentiation by students between specific and general concepts; for example, students can be required to subsume specific concepts such as "food," "shelter," and "clothing," under a more general concept such as "basic needs." When students can accomplish this type of subsumption and can verbalize the reasoning behind it, they understand that some concepts are more general than others and can use the concepts accordingly.

Power

The power of a concept refers to the extent to which that concept facilitates, or is essential to, the attainment of other concepts (Klausmeier, Ghatala, and Frayer 1974). Examples of powerful concepts include those "big ideas" or fundamental concepts of the disciplines referred to by Bruner (1960) and the construct of the advance organized proposed by Ausubel (1966). A powerful concept in the social studies is "revolution." The understanding of this big idea enables students to acquire both lower-level concepts such as those related to specific revolutions, as well as higher-order concepts such as "change" and "conflict." Teachers need to structure their teaching in terms of powerful concepts and organize learning experiences that teach these concepts.

The concept of "pattern" is a powerful one that is applicable to the social and physical sciences. When students have internalized the concept, they can use it to acquire lower-level concepts such as those related to simple mathematical patterns and, eventually, highly abstract patterns such as those of societal behaviors. Students should experience, and verbalize in some way, patterns that range from the concrete (blocks, colors, shapes) through the symbolic (math, language) to the abstract (genetic, physical force, historical). Many current curricula include exposure to the concept of pattern at every level; what is lacking is the verbalization of the concept and the conceptual teaching approach whereby connections between patterns of various types are established inductively by the students.

Structure

The *structure* of a concept refers to the relatedness of its defining attributes (Klausmeier, Ghatala, and Frayer 1974). The teaching requirement related to concept structure is to develop students' ability to recognize defining attributes and their relatedness. A concept such as "the water cycle" is defined by its attributes and/or elements (evaporation, condensation, water vapor, liquid water, ice) and their relatedness. Students can be asked to name specific information they have acquired about the water cycle, to form groups of items (elements or attributes) because they are alike in some way, and to label these groups of items. As they provide the reasons for grouping and for labels, students are verbalizing the relatedness of the attributes and thus exploring the structure of the concept.

Instance Perceptibility

Instance perceptibility of a concept refers to the extent to which instances of the concepts can be sensed. For example, "plant" has many instances to be experienced, while "eternity" has none. The implication for teaching is that teachers should consider the developmental level of students as well as instance perceptibility of the concept. In other words, young children can develop only those concepts that have high instance perceptibility, such as "plants," "animals," "family," and "friends"; concrete objects and personal experience are the basis of concept formation at early ages. Maturation allows the movement from the concrete to symbols or representations and finally to abstract concepts with little or no instance perceptibility, such as "social order," "government," "biological order," and "interdependence."

Instance Numerousness
Most concepts have instances, but the number of instances range from one to an infinite number. "The Earth's moon" has one instance, "the Earth's continents" a small number, "drops of water" a large number, and "integers" an infinite number (Klausmeier, Ghatala, and Frayer 1974). In-school application of instance perceptibility requires that teachers be aware of the level of (a) availability and (b) student experience with instances of specific concepts. Children living in the desert may need to be provided with numerous examples and experiences with attributes of the concept "ocean." While some locales provide high instance numerousness of "ocean," others necessitate planned experiences and presentation of information.

Concept Formation and Development

Forming a concept involves organizing information about an entity or an idea and associating that information with a label or word (Marzano et al. 1988). Concept formation requires the discrimination of elements or properties of objects or events. The process entails both separating and uniting and analyzing and synthesizing elements and information. Concept formation is a sequential process in which each step is a necessary prerequisite for the next one (Taba 1966). When toddlers begin to form the concept "dog," first they must separate dog characteristics and behavior from characteristics and behaviors of other living things, then bring together characteristics and behaviors of several instances of "dog." Their pool of information is analyzed for pertinent elements; these elements are synthesized to form the concept. As maturation and life experience provide more capabilities and experiences, concepts continue to develop (expand and be refined) and can be used in thinking about the physical and social world (Rampaul 1976).

Klausmeier (1985) found four levels of concept formation: concrete, identity, classificatory, and formal levels. Attaining a concept at the *concrete level* entails noticing or attending to something one or more times; discriminating it from other things; remembering it; and later attending to, discriminating, and recognizing it as the same thing. A child attends to a kitten, discriminates it from other objects, represents the kitten internally, retrieves an earlier representation of the kitten, and recognizes it as the same thing attended to earlier. The child knows the concept of that particular kitten at the concrete level.

When the child recognizes the kitten in a different context, the *identity level* has been attained. Whether the kitten is inside or outside the house, on the floor or on the furniture, it is recognizable to the child at the identity level.

The *classification level* requires the learning of at least two examples at the identity level. When the child sees the first kitten as equivalent to a different kitten, the concept is attained at a beginning classificatory level.

The *formal level* of concept development includes the following capabilities: (a) Examples of the concept can be identified accurately; (b) the concept and its distinguishing attributes can be named; (c) a societally accepted definition can be provided; and (d) indications of how examples of the concept differ from nonexamples can be provided. Using the previous example, the formal level would be reached when the concept of "feline" is attained, with all the above criteria met.

Based on extensive research in classroom settings, Taba and colleagues (1971) proposed the following five steps as necessary for forming, clarifying, and extending or expanding concepts:

1. Enumerating items
2. Finding a basis for grouping similar items
3. Identifying common characteristics of items in a group and labeling the group based on these characteristics; subsuming other items under the labels
4. Regrouping items and labeling new groups
5. Summarizing the information into one sentence

Klausmeier's (1985) first steps (concrete and identity) are at a more basic level than Taba and colleagues' five steps (1971), probably reflecting the classroom and curricular emphasis of Taba's work. In a classroom setting, students have attained the concrete and identity levels for many concepts; therefore students can, as a group, enumerate, group, and label related items. Some members of the group may be functioning at the identity level, while most should be at the classificatory or early formal level for concepts under consideration. The five steps outline a sequence of experiences that will enable students to move through the four levels identified by Klausmeier.

PRINCIPLES

Principles are the major organizing factor in intellectual functioning. They are necessary for interpreting and organizing phenomena in the physical and social world and for solving problems (Gagné 1966; Klausmeier 1980). Principles are generalizations in that they apply to more than one situation. However, principles describe the ordered relationship of a limited number of concepts and can be considered rules governing the relationship between these concepts. Principles are *always* applicable; generalizations are *usually* applicable. If students are to understand and apply principles, they must have experiences that allow them to derive principles as well as to apply them in a variety of situations. Facilitating the acquisition of principles by students in a classroom is an important teacher role.

Deriving Principles

A principle is formed when the learner recognizes a relationship that applies to multiple examples (Marzano et al. 1988). Evidence of understanding a principle is the demonstrated ability to make well-supported and qualified inferences in new or changed situations (Seiger-Ehrenberg 1985). Students demonstrate understanding of the principles of vibration and sound when they can make predictions regarding the effects of loosening or tightening the strings of a musical instrument. They have a mental image of the relationship between vibrations and the pitch of the resulting sound. This mental image enables them to make logical predictions and projections.

Understanding the concepts embedded in a principle is necessary but not sufficient for understanding the principle (Klausmeier 1980). Principles go a step beyond concepts in complexity and theoretical sophistication. They may require a capability to demonstrate a sequence of behavior, each element of which may involve a concept (Gagné 1966). To construct a paper airplane that will fly a maximum distance, students take the following steps:

1. Choose appropriate paper, which requires understanding the concepts of weight, size, and flexibility and the principles governing flexibility of paper and folding, as well as those governing weight and flight.

2. Fold the paper, which requires understanding the concepts of flight, lift, and aerodynamics and the principles governing shape and lift and shape and flight.
3. Test the craft, which requires understanding the concepts of observation; recording of data, speed, and time; and the principles governing weight, shape, and speed.
4. Modify the design and/or try new designs, which builds on the concepts and principles applied in the preceding steps.

This sequence of behaviors requires comprehension not only of the concepts, but also of the relationships between them—the *principles* involved.

Teaching and Principles

While Klausmeier (1980) states that students develop the understanding of principles, taxonomic relationships, and problem solving during most of their school years, teachers may have concerns about how to ensure and/or facilitate such development. Two words in the prior statement are key to such facilitation: *develop* and *understanding*. Students first must develop and expand the concepts included in and related to a specific principle, then have a series of experiences that illustrate the principle and therefore increase their understanding (Katz 1976).

If comprehension of the principles that govern interdependence were a teaching goal, the following might be included in lesson plans:

- Setting up a class ant farm, a terrarium, and/or an aquarium
- Showing films about animals in natural habitats
- Student collection of current articles on the effects on humans of dwindling fish and animal populations
- Student-generated diagrams showing on whom and what a day's food and clothing depend
- Guided discussions designed to develop key concepts, examine cause-and-effect relationships, and provide opportunities to make and support related inferences

These activities are designed to enable students to derive the principles governing the relationships between food supply and populations, plants and animals, predator and prey, and the needs of plants and the needs of animals. By building on concrete experiences, providing information, and guiding discussions so that students process the information in ways that lead to the derivation of principles, the teacher sets the stage for the sequential, inductive learning of the principles of interdependence.

CONCLUSIONS

Drawing well-founded conclusions is an important developmental step in becoming an effective thinker. *Conclusions* are inferences that go beyond the information given (Taba 1966), inferential beliefs derived from premises or prior information or conclusions (Costa 1985b; Ennis 1985a). Conclusions require the synthesizing of inferences (Maker 1982a) to produce a higher-level (more abstract) inference.

An example of asking students to infer conclusions follows. On the sudden death of the class's pet hamster, students can be asked to infer possible causes. Based on the inferred causes and their reasons, they can be asked to conclude what they believe is the most likely cause of the untimely departure. This task necessitates examining the possible causes known or suggested, synthesizing the known information, and making an inference based on previous inferences. In this example, the conclusions are removed at least two steps from the data (the physical evidence), and therefore students who respond are thinking at an abstract level.

Classrooms offer many opportunities for developing student ability to draw warranted conclusions. When teachers understand what conclusions are and the importance of the skill, they find ways to incorporate the necessary practice into the curriculum. A few examples of situations in which students can be asked to make a conclusion follow.

After a particularly successful or unsuccessful recess period (as determined by the quality and quantity of social interactions), elementary school students could be asked to (a) list specific events that occurred, (b) infer causes or effects (and provide reasons that support the inferences), and (c) draw a conclusion regarding the most important cause or effect of the success or lack of success of the recess.

At the culmination of a unit of study on Japan, students could be asked which of the elements studied has influenced Japanese culture the most (e.g., geography, historical events, natural phenomena). Students always should be asked to provide examples or reasons to support such inferences.

Middle school students might survey their peers' attitudes toward a proposed schedule or rule change. If the data indicate the majority of their peers are not in favor of the change, the students could brainstorm alternatives, ways to lobby against the change, or elements for a public relations campaign. Conclusions could be made regarding the most viable alternative, most effective lobby, or the most important campaign components.

Literature at any level offers opportunities to draw conclusions concerning characters, plots, writing style, or other elements of writing. High school students can draw conclusions about the influence of specific literary works on, for example, the Civil Rights movement.

GENERALIZATIONS*

A generalization is a broad statement that applies information gained from experiences with a limited number of phenomena to a class of phenomena in general. After two weeks in Arizona in July, a visitor might make the general statement that deserts are hot. This statement is based on a finite number of experiences and is applied to a broad category (deserts). This generalization requires classification of information (daytime temperatures, type of vegetation), understanding concepts ("desert," "hot"), and drawing conclusions ("the Arizona desert is hot in July"). Some generalizations also may require the derivation of principles. If the sample generalization had related vegetation type to temperature, deriving related principles would have been necessary.

The skill of generalizing should be a cognitive goal for students. Forming good generalizations is the most difficult of the developmental skills, but students can learn to make and recognize sound generalizations and in so doing become more effective thinkers.

Generalizations in Curricula

The use of generalizations to plan curricula provides a focus for a unit or an entire text, as well as a broad base and comprehensive approach to the planning process. However, generalizations also should play an important role for students on an individual level. As part of the process of searching for meaning in social studies, English, science, and mathematics, students need to be able to generalize from the data. Therefore, they should be given many opportunities to generalize about what they read, see, and hear and to test their generalizations against standards of accuracy and relevance.

Development of the cognitive skill of making warranted conclusions and generalizations can be brought about through the use of sequential, appropriately focused questions. Students should have opportunities to spend significant amounts of time developing their

*Unless otherwise noted, the information in this section is drawn primarily from materials developed by the Institute for Staff Development (1971a, b, and c).

own generalizations rather than concentrating on the memorization of generalizations that are the end products of someone else's thinking.

The task of making generalizations involves four basic operations (Taba, Levine, and Elzey 1964):

1. Assembling concrete information, either by recalling previously learned information or by identifying specific points from new data
2. Explaining or giving reasons for certain events, such as providing reasons for heavy immigration to the United States from certain other countries
3. Relating different points of processed information, such as comparing the proportion of college graduates who are members of ethnic minorities to those who are Anglo-American, and relating this information to socioeconomic status of the groups
4. Formulating a generalization or an inference based on the data and its processing

Students should use these steps frequently in every content area and in reference to social interactions as well. Teachers can structure individual lessons, instructional units, and impromptu discussions to incorporate the steps into the curriculum.

Helping Students Improve Their Generalizations

Criteria to use in evaluating student generalizations are inclusiveness, precision, and tentativeness. *Inclusiveness*, for example, is incorporating in a concept word as many elements as are appropriate and possible; *precision* is introducing important shades of meaning to ideas while avoiding vagueness; and *tentativeness* is recognizing inevitable restrictions on data. For example, the generalization "The usual result of increased birth rates is a decreased standard of living" is inclusive ("birth rates," "standard of living"); precise ("result," "increased," "decreased"); and tentative ("usual").

Students should become aware of the criteria for evaluating generalizations. Teachers can help their students develop effective generalizing skills in the following ways:

- Focus on one criterion at a time, such as tentativeness. Point out words such as *most, usual,* or *some* and how they make a statement tentative (and more accurate).
- Present sample generalizations, pointing out the elements that make the statements tentative and explaining why this is desirable.

- Present sample generalizations and have students restate them in more tentative ways.
- Collect generalizations made by students. At a later date, have students decide whether the statements need to be more tentative and if revisions are necessary.
- Request that students bring in generalizations from newspapers or other sources. Let the class decide whether the statements need to be more tentative and revise them if necessary.

Follow the same procedures to teach the other criteria. Encourage cumulative learning by having students consider all the criteria they know at a given time in evaluating their own and others' general statements.

CHAPTER SUMMARY

Human growth and development occur on a continuum, and cognition is part of this growth and development. The processes discussed in this chapter—classification, concept development, deriving principles, drawing conclusions, and making generalizations—are sequential and continuous. School curricula must include repeated practice in the processes, which can and should be used at a variety of levels, in different content areas, and as needed to engage in the complex thinking strategies and in solving undefined or real-life problems. The discussion and examples in this chapter are designed to help teachers provide the necessary practice and direction so that their students can become effective thinkers.

3

The Complex Thinking Strategies

No idea stands alone; rather each is part of the vast web of knowledge. No thought exists or operates in isolation; each is part of a web of dynamic and interactive processes. As Beyer (1987) reminds us, thinking is the combination of many parts and procedures, and the whole is greater than the sum of the parts.

Defining, delineating, and attempting to show relations between complex thinking strategies may be presumptuous as well as a gargantuan task. However, the purpose of this chapter is just that—to bring the reader to an understanding of the components of each strategy, how each relates to other complex strategies, and how these can be brought into every classroom. Each of the complex thinking strategies—solving defined problems, creative/productive thinking, critical thinking, evaluation, and decision making—will be discussed, with examples of classroom applications.

Teachers must understand the roles of transformation and application before they can teach complex thinking strategies, so, these components of the Spiral Model are discussed before coverage of the complex thinking strategies. The final section of this chapter is devoted to undefined or real-life problems. A rationale for their inclusion in the curriculum is suggested and examples of their application are provided.

TRANSFORMATION AND APPLICATION OF THE DEVELOPMENTAL THINKING PROCESSES

Transformation is the selection and manipulation of pertinent information and processes for a cognitive task. During transformation necessary elements are synthesized, resulting in a product unique to an individual. Identical information and previous cognitive experiences will not produce identical approaches or responses, but rather transformations that are distinctive even if similar.

Application is the step wherein the transformed information and processes are brought to bear on a complex thinking strategy. Application is the connecting point between developmental processes and complex strategies, where proposed plans, solutions, and ideas are put to work on the task for which they were transformed.

The complex thinking strategies by definition require two or more of the developmental processes for their execution. The role of transformation and application is critical: The most pertinent and efficient processes or parts of processes must be selected, blended, and applied to specific situations.

The teacher's role in the inductive approach to teaching thinking is to ensure that students have the necessary developmental processes in place *at a level appropriate for the task,* and then to ask a critical question or devise a critical learning situation. Learning activities should follow a developmental continuum of cognition in which the prerequisite skills and processes are transformed and applied in complex thinking strategies to high-level tasks. Directive teaching methods make this sequential development obvious, but it is no less necessary when using the inductive approach.

COMPLEX THINKING STRATEGIES

The complex thinking strategies require the use of developmental processes and purposeful, goal-directed thinking. Each of them also calls on one or more of the other complex strategies and is necessary for solving real problems.

Solving Defined Problems

Solving defined problems involves using the appropriate enabling skills and developmental processes to resolve a known or defined difficulty. This requires assembling facts, determining what additional information may be needed, inferring or suggesting alternate solutions and testing them for appropriateness, eliminating discrepancies in the solution, and checking solutions to determine their effectiveness (Presseisen 1985a).

Getzels (1975) delineated two types of problem situations: presented and discovered. Presented problems have a known formulation, a known method of solution, and a known solution. Discovered problems do not yet have a known formulation, method of solution, or solution. Further development of this concept led to the conceptual distinction between types of problems discussed in Chapter 1. This distinction is based on (a) how clearly and completely the problem is stated at the beginning, (b) how much of the method for reaching the solution is available to the solver, and (c) how general is the agreement about an acceptable solution (Getzels and Csikszentmihalyi 1967). Maker (1986) and the author of this text have expanded Getzels and Csikszentmihalyi's idea, suggesting two additional major types of problems, as presented in Chapter 1. An earlier figure is repeated here as Figure 3-1 for the reader's convenience.

The term *defined problems* as used here refers to problem types I, II, III, or IV. However, because Type I and Type II problems require only memorization and application of memorized steps or techniques, types III or IV will be used for examples. Type III and Type IV problems require the developmental processes and the use of (other) complex thinking strategies for their solution.

Curricula may include any problem type. Typically, however, the majority of problems students are required to solve are Type I or Type II. A page of multiplication problems to complete poses a Type I problem; answering comprehension questions at the end of a text chapter is a Type II problem.

To incorporate higher and more complex thinking with curriculum content, Type III and Type IV problems can be used. For example, students in the intermediate grades usually have some degree of understanding about the food chain and ecological systems (concepts). A problem-solving approach could be used to increase their understanding and develop their thinking abilities. A Type IV problem could be based on the following situation: "Upper Nirvana is a 200-square-mile island in the tropics. It is heavily forested and has numerous native vertebrates—birds, bats, lizards, and small mammals—but no snakes are native to the island. A small, aggressive, venomous tree snake is introduced to the island, where it has no natural enemies." The assignment could be to develop fully a pre-

FIGURE 3–1 Types of Problem Situations

TYPE	PROBLEM		METHOD		SOLUTION	
	Presenter	*Solver*	*Presenter*	*Solver*	*Presenter*	*Solver*
I	K	K	K	K	K	U
II	K	K	K	U	K	U
III	K	K	R	U	R	U
IV	K	K	U	U	U	U
V	U	U	U	U	U	U

K = Known   U = Unknown   R = Range

diction of what will happen on this island in twenty to thirty years. Each projection must be supported by evidence or reasoning, and a variety of aspects of the situation—the ecological system, wildlife, effects on people, and other dimensions—should be included. Students could be asked to present their predictions to the class.

During completion of this assignment, processes similar to the following could be expected to occur.

- The expansion or refinement of concepts of tropical venomous snakes, tropical islands, ecosystems, and food chains, as students gather information on these topics
- The derivation or expansion of the principles of predator–prey relationships
- The drawing of conclusions regarding which principles will predominate in this situation
- Generalization about the effects of introducing a foreign element into an ecosystem

Other complex strategies are required for this cognitive task, including evaluation, making decisions, and creative/productive thinking.

In this example, the curriculum content provides the context for the thinking, and the problem type determines the processes that will be used. The teacher has provided or overseen the development of a knowledge base, then asked the critical question "What do you predict will happen in twenty years?"

While open-ended problems such as this are defined problems, they allow and require the use of developmental processes and (other) complex thinking strategies. When teachers understand the concept of problem types, Type III or Type IV problems can be posed or found in every content area. In math, students can collect and analyze data, using graphs to depict the results of their analyses; in social studies locate examples of, classify, and generalize about the infusion of foreign cultures into the local community; in science investigate the impact of civilization on indigenous flora; and in language arts learn about and write samples of different types of poetry (such as sonnet or haiku). Each of these activities is based on solving a defined, but open-ended problem (Type IV). Each also requires the transformation and application of various developmental processes.

The teacher's role in problem solving in the curriculum is to check for or develop the necessary knowledge base (concepts and principles) for solving the problem, ensure that students can use the developmental processes, teach a problem-solving method, and develop the problems.

Students need experience in classification before beginning to solve open-ended problems. A solid information base and facility in the developmental processes set the stage for concept expansion, derivation of further principles, drawing conclusions, and generalizing at higher and higher levels on topics related to the focus.

Direct teaching of problem-solving steps will help students be more comfortable with their task. For example, the five steps of "Creative Problem Solving" (Noller, Parnes, and Biondi 1976) could be presented to students, used to solve an imaginary problem, posted on a chart in the room, and applied to problems that arise in the classroom. The five steps are:

1. Data finding—determining the who, what, when of the situation
2. Problem finding—narrowing down elements and factors to define the major problem
3. Idea finding—generating many possible solutions
4. Solution finding—choosing the best solution
5. Acceptance finding—developing an effective plan of action.

When the problem is defined, step 2 can be omitted; step 1 is necessary with all problems; steps 3, 4, and 5 are necessary to solve all open-ended problems.

Creative/Productive Thinking

Agreeing that the ultimate criterion of creativity is output (Perkins 1985), the author chooses to link productivity and creativity—if nothing is produced, be it an idea or a sonata, one is hard pressed to postulate the presence of creativity. Based on the work and ideas of others (Beyer 1987; Costa and Presseisen 1985; Halpern 1984; Marzano et al. 1988; Perkins 1985; Presseisen 1985a), the following definition was formulated. *Creative/productive thinking is divergent productivity, the synthesis or generation of new, original, novel ideas or products.*

Since "creative results do not just bubble up from some fecund swamp in the mind" (Perkins 1985, p. 59), educators need to find ways to encourage creativity. Beyer (1987) lists the following characteristics of creative people:

• Guided or driven by the desire to seek the original
• Value mobility
• Revel in exploration
• Require flexibility
• Honor diversity

These characteristics can serve as guidelines for creating classroom environments that foster creativity.

New, original ideas and products must be valued if creative production is to be fostered. This valuing can be expressed through the display of student products and through teacher attitudes toward and questions about unusual ideas. Additionally, students must be allowed appropriate mobility and opportunities for exploration. Flexibility and diversity must be modeled for and encouraged in students.

Another way to demonstrate that creativity is valued is to give each student an "idea trap," a blank notebook. When students have an idea that cannot be dealt with at the moment, they write the idea in the idea trap (F. A. Kaufmann, personal communication, October 17, 1988). At least once a week time should be allowed for students to go through their traps to see which ideas need more thinking about and/or which ones are ready to be shared with another person or the group. Idea traps dignify students' ideas as worthy of being recorded and thought about more thoroughly, and they allow teachers to proceed with a lesson or go on to the next activity without crushing budding creativity.

Mobility usually is thought to mean physical mobility, wherein students are moving inside and outside of the classroom. This is not always possible or desirable, but mobility of sources and ideas may be more feasible. Mobility of ideas means that new or different ideas are welcome in a classroom; the teacher and the students maintain open minds and in fact seek different opinions or information even when they have tentatively formed their own opinions. Mobility of sources entails calling on nontraditional sources of information, such as parents, grandparents, or others who have a hobby related to what is being investigated, or other members of the community who may not have excessive formal schooling, but who are knowledgeable in an area of interest.

Exploration is essential to creativity, and it is perhaps the hardest condition to provide in a classroom. However, teachers can encourage the exploration of ideas through their attitudes and through open-ended questions and activities. Also, ordinary activities can be approached in an exploratory manner, as when kindergarten students are invited to explore different colors, brush strokes, and techniques of water coloring, rather than being instructed to paint a certain object or scene. Students at all ages love exploring the world around them through hands-on science investigations. When budgetary constraints prohibit field trips, one can use films, guest speakers, and videotapes to explore topics and ideas in the classroom. The attitude of the teacher can establish a classroom as one in which learning is seen as a gigantic exploration of ideas and topics; such an attitude is contagious, and helps provide a setting for creative production.

Asking students to find a way to demonstrate to others what they have learned on a topic offers opportunities for creative/productive thinking. If students are expected, say, to share what they have learned about the effect of climate on lifestyle, they classify information about weather and climate and ways of living for a variety of areas, expand or develop related concepts, derive principles that connect certain concepts, reach conclusions, and generalize about types (categories) of climates and lifestyles. When deciding on presentation mode and medium, they will examine critically and evaluate options, make decisions, and solve both defined and undefined problems. These processes and relevant information will be transformed and selectively applied to the creation of a way to share the information. Each product will be unique, both in format and in underlying cognitive processes. The information will be processed to a greater depth (and thus remembered longer and retrieved more readily) than if the students had read textbook material and answered questions at the end of the chapter. Students usually enjoy well-planned activities that require creative/productive thinking more than they do traditional exercises, and they typically learn more as well.

The teacher's role in creative/productive thinking is to create an environment in which thinking *and* creativity will flourish. This environment includes the encouragement of divergence, mobility, flexibility, and exploration.

Critical Thinking

Critical thinking is reasonable, reflective thinking focused on deciding what to believe or do (Ennis 1985b). It involves using basic thinking skills and processes to analyze arguments and generate insight into particular meanings and interpretations; to develop cohesive, logical reasoning patterns and understand assumptions and biases underlying particular positions; and to attain a credible, concise, and convincing style of presentation (Costa and Presseisen 1985; Presseisen 1985b). Critical thinking is used to judge the authenticity, worth, or accuracy of ideas or arguments; it is objective and value-free; each component contains analysis and evaluation (Beyer 1987). People use it to solve problems, make decisions, and learn new concepts (Sternberg 1986).

The processes of critical thinking, such as raising questions, breaking complex ideas into components, drawing on prior knowledge, translating complicated ideas into examples, and making hypotheses (Heiman and Slomianko 1986) should be included in curricula at all levels. Ennis (1985b) believes that critical thinking consists of an integration of specific dispositions, such as seeking reasons or trying to be well informed, and sets of general abilities, such as thinking and speaking clearly and making inferences. He identifies three dimensions of logical thinking: logical, criterial, and pragmatic. The logical dimension is related to judging alleged relationships between the meanings of words and statements, the criterial to judging statements covered by the logical dimension, and the pragmatic to the purpose of the judgment and whether the judgment is good enough *for the purpose.*

In the statement "You can't win if you don't play" which is used to advertise the state lottery in Arizona, these dimensions can be identified thusly:

• Logical—What do the words mean? Does the statement make sense?
• Criterial—On what basis should we judge the accuracy or truthfulness of this statement?
• Pragmatic—How accurate and truthful do commercials have to be?

Students of all ages are familiar with commercial advertisements, especially those appearing on television. The examination of such advertisements provides a way to give practice in critical thinking. Students watch television, and many commercial advertisements are misleading and consist mainly of drivel. Educators can "join them" rather than "fighting them," and use the students' knowledge to learn to think critically and to recognize the advertisements for what they are.

At the elementary level, students can analyze the explicit and implicit assumptions in, for example, commercials for toys. Explicit assumptions may include assumptions such as (a) having the toy will make a child happy and (b) being the first on the block to have the toy will make a child ecstatic. An implicit assumption might be that parents want their children to be happy and therefore will want to purchase the toy.

Students also can look for evidence to support or refute claims made in the commercials and can evaluate commercials by making a judgment of their truthfulness and accuracy.

The developmental processes used include classifying various commercials into groups, developing and expanding concepts regarding the use of language and images to persuade, deriving principles of persuasive techniques, drawing conclusions about specific advertisements, and making generalizations about toy commercials overall. Complex strategies used in this critical-thinking task include evaluation, decision making, and solving defined problems.

At the middle school level, commercials advertising a specific cola could be analyzed for unstated assumptions and the validity of explicit claims (e.g., discerning people insist on this cola) and implicit (e.g., drinking cola is fun and is necessary for a good time). In the course of such an assignment, students would classify soft drink commercials based on similarities, develop concepts and derive principles related to persuasive techniques, make conclusions about such commercials, and generalize about television advertising. Such an assignment also would require the use of complex strategies such as evaluation, decision making, and solving defined problems.

High school students could examine political campaign advertisements for factual content, unstated assumptions, bias, logical fallacies, and logical inconsistencies and determine the strength and validity of the claims made. These students would classify claims and assumptions, develop and expand concepts and derive principles related to persuasive techniques, make conclusions about individuals' campaigns, and generalize about political campaigns. They also would use complex strategies such as evaluation, decision making, and solving defined and undefined problems.

The teacher's role in critical thinking is to instruct and provide practice for students in raising questions, identifying unstated assumptions, detecting bias, distinguishing between verifiable facts and value claims, determining factual accuracy and credibility of sources, identifying ambiguous claims or arguments, identifying logical fallacies, recognizing logical inconsistencies in reasoning, and determining the strength of an argument or claim (Beyer 1987). Young students can learn to examine critically statements or ideas in light of only one or two considerations. For example, primary students might focus on distinguishing between verifiable facts and value claims. Intermediate students can process three or four considerations, and high school students can learn to examine ideas or statements in light of all the considerations mentioned above.

In Figure 3-2, the Arizona state lottery advertisement, "You can't win if you don't play," is used as the basis for sample questions that might trigger critical thinking. The left column lists critical thinking skills, and academic levels are listed across the top. Sample questions appear in the space denoting the intersection of a skill and an academic level. All questions asked at the primary level also can be asked at intermediate or high school levels, and all at the intermediate level also can be asked at the high school level.

FIGURE 3–2 Critical Thinking

	COMMERCIAL: "You can't win if you don't play."		
Skill	Primary	Intermediate	High School
Raising questions		Who pays for the commercial? How are lottery monies allocated and spent?	
Identifying unstated assumptions		On what assumptions is this slogan based?	
Detecting bias		Why is this commercial aired? Who benefits most from the sale of lottery tickets?	
Verifiable facts versus value claims	How many people play the lottery? How many win?	What are the odds of winning the lottery?	What is the probability of a single ticket winning the lottery?
Factual accuracy and credibility of source		Who pays for this commercial?	
Ambiguous claims or arguments			
Logical fallacies	What do the people who made this commercial want you to think?	Is the reverse of this statement true? Why? Why not?	
Logical inconsistencies			
Strength of argument	What are reasons to buy a ticket? *Not* to buy a ticket?		How valid are the assumptions? Based on verifiable fact, how sound an investment is a lottery ticket?

Critical thinking is considered essential for democratic citizenship (Goodlad 1984); the goal of teaching critical thinking is to develop people who are fair-minded, objective, and committed to clarity and accuracy (Ennis 1985). In fact the teaching of critical thinking seems to be one of the few areas of teaching that seldom comes under fire from public education's critics. People with a well-rounded repertoire of thinking strategies are comfortable with and proficient in the use of critical thinking.

Evaluation

Evaluation is examination or judgment about the value of items, events, or phenomena in terms of external or internal criteria (Bloom 1956; Costa and Presseisen 1985). The criteria, or standards, are used for appraisal of the extent of accuracy, effectiveness, economy, or satisfactoriness. The judgment may be quantitative or qualitative, and the criteria may be developed by, or provided for, the evaluator (Bloom 1956).

Evaluation can be taught formally and informally in the classroom. Students can be instructed and given practice in developing criteria and applying them, and they also can be asked how they came to decide on particular extracurricular activities or modes of behavior. Obviously, evaluation and decision making are (and should be!) closely related. Objective evaluations are an important part of sound decisions.

Students should be asked to evaluate information, courses of action, sources of information, and their own academic progress. For example, students in the primary grades can evaluate stories they write, based on these criteria: (a) Story has two or more characters; (b) story line has a beginning, an interesting event or problem, and resolution of the problem; and (c) the setting of the story is mentioned or described.

At the intermediate and middle school level, students may be able to evaluate ideas such as suggestions for fund-raising activities. The students themselves may be able to generate criteria, such as: (a) Activity is legal; (b) activity is within the capabilities of the students involved; and (c) amount of money raised is adequate for time and effort expended.

High school students can evaluate possible college choices or occupation options. They should generate criteria, which for occupation options might include: (a) number of years of training or schooling required; (b) potential salary; and (c) job location. Applying relatively objective criteria to a decision that typically might be governed primarily by emotion may not only help students with the decision, but also illustrate a method to be applied to future decisions. Through applying evaluative strategies frequently and in a variety of different contexts, students will become adept at evaluation.

In the preceding examples, the primary students transform and apply concepts such as characters, setting, and parts of a story, and they make decisions as to whether or to what degree the story meets the criteria. The middle school students might classify activities to develop a list of possible fund raisers, expand concepts related to raising funds, and come to conclusions regarding likely possibilities. These components would be transformed to apply specifically to this evaluation task, before a decision would be made.

The teacher's role in teaching evaluation is to find the opportunities that arise within the written curriculum and everyday events for students to evaluate information, ideas, sources, plans, and behavior. Evaluation can be taught and practiced in a variety of contexts in ways that seem natural and nonacademic to students.

Decision Making

When making decisions, we use thinking processes to choose one or several options after consideration of facts or ideas, possible alternatives and their advantages and disadvantages, probable consequences, and personal values (Costa and Presseisen 1985; Presseisen 1985b). Making a decision always involves two or more competing alternatives that may or may not be obvious to the decision maker (Halpern 1984), and it may include choosing from a number of acceptable alternatives when no single, objectively correct alternative exists (Beyer 1987). Additionally, a decision may require the simultaneous evaluation of alternatives, the use of qualitative as well as quantitative criteria in analyzing the alternatives, and repeated reference to values in applying the criteria (Beyer 1987).

In a society that changes rapidly, people cannot depend on routine behavior or tradition in making decisions. In a nation whose future depends on the expressed will of the people, the capability to make intelligent and independent decisions is of paramount concern (Isham 1982). Many educators believe that decision making should be the focal point of education, along with the thinking skills that serve it and the knowledge base that supports it (Marzano et al. 1988). No matter what career or occupation is engaged in, success depends on decision-making skills and expertise (Nardi and Wales 1985). Therefore, educators should teach at least one decision-making process and provide students with academic and real-world instances in which to practice decision making.

In the primary grades, four decision-making steps can be taught:

1. State the goal or problem.
2. Consider the options.
3. Prepare a plan.
4. Take action (Nardi and Wales 1985).

As students mature, their decision making may include six steps:

1. Define the goal or problem.
2. Identify alternatives.
3. Analyze the alternatives.
4. Rank the alternatives.
5. Judge the highest-ranked alternative.
6. Choose the "best" alternative (Beyer 1987).

Decision-making steps can be taught directly and practiced in class discussions, with questions being asked to guide students through the steps. Literature and stories from the basal reader can be used as a focal situation. In the book *Old Yeller*, Travis and Little Arliss have an argument, and Travis has to decide what he is going to do. The teacher can state the goal, that Travis has to make a decision. Then, through questioning a small group or the whole class, the teacher can lead them to consider the options (What could Travis do? What else could he do?); and prepare a plan (If he decides to make friends with the dog, how can he go about doing that?). When literature or hypothetical situations are used, the goal is stated and no action is taken, so only two steps are necessary for primary students: consider options and prepare a plan. At more advanced grade levels, hypothetical situations require identifying, ranking, and judging alternatives before choosing the best one.

Students should be provided opportunities to define goals (What do you have to decide?), identify alternatives (What things *could* you do?), analyze alternatives (What might happen if you decide to use your money for a trip? Why would that happen? How is that different from what would happen if you decide to put it in a savings account?), rank the alternatives (Which of these choices do you think is the most desirable? Why? Next desirable? Why? . . .), judge the highest-ranked alternatives (How good is the decision to take the trip? Why do you say it is the best option?), and choose the best alternative (Remembering all the things we have said, what do you think is the best choice? Why?). Through a sequence of questions, students are led through the necessary steps. With repeated experience, students can internalize this approach to decision making and use it independently in their personal lives and for school-related tasks.

In the last example, students select and transform pertinent concepts or parts of concepts to apply to their thinking; make conclusions about good, better, and best choices; and generalize when they predict the consequences of various options. Each piece of information and each process is tailored, or transformed and applied, to the task at hand. Decision making includes judgment of the highest-ranked alternatives, which is evaluation; it also may include creative/productive thinking when alternatives are generated.

Students can be encouraged to use decision-making steps through informal as well as academic interactions. When students tell teachers about personal goals or opportunities, social interactions, or decisions they must make, the teachers can ask the questions mentioned above to aid the students' decision-making process. Planning class parties, outings, or projects also requires decisions and should be approached through the same steps.

The study of famous people or current events offers opportunities to practice the decision-making process. For example, President Truman's decision to drop the atomic bomb on Hiroshima during World War II can be examined in light of options, consequences of alternative solutions, and a ranking of alternatives. Students can investigate the situation and use the steps in writing a position paper or an essay or engaging in a debate, taking a stand on the "best" alternative.

The teacher's role in teaching decision making is to instruct students in the steps of an appropriate decision-making process and to help them practice consistently through reminders, guided questions, and learning situations that require decisions. The steps should be taught through direct instruction and applied across situations and disciplines and to all types of decisions (personal, interpersonal, academic, social) for maximum internalization by students. The teacher needs to check the knowledge base before students are asked to make a decision and should assist students in acquiring more knowledge if necessary. Above all, the teacher must be aware of the importance of decision-making expertise and pose learning experiences or critical questions that require students to use this strategy.

UNDEFINED OR REAL-LIFE PROBLEMS

Undefined or real-life problems are at the top of the Spiral Model of Thinking, indicating the level of sophistication and complexity of the cognitive processes required for their solution. The ability to solve problems is a prerequisite for human survival (Rowe 1985), but strategies needed to solve personal and professional problems are not routinely taught.

Students encounter a variety of problems in their lives, including (a) a need to find answers, (b) puzzling situations, (c) value-based problems, and (d) situations requiring innovation (Costa et al. 1985). The preponderance of well-structured problems in schools imposes a severe limitation on the development of student skills, because personal problems and important social, political, economic, and scientific problems are ill defined (Marzano et al. 1988). To help students cope with current and future situations, school curricula should include all types of problems, from defined problems with one correct solution to undefined problems with many possible methods of solution and solutions.

Curricula typically include many Type I and Type II problems, and the inclusion of Type III and Type IV problems already has been discussed. The following section is designed to illustrate how Type V—undefined or real-life—problems can be incorporated into the curriculum.

Type V Problems in Curricula

Developing curricula based on the solution of undefined problems requires a mindset change. Instead of thinking in terms of providing information and learning experiences that will result in the mastery of content, the teacher must become sensitive to discovering problem situations related to curriculum content. Content will be mastered through solving a related problem, but the approach is different. The mindset of the teacher who understands the five problem types and wants to incorporate Type V problems into the curriculum is manifest by this question: "What problem situations related to [e.g., the Western Hemisphere, or the food chain] have the potential to interest the students and require that they acquire the appropriate factual information?"

Some topics and grade levels lend themselves more readily to the use of Type V problems than do others. Health, science, and social studies at almost any level include numerous problem situations, while the study of mathematics at elementary and junior high school levels encompasses primarily problem types I and II. Extracurricular activities and situations are fraught with real problems, and planning class parties or student presentations also requires the solution of real problems.

An example of using a real problem to accomplish curriculum objectives follows. A fifth-grade classroom was in a particularly bad physical location. When it rained, water ran into the room and students had to walk through mud coming to and going from the classroom. During dry spells the wind blew dust into the room. The area nearby was unkempt, and grass, bushes, and trees had died from neglect. In the words of one observer, the area was the "aesthetic pits." Budget problems prohibited the school district from landscaping, making repairs, or maintaining the grounds.

The teacher assigned to this classroom viewed the unpleasant situation as a learning opportunity, a real problem that students could define and solve in a variety of ways. In response to student complaints the teacher suggested that they might want to do something about the area. The ground rules were that the budget was zero, the students were the work force, and the sky was the limit.

The students decided to hold a design contest, which required measuring the area accurately and making scale drawings. Ultimately they solicited and received from the community donations of necessary materials and a landscape architect's time. The student labor force measured, ordered pipe, and dug trenches for a drainage and diversion system. A number of decisions had to be made, such as the type of benches to use and what shrubs to plant. As plans were developed, the school principal, PTA, and the school district's engineering office had to approve them.

The solution to this problem was to create a delightful area based on the winning design, which included benches, a bricked area, and low-maintenance, drought-resistant shrubs. It is a source of pride for the entire school, and certainly for the fifth-grade class (J. A. Klipp, personal communication, February 14, 1989).

Through guided discussions, instruction, and independent and small-group investigation, the fifth-grade class (a) learned about the political structure of the school district, (b) gained understanding of basic economic principles, (c) contacted people in the business sector, and (d) developed workable solutions to problems. They classified elements of the problem and people who could help them, expanded their concepts of governmental structures, derived economic and human relation principles, drew conclusions about proposed solutions, and made generalizations regarding the relationship of property taxes and school maintenance. In defining and solving the problem they evaluated information and solutions, made decisions about actions, critically examined arguments and official positions, and were creatively productive in devising and implementing their solution.

A real problem may not exist for every concept to be taught, nor may presenting a related undefined problem situation always be possible. Teachers must become aware of how valuable undefined problems are in terms of the thinking required, learn how to use them in the curriculum, and be flexible and willing to take the risk— to seize the moment, even if it is out of sequence according to the written curriculum. If the teacher in the preceding example had waited until the district curriculum prescribed the study of local governmental structures, the students would have missed a rich learning experience and would have spent the year in unpleasant physical surroundings. Because she saw the situation as a learning opportunity as well as a way to remedy an undesirable condition, her students developed cognitively and personally. Real problems are "messy" to deal with, and certainly to include in the curriculum, but the benefits for the students are worth the extra effort.

The teacher's role in using undefined or real-life problems in the curriculum is more difficult to define than with the complex thinking strategies. Teachers need to be aware of the value of allowing students to solve this type of problem, and they need to be willing to be flexible and nontraditional in their approach to teaching. For this approach to curriculum, the attitude toward and expertise in using undefined problem situations as learning experiences become paramount. Teachers who use this approach successfully dignify students with their confidence and make learning meaningful.

CHAPTER SUMMARY

This chapter includes a discussion of the complex thinking strategies, examples of their use in the curriculum, and explanations of the transformation and application of developmental processes. Undefined or real-life problems and necessary teacher attitudes and mindset also were discussed. Using a problem-solving approach to developing curriculum is one way of incorporating higher levels of thinking into prescribed content. Problem types III and IV are adapted easily to many curriculum concepts; Type V problems are more difficult to include on a regular basis, but they are equally (or perhaps more) important to the development of complex thinking strategies.

PART TWO

TEACHING
AND
THINKING

4

Curricula for Thinking

The ultimate purpose of education is to prepare students to lead productive lives, both during and following their formal education. In this era of rapid change and proliferation of information, designing curriculum is a challenging task indeed. If productive adulthood is the goal of education, the criteria by which curricula are judged must be usefulness, practicality, and transfer. Educators must include content and processes that transfer across disciplines, are widely applicable, and are important for students to know. Additionally, teachers must be mindful of their accountability and the annual media coverage of those venerable spring rites, achievement tests.

One effect of the information explosion and other rapid changes is the need for increasingly efficient teaching and learning. Time in school must be used effectively, with waste held to a minimum and students receiving maximum benefit. One way to use time efficiently is to teach curriculum content and processes simultaneously. This is not only a judicious use of time, but may result in enhanced learning, as well.

While the author believes that all curriculum should be designed to teach both content and process objectives, she recognizes individual differences among teachers. This belief and recognition are reflected in the balance of this chapter, in which general principles for curriculum development are presented, general considerations in planning curriculum are discussed, and three approaches to planning curriculum are explained. These approaches are the content, problem-solving, and cognitive process approaches to planning curriculum. Examples of the approaches and suggestions for their use are given.

PRINCIPLES FOR CURRICULUM DEVELOPMENT

Based on personal experience, the research and literature on teaching and thinking, and learning theory, the author has formulated seven principles of curriculum development. These principles serve as the foundation of curricula, regardless of the approach taken. Readers will note repeated reference to the work of Hilda Taba in this section. While Taba's work was completed over twenty years ago, it is still theoretically sound, and the scope and comprehensiveness of the supporting research have few, if any, parallels. The statement has been made that most prominent social studies professionals stand on Hilda Taba's shoulders (Isham 1982). Her work and findings are generic and widely applicable, and curricula across the disciplines would do well to rest on the same shoulders, the same maxims, and expansions of the same research base.

Curriculum Development Principles

Principle 1. Students should learn curriculum content and thinking processes and strategies simultaneously. Many educators, researchers, and theorists believe that thinking skills cannot and should not be taught separately, that content matter is essential for instruction and practice if transfer is to occur (Glaser 1984; Marzano et al. 1988; Taba, Levine, and Elzey 1964; Taba 1966). Further, some researchers suggest that knowledge of specific content domains is a crucial dimension of development in its own right, and that changes in such knowledge may underlie other changes previously attributed to the growth of capabilities and strategies (Siegler and Richards 1982). Advances in developmental theory suggest that thinking abilities are not simply added to domain-specific abilities. Rather, competencies in a domain and the ability to think about that domain seem to develop hand in hand (Bransford et al. 1986). Additionally, recent work on problem solving done in knowledge-rich domains shows a strong interaction between the structure of knowledge and the cognitive processes used (Glaser 1984).

Principle 2. Curriculum content should be valid and significant and represent an appropriate balance of breadth and depth (Taba 1962). Content is valid and significant when it reflects contemporary knowledge in a subject matter area; the breadth and depth must be sufficient to develop the desired understanding by students. Class time is too precious to waste; content must be selected carefully, including important information with the most potential for transfer to the solution of current and future problems. In other words, the main ideas should be few and important, but combined in every way possible. Students should make these main ideas their own and understand applications in the circumstances of their lives (Whitehead 1929).

Principle 3. Facts should serve to illustrate main ideas or form concepts. Specific knowledge should be sampled and used to develop important ideas rather than just memorized or "covered" (Taba et al. 1971). The goal of this type of curriculum organization is to replace the concept of coverage of detail without reducing the essential ideas of the content, to focus on fundamental ideas while judiciously sampling details that develop these ideas (Taba 1975). Given a rapidly expanding and changing information base (e.g., changes in the names of cities or countries and scientific or technological discoveries), having students learn a set of "facts" is not a good use of instructional time. Rather, facts should be processed within large or main ideas that have wide applicability.

In 1929, Alfred North Whitehead observed that traditional schooling tends to produce *inert knowledge*, knowledge that is accessed only in a restricted context, even though it is applicable to a wide variety of domains. This situation still prevails, as evidenced by media reports of employers having to train college graduates to apply (access and use) information and processes they "learned" in school. Teaching facts separate from a conceptual structure can lead to inert knowledge, failure to access information, and poor generalization of learning (Bransford et al. 1986).

Content fields should not be viewed as hoards of knowledge to be transmitted, but as ways of understanding a limited number of basic and important ideas. Based on this view, the curriculum question becomes not what array of facts should be packed into students, but rather what basic ideas need to be understood, what questions need to be asked and answered, and how these fit into reaching curriculum goals (Taba 1962).

Principle 4. Within the curriculum, ideas or content should be sequenced in order of complexity and abstractness, and cognitive processes should be sequenced in the order of increasingly demanding intellectual rigor (Collins and Brown in press, cited in Marzano et al. 1988; Taba 1962). Learning should begin with concrete experiences and simple ideas that can be expanded to increasing levels of abstractness and complexity; thinking must develop in an orderly sequence, based on student age, experiences, and developmental level. This principle relates to schema (see Principle 5) and developmental learning theories and to research on learning.

Principle 5. Curriculum content and processes should be learnable and adaptable to student experiences and appropriate to the needs and interests of the students (Taba 1962). This principle is expressed less elegantly by the teaching adage "Take the students from where they *are.*" Student age, background, experiences, and schooling level must be considered for development of appropriate curriculum.

Theory and research underline the importance of background knowledge. Schema theory furnishes a powerful rationale for linking student background and subject area knowledge (Marzano et al. 1988). A *schema* is a modifiable information structure that represents generic concepts stored in memory (Glaser 1984). For example, elementary school students have a schema related to sharing and a "fair share." Such concepts as equality, taking turns, and sharing might be included in the related schema. When introducing the concept of division, the teacher should build on these existing schema, which will make the concept learnable, and adapt the activities to fit the students. Adaptation may include several experiences of dividing concrete objects into two, three, four, or more fair shares. After existing schema are verified, the concept of division can be expanded by adding (through experiences with concrete objects) the concept of "remainder." In this way, teachers meet the needs of students, teaching requirements, and sound curriculum principles.

Principle 6. Curriculum should be balanced to accommodate a variety of learning modes and styles (Taba 1962). McCarthy (1986) identifies four basic types of learners. Type One people learn by listening and sharing experiences, need to be personally involved in their learning, and are imaginative thinkers. Hands-on experiences, wherein students manipulate artifacts or data and discuss their observations and reactions, and simulations of real situations should be included in curricula to provide for Type One learners.

Type Two learners are abstract and reflective, and value sequential thinking and details. These students enjoy traditional classrooms and are well served by typical school activities such as lectures, educational films, and reading from textbooks.

Type Three students are theory testers. They are practical, perceiving abstract ideas and checking to see if they work. These learners need to experiment with materials and ideas, to use kinesthetics in finding which ideas to retain or expand and which to discard.

Type Four learners learn by trial and error and believe in self-discovery. They need opportunities to try things for themselves and modify their ideas according to their experiences.

Students in any classroom represent degrees and combinations of these learning styles. If each student is to have meaningful experiences, curricula should include activities and approaches that accommodate these differences. A variety of activities also helps motivate students and keeps learning interesting.*

Principle 7. An evaluation plan should be designed as an integral part of the curriculum. This principle is applicable whether the curriculum includes an entire year's learning or one instructional unit. Evaluating student progress and the effectiveness of materials and activities is critical to effective teaching. Often evaluation either is omitted, "tacked on" as an afterthought, or left to a standardized test. Designing the evaluation when the curriculum is written helps the teacher clarify the relationship between the learning objectives and the planned activities. Evaluation procedures should yield information that exposes gaps in student knowledge or abilities and assists the teacher to be more effective with these students and when teaching a similar unit or group in the future.

Developing curriculum or adapting the curriculum that exists in textbooks requires dedication, time, and guidance. The seven principles outlined here provide the guidance; the dedication and time will be provided by inspired teachers everywhere.

PLANNING CURRICULUM

Every teacher plans curricula, both formally (instructional unit plans) and informally (impromptu activities that fill an immediate need), and all teachers have customary procedures they use when planning. Certain steps facilitate the planning of learning activities that incorporate principles of sound curriculum development and meet specified objectives. Use of the following elements and procedures increases the likelihood that resulting curricula will meet designated goals and objectives.

Planning Generalizations

A *planning generalization* is a broad and abstract statement of the key ideas or concepts to be taught. It provides an overarching structure for curriculum; the key concepts are the supporting columns, and the supporting facts and details are the bricks and mortar. The

---

*The reader is referred to McCarthy 1986; McCarthy and Leflar 1983; McCarthy, Leflar, and McNamara 1987; and McCarthy, Samples, and Hammond 1985 for further information on accommodating student learning styles in the curriculum.

generalization gives definition and direction to the mastery of the important concepts, which are supported by pertinent facts and details. Planning generalizations should be inclusive and comprehensive, and preferably interdisciplinary. They establish the parameters of instructional units and enable the teacher to see and help students make connections between related ideas or elements, to conceptualize the "big picture."

A generalization such as "Animals, plants, and human beings are interdependent, within and across species," for example, might be formulated to include important concepts from social studies and science texts. This generalization is interdisciplinary, because the concept of interdependence spans several disciplines; it is inclusive, as indicated by categorical words such as "animals" and "plants"; and it is abstract due to the inclusion of the abstract concepts of "interdependence" and "species."

This generalization includes teaching concepts such as the following:

- Family roles and responsibilities
- How families meet their basic needs
- Organization of communities
- Trade between communities, states, and nations
- Organization of government and social services
- Food chains
- Ecological systems
- Environmental balance

Figure 4-1 contains a diagram of the structure of social studies and science curriculum that might be developed based on the interdependence example. The generalization at the top of the figure is the overarching theme that unifies the learning. Basic concepts are under the generalization and are enclosed in a solid oval. Under these are subconcepts, enclosed within smaller ovals, and facts, enclosed in solid rectangles. The facts of the disciplines are the foundation of the curriculum; the generalization offers an organizational structure for planning interdisciplinary curriculum.

When a teacher has formulated or internalized a good teaching generalization, each concept taught will be presented as part of an integrated whole, because the generalization pulls concepts together in the teacher's mind. Learning to develop and use teaching generalizations requires hard work and practice. However, once the habit is formed, teaching becomes more effective and teachers find they cannot conceive of planning curriculum any other way.

FIGURE 4–1 Diagram of Interdisciplinary Curriculum

GENERALIZATION: Animals, plants, and human beings are interdependent within and across species.

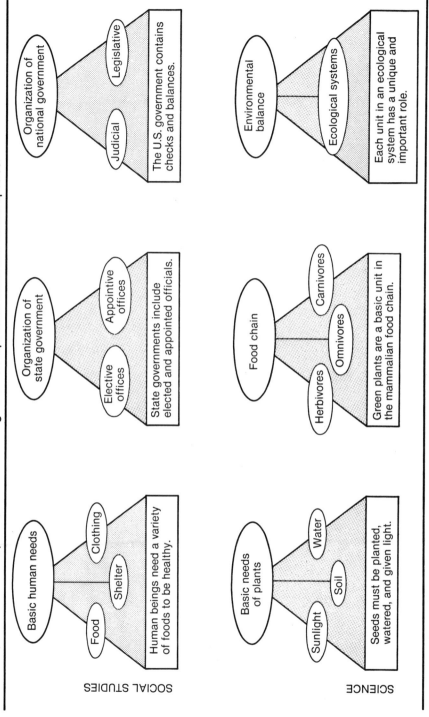

Some, but not all, textbook series provide a conceptual organization or scope and sequence of the text contents for the teacher. When none is provided, teachers can use the important ideas to develop a teaching generalization that will guide their curriculum planning. For example, the teacher's editions for *Principles of Science* (Charles E. Merrill Publishing Company, 1983) do not offer a conceptual organization or scope and sequence chart. However, a teaching generalization can be developed. The second book of the series devotes two units to the human body and health. By selecting key concepts and important issues from the text, one could develop the generalization "Human health and well-being depend on internal systems and external factors. Healthy practices are based on knowledge and informed choices."

People on Earth: A World Geography (Scott, Foresman and Company, 1983) does not include a conceptual organization chart for teachers. However, examining the table of contents reveals that a number of the chapters can be clustered to form a conceptual teaching structure. If the concept of cultural patterns was determined to be important, details and facts about the cultures of the United States, Europe, Asia, and Africa could be used to support the concept. The following generalization might be formulated as an overall teaching structure: "Human cultural patterns are affected by climate, heritage, history, and geographic factors. Cultures are different from and similar to each other." This generalization provides guidance in selecting facts and details about each culture, as well as suggesting appropriate processes (generalizations about cause–effect relationships) to be included.

In *Our Regions* (Holt, Rinehart and Winston, Publishers, 1983), lists of concepts for each unit are included, but no overall conceptual organization is given. However, some of the unit concepts lend themselves to expansion. For example, "People's lifestyles and occupations are determined by the climate and landforms where they live" is listed as a unit concept. A teacher could develop a generalization such as "Human culture is related to environmental factors." A sampling of facts and details about several regions and peoples quite different from each other provides the knowledge base. From this base, related concepts can be developed, enabling students to generalize about the effects of differences in land and climate on the way people live and work.

The syllabus for a secondary literature class might be structured based on the generalization "The written word may take many forms, each with differentiating characteristics, purposes, and form. Mood and intent may influence choice of form." To develop the concept of what differentiates a novel, short story, or narrative poem from, for example, a sonnet or a historical narrative, students could sample various types of literary forms and identify similarities and differences. Teaching from this generalization provides a thread of continuity that may enable students to see connections between different literary forms.

Using planning generalizations such as the examples given here as a way to organize curriculum requires knowledge and practice. However, the benefits to student learning and teacher satisfaction are significant. Once educators master the technique, they wonder how they ever managed to teach without this organizational aid to the conceptualization and implementation of curriculum.

Evaluation

When the approach to a unit and the content and process objectives have been selected, a plan for evaluation should be developed. Questions to guide evaluation include the following:

- What factual information should students acquire, and how will this be measured?
- What thinking processes are to be learned or practiced, and how can these be evaluated?
- What level of expertise (e.g., in scientific processes) should be demonstrated, and how will this be ascertained?

The most common form of evaluation in schools is a written test or examination. Questions on such tests should be open-ended, requiring higher levels of thinking *and* facts, details, or reasoning to support answers.

With instruction, guidance, and consistent standards of excellence to strive toward, students can demonstrate mastery of information and thinking processes and/or strategies. For example, a graph of survey results presented to the class can include the questions asked in the survey, explanation of the graph, conclusions about the data, and support for the presenter's conclusions. Student- and teacher-developed criteria can be used by the teacher, students, and peers to evaluate the product. Other possible products include essays, models, dramas, demonstrations, monologues, and a written or oral stance on an issue, such as a position paper or a debate.

The advantage of designing the evaluation procedure before teaching the unit is in helping the teacher to clarify what is to be taught and how it can be taught most effectively. Being aware of this direct relationship may help teachers reach unit goals.

A Planning Matrix

A matrix or grid can be used to check for the inclusion of critical elements of curriculum. Figure 4-2 is a partially completed matrix based on one of the examples used for a content-based approach to planning curriculum. In this matrix the teaching generalization appears at the top, and important concepts and science processes are listed under "Teaching Objectives," along the left side of the matrix. Learning activities are listed in the second column, adjacent to the concept they teach, and necessary thinking processes or strategies used in the activities appear in the third column. In the final column are listed the sources of data for evaluation, but no specifications as to how the data will be used. The science processes students will use during the activities are marked with a check. The matrix is not complete; concepts 2, 3, and 5 have not been planned. Learning activities and ways to gather evaluative data need to be formulated for these concepts.

Individuals may devise simple systems that use numbers, checks, or symbols to indicate concepts, activities, processes, and evaluative measures. The importance of the planning matrix is that it provides a visual way to check for gaps in content or process development and for the gathering of evaluation data for each objective. The blank matrix given in Figure 4-3 can be duplicated and used as an aid to planning.

APPROACHES TO PLANNING CURRICULUM

"As individuals acquire knowledge, they also should be empowered to think and reason" (Glaser 1984, p. 103). This statement captures the essence of the philosophy of various educators, researchers, and the author of this text. From this philosophical base, several organizational strategies for developing curriculum are possible. Three of these approaches, the content, problem-solving, and process approach, will be discussed. Each offers the integration of content with thinking processes and includes problem solving. They differ primarily in their approach to planning the curriculum.

A Content-Based Approach

Content-based curriculum planning usually is based on district-adopted textbooks. Therefore the examples in this section are based on texts from several publishers. An attempt has been made to provide examples at a variety of levels.

FIGURE 4–2 Curriculum Matrix
TEACHING GENERALIZATION: Living things are interdependent with one another and their environment.

TEACHING OBJECTIVES	LEARNING ACTIVITIES	THINKING PROCESSES OR STRATEGIES USED	EVALUATION
Concepts 1. Needs of living things	Grow plants; experiment; classroom pets; personal pets; survey of experts; classification/naming class discussion; presentations	Classification, concept development, conclusions, generalization, decision making	Student logs and graphs of plant growth; amount of useful information from experts; taped class discussion; self-, peer, teacher evaluation of presentations
2. Interdependence of living things			
3. Relationship of living things to environment			
4. Characteristics of green plants and their role in the food chain	Classification discussion, individual & group observations, making charts	Classification, concept development, generalization	
5. Causes and effects of extinction			
Science Processes 1. Observation ✓ 2. Compare/contrast ✓ 3. Investigation ✓ 4. Exploration of relationships ✓ 5. Seeking evidence ✓			

FIGURE 4-3 Curriculum Matrix Form

TEACHING GENERALIZATION:

TEACHING OBJECTIVES	LEARNING ACTIVITIES	THINKING PROCESSES OR STRATEGIES USED	EVALUATION

To develop or adapt curriculum content, generalizations or conceptual patterns to be taught must be identified or developed. Many textbook series include these as part of the scope and sequence provided near the front of the teacher's manuals. For example, *Concepts in Science* (Harcourt Brace Jovanovich, 1980) includes six conceptual schemes that are taught at the six elementary levels. Conceptual Scheme D is "Living things are interdependent with one another and with their environment." At Level II the concept to be taught is "Living things depend on their environment for the conditions of life." Four units in the text are related to this concept: *Plants—Alive and Growing, Animals—Alive and Growing, Caring for Plants and Animals,* and *Caring about Living Things.* In the content-based approach to planning curriculum, one unit can be planned to develop the fundamental ideas, with details of each unit being sampled to support the important ideas. The fundamental ideas of the four units include the following:

1. Needs of living things
2. Interdependence of living things
3. Relationship of living things to their environment
4. Characteristics of green plants and their role in the food chain
5. Causes and effects of extinction

The scientific processes suggested in the text include the following:

1. Observation
2. Making comparisons and contrasts
3. Investigation
4. Exploration of relationships
5. Seeking evidence

All of the developmental processes and most or all of the complex thinking strategies can be incorporated with the content of a unit based on these ideas and processes.

As an introduction to a unit on living things at the second-grade level, students could plant various seeds in containers in the classroom or a small garden plot and keep logs of observations of the growth and development of the plants. When these plants are mature, a nature walk could be taken to observe and collect, if possible, other plants or parts of plants. Following this, the teacher could lead a class discussion in which characteristics and parts of plants are listed, classified based on similarities, and names developed for the categorical groups. This classification and naming activity will develop concepts of plant structure and possibly plant function (e.g., food for horses, cows, people). At this time the teacher might choose to instruct students on scientific names for types of plants and plant parts.

A focus on animals could complement the focus on plants. Keeping appropriate animals in the classroom, and asking students to enumerate responsibilities related to the care of family pets would build a knowledge base on animal needs.

At this point the teacher could ask the class how they can find out what plants and animals need to be healthy (Type IV problem). The group might suggest experimenting with growing conditions for plants and asking experts for information regarding animals. (This suggestion might be made right after animal experimentation is ruled out!) Small groups then could design experiments on plants and questions to ask experts (e.g., veterinarians, pet store owners, breeders) regarding the needs of fish, cats, dogs, rodents, and reptiles. The groups should share their survey questions and ideas and plans for experiments with the entire group before implementation.

Students conducting plant experiments should develop or be given a structure for observing and recording experimental conditions and results. Those collecting information on animals might tape record interviews, or draft a willing adult to take notes on responses.

When each group has gathered its data, the groups need to compare and contrast their information, inferring possible reasons for differences and making conclusions about the most reliable or valid sources (critical thinking). Each group should present a synthesis of its investigation results to the entire class. If students are given support and parameters but not specific directions, designing the presentation can be a Type V problem. Such a task requires evaluating, selecting, and developing the format and media of the presentation.

If students, classroom conditions, or teaching style prohibit a substantial amount of small-group work, films and/or filmstrips can be used to provide information. The entire class can watch these, with half of the class being responsible for becoming "experts" on animals and the other half "experts" on plants. Directed discussions, group or individual charts, and graphs can be used to illustrate similarities and differences, comparisons and contrasts, conclusions, principles, and generalizations related to living things.

After students have gathered information from other sources, they might be directed toward pertinent sections of their science textbook, to see how their findings compare to the book. They may discover, as have others before them, that the text offers a predigested diet, giving answers rather than raising questions, and presenting organized thought rather than stimulating them to think (Taba 1962). If so, they may conclude that books are only one, and sometimes not the best, source of information.

Similar activities and approaches can be developed to teach and explore further the fundamental concepts 3 through 5 and scientific process 4.

Most classroom teachers use a content approach to planning curriculum, since textbooks, achievement tests, parents, and administrators usually are concerned with the acquisition of information. The content approach should incorporate thinking processes and strategies into the teaching of content and should include problem solving. This approach merely means that the content is selected first, and the thinking processes and problem-solving experiences are chosen according to the structure of the content. The processes and experiences selected are those believed to be most likely to result in student mastery of prescribed content.

Problem Types as a Way to Structure Curricula

In the problem-solving approach, every curricular experience can be seen as a Type I, II, III, IV, or V problem, and an effort is made to include all five types of problems in the curriculum. To refresh the reader's memory, Type I problems are presented to the student, and the method of solution is known by both student and presenter; the (one) correct solution also is known to the presenter. An example of a Type I problem is instructing students in the formula for finding the area of a rectangle, then asking the area of a rectangle when $a = 3$ and $b = 4$. The primary mode of thought for Type I problems is memory and retrieval (Getzels 1975). A formula is applied to a problem similar to the exemplar; this is a low level of application and it does not require the transformation of processes or information.

Type II problems are presented to the student, and an accepted method of solution and correct solution exist. To continue with the preceding example, students might be asked, without prior instruction, how to go about determining the area of a rectangle. The primary mode of thought required for Type II problems is reason or convergent thinking, in addition to memory and retrieval (Getzels 1975). The thinking is convergent because it must result in arriving at the accepted method and (correct) solution.

Type III problems are presented problems, and they have known, most acceptable, or ranges of correct solutions. However, several methods of solution are possible. Posing a Type III problem related to the area example might involve asking students how they might find the area of a parallelogram that is not a rectangle. The students do not have the accepted formula and may devise a variety of ways to reach the correct answer. Solving a Type III problem requires hypothesizing (generalizing) possible solutions, trying them out, evaluating the results, and making decisions.

Type IV problems are presented, but the method(s) of solution and solution(s) are unknown to presenter and solver. An example of a Type IV problem is asking students what important questions might be asked about the area of geometric figures. Type IV problems require the same processes as III—hypothesizing possible solutions, trying them out, evaluating results, and drawing conclusions and/or making decisions.

Type V problems are actually problem situations; the problem, method of solution, and solution are unknown to presenter and problem solver. Asking students to pose an important problem about a rectangle and to solve it is a Type V problem. Students must sense or imagine the unidentified problem in the situation, formulate the problem, attempt to develop solutions (Getzels 1975), evaluate results, and draw a conclusion and/or make a decision.

Generally, the problems used to teach students to think do not correspond well with the "real world." In the real world, the first and sometimes most difficult step is the recognition that a problem exists. Solving problems already identified and posed does not train students to find, select, and define problems on their own. Everyday problems are harder to define than to solve, are ill-structured, lack clear information on what additional knowledge is needed or where to find it, frequently are unclear, and have solutions that depend on and interact with the problem context. Additionally, everyday problems generally do not have one right solution, and the solutions have consequences that matter (Sternberg 1985a). These characteristics of real-life problems contrast starkly with the problems commonly found in textbooks and school curricula, where the problem is clearly defined and presented in isolation from other similar problems or a meaningful context, one acceptable solution and one answer exist, and the consequences of solutions are most closely related to grades.

A problem-solving approach to developing curriculum begins with the problem types and fits the content and processes to be taught into a problem-solving format. School curricula typically consist primarily of Type I problems. However, Sternberg (1985b) believes that unless the thinking required and the problems solved in school reflect the realities of everyday problem solving and decision making, students will not apply what they have learned to their lives. This belief implies the need for problem types II, III, IV, and V in the curriculum.

An example of curriculum planning from a problem-solving approach follows. At the middle school level, a Type IV problem could be used to teach the concept of different values among people in different periods of time (Taba et al. 1971). The question "How can we find out what people valued or believed important in Ancient Greece, Colonial America, and contemporary United States?" defines the problem. The problem has been posed, but the methods to be used and the resulting data are as yet unknown to teachers and students.

In this example the process objectives will determine what is done with data that are gathered. For example, information about the values of different societies could be used to refine classification behaviors; develop concepts about values, periods of time, or relationships between the two; and derive principles, draw conclusions, and/or generalize about societal values. If developing evaluation strategies is a goal, students could develop criteria and evaluate the values of the various groups.

Solving Type V problems is an important aspect of student education, but real-life problem situations are not always compatible with curriculum content objectives. Therefore, teachers need to be alert to potential problem situations their students are interested in and may be able to solve. As alluded to earlier, student presentations at the culmination of an instructional unit may be Type V problems, if the parameters are very general, such as "Find a way to share what you have learned." Planning classroom celebrations; devising classroom rules; or dealing with playground, cafeteria, library, or classroom situations can become Type V problems. For example, the noise level or degree of waste in a school cafeteria troubles many youngsters. Given the opportunity, guidance, and support, they can define the problem, investigate the causes, and propose and evaluate solutions, implementing the most workable.

While problems such as cafeteria situations may not seem related to academics, math and writing skills are inherent to many investigations and solutions, and other content area skills can be tapped, as well. Students tackling the problem situation of school cafeteria waste need to devise some measure of the waste, and perhaps compute the dollar amount indicated. Developing (and writing) questions for surveys and interviews to obtain the perspective of cafeteria workers, custodians, students, teachers, and the principal sharpen communication (language arts) skills, as will presenting a proposed solution to appropriate administrators.

Most teachers agree philosophically with having students solve real-life problems but are concerned about taking time from content areas. The key is to recognize not only the value of the problem-solving processes, but that of *applied academics* within a real context.

No mention has been made in this chapter of problem-solving heuristics. Space prohibits the examination of various problem-solving techniques, but the author suggests that teachers become familiar with and use consistently one heuristic, such as Parnes's (1981) Creative Problem Solving or other, similar methods. A body of research supports the use of problem-solving techniques, but none exists regarding the sequential use of problem types. Based on arm-chair logic, a sequential approach (Type II, then III, IV and V) is defensible as offering increasing degrees of openness and complexity. However, teachers may prefer to be more random in the selection of problem types and to let situations and content or process objectives determine the order of problem types.

Teachers can use the problem-solving approach to provide for a wide range of abilities in a classroom. Types III, IV, and V offer opportunities for slow students to work at a comfortable level and gifted or high-achieving students to conceptualize and produce at levels commensurate with their ability.

The problem-solving approach to curriculum can be used by those who find it innately appealing and a good match with their teaching style, those who believe that teaching problem solving is a primary goal of education, or those whose students have an especially broad range of learning needs and abilities. As with other approaches to curriculum planning, the principles for curriculum development should form the foundation, and the content and the thinking processes to be learned should be an integrated whole that fits into the problem-solving format.

A Process Approach

A process approach to curriculum planning begins with process objectives; that is, one or more developmental processes or complex strategies to be taught. Content that fits best with the designated thinking objectives is selected, and learning activities are designed accordingly. Problem solving may be used as the context for some of the activities.

For example, kindergarten teachers might want their students to become proficient at classification. Initial tasks should be simple, using attribute blocks or similar concrete objects. Students can be instructed to classify by specified shape, color, size, or thickness

(Type I problem). Later, students can group buttons, objects from the teacher's desk, or even classmates on the basis of some similarity (Type IV). Other possibilities include objects that sink/float, leaves, animals, or pictures. After repeated practice, some students may be able to classify abstractions, such as stories they have heard, according to whether they have animals, machines, or people as characters, or as "funny," "scary," or "happy."

At the intermediate level, learning to generalize is an important achievement that can be accomplished best if practiced in various content areas and settings. General statements should be asked for when students have accumulated some knowledge from which to generalize. This may be at the end of a class discussion, the culmination of an instructional unit, or whenever available information can be used as a basis for a generalization. For example, after learning about several types of heavenly bodies, students could be asked to make a general statement about bodies in space. Additional sources for generalizing can be found in math—common fractions or decimal fractions; in social studies—regional differences; in language arts—communication; after recess—student behavior; or after a teacher's absence—the effect of having a substitute teacher or the effects of student misbehavior when a substitute teacher is in charge. Forming a generalization does not require exhaustive information, merely a sample or variety of details that can be synthesized to become the basis for a general statement.

At the secondary level, if students are not adept at critical thinking, a teacher might plan curriculum to develop this strategy. In any content area, students could be required to examine critically and evaluate the logic of information, sources, or viewpoints.

The examples provided here do not imply that kindergartners cannot think critically or that high school students do not need practice in classification. As stated previously, advanced maturation and experiences require and make possible executing the same processes or strategies at increasingly sophisticated levels. Students of all ages should have experiences with all the developmental processes and the complex thinking strategies *at the level of their development*. Increased facility will come through repeated practice with increasingly abstract and complex content; growth will result from new applications that require students to stretch.

Teachers who use the process approach as their primary approach to planning curriculum include teachers of classes for gifted students, where higher thinking levels are program objectives; resource teachers who are designated as thinking strategy specialists; or any teachers who want to emphasize processes.

As with the content and problem-solving approaches, the process approach to planning curriculum integrates content with the thinking processes and may include a conscious effort to vary problem types. This approach is different from the other two merely in the point of departure; the process objectives are the first consideration, with content being selected based on its suitability for teaching specific processes.

CHAPTER SUMMARY AND CONCLUSIONS

The purpose of this chapter is to illustrate for practitioners how the Spiral Model applies to curriculum. Drawing on literature, research, learning theory, and personal experience, the author proposes seven principles of curriculum development and discusses critical components of and steps for planning curriculum. Three approaches, the content, problem-solving, and process approach, are suggested as ways to frame curriculum development. The examples provided are at various levels, and they incorporate the curriculum development principles.

Reading *Aims of Education* and other essays by Alfred North Whitehead published in 1929; books, chapters, and articles by Bruner and Taba from the 1960s and 1970s; and articles currently appearing in newspapers and magazines makes one feel that education has progressed little or not at all in this century. Students still are expected to memorize and repeat the results of others' thinking, and educators still are calling for reform, pointing to a changing world and its as-yet-unknown needs.

This chapter, however, is offered to the eternal optimists that most educators appear to be. It brings together what the author knows and believes about curricula, and it is presented with the hope that education is on the threshold of changes that will benefit individual students and society as a whole. May the readers take the principles, the approaches, and the examples and meld them into revolutionary teaching practices that promise a brighter tomorrow.

5

Questions as a Teaching Tool

Overwhelmingly, questions are named as the most frequently used teaching technique, both in the classroom as initiated by teachers, and in textbooks (Carin and Sund 1971, 1978; Chaudhari 1975; Dillon 1982; Feldhusen and Treffinger 1980; Taba, Levine, and Elzey 1964; United States Department of Education 1986). Questions not only are used frequently, but they also are viewed as singularly effective in promoting knowledge acquisition and in developing the higher levels of thinking (Feldhusen and Treffinger 1980; Gallagher, Aschner, and Jenné 1967; Hunkins 1968, 1989; Manson and Clegg, Jr. 1970; McKenzie 1972; Taba, Levine, and Elzey 1964). Not surprisingly, effective questioning is equated with effective teaching (Chaudhari 1975). Socrates is noted for asking questions to induce thinking and to lead the learner to new discoveries (Carin and Sund 1978), but questioning was a common teaching technique even before Socrates (United States Department of Education 1986).

Belief in the importance of questions and the ability of teachers to learn and implement improved questioning and discussion techniques provides the rationale for this chapter and the next. The information herein is designed to provide the rationale and principles that will motivate and enable teachers to move away from mind-shrinking questions. Such questions set students up to say exactly what the teacher wants them to say, rather than inviting invention, discovery, and the creative use of previous knowledge (Taba, Levine, and Elzey 1964). To this end, a sampling of research on questioning, principles of effective questioning, questions in the curriculum, and student questions will be discussed.

RESEARCH ON CLASSROOM QUESTIONS

Mary Budd Rowe (1974a, 1974b), who coined the term "wait-time," conducted an extensive study of classroom discussions that spanned six years. This study was initiated to discover the reason for the disappointing quantity and quality of inquiry generated by students in elementary science programs. Teachers with a strong science background were as unsuccessful with these programs as those who had less training in science. Initial observations indicated that, regardless of training, the patterns of teacher questions and student responses were remarkably alike; the typical interchanges resembled an inquisition rather than a joint investigation or reasonable conversation. Analysis of a set of 300 taped classroom discussions revealed that teachers were waiting an average of 1 second after asking a question before reasking the question or calling on another student, and allowing only 0.9 second after a student response before reacting or asking another question (Rowe 1974a).

An analysis of over 900 taped discussions conducted by teachers trained to wait for 3 to 5 seconds following questions and after student responses showed changed values on ten student variables (Rowe 1974b):

1. The length of response increased.
2. The number of unsolicited but appropriate responses increased.
3. Failures to respond decreased.
4. Student confidence (the lack of which is indicated by inflected responses signaling a question on the part of the student) increased.
5. Incidence of speculative responses increased.
6. Incidence of child–child comparisons of data increased.
7. Incidence of evidence-inference statements increased.
8. Frequency of student questions increased.
9. Incidence of responses from students rated by teachers as relatively slow increased.
10. Variety of type of student responses increased.

Servo-chart plots of classroom discussions showed that students typically speak in bursts, with 3 to 5 seconds between bursts being fairly common. (A servo-plot charter consists of an instrument that marks paper as it rolls by, in response to sound or other phenomena.) A wait-time of 0.9 second after a student response or unanswered question apparently prevents completion of thoughts (Rowe 1974a).

Further, Rowe (1974b) notes that in classrooms where the teacher engages in frequent positive reinforcement, verbal performance of students was negatively influenced, even when significant wait-time was allowed. Studying reward patterns revealed the following (Rowe 1974b):

- Overt verbal rewards constitute as much as one-fourth of the total speech output of some teachers.
- Task persistence was greater where overt verbal rewards were fewer.
- Students who function at relatively lower levels generally received more verbal rewards than top students, but the pertinence of the rewards tended to be unclear.
- Students functioning at lower levels received more negative sanctions than students at higher levels.
- When overt verbal rewards are high, three student behaviors that are indicative of low confidence are exhibited more frequently. These behaviors include (a) eye-checking with the teacher (seeking affirmation), (b) inflected speech (asking rather than telling responses), and (c) shorter task persistence.
- The number of alternative explanations was markedly reduced.

A number of researchers report that higher-level questions facilitate the development of the higher cognitive processes in students (Batson 1981; Hunkins 1968; Hyram 1957; McKenzie 1972; Taba 1966; Watts and Anderson 1971). In addition, the average student who encounters a predominance of higher-level questions during instruction will score at the 77th percentile, in contrast to scoring at the 50th percentile when higher-level questions are not emphasized (Redfield and Rousseau 1981).

Gallagher, Aschner, and Jenné (1967) and Taba (Taba, Levine, and Elzey 1964; Taba 1966) analyzed taped classroom discussions of trained and untrained teachers. Based on tapescripts and observations, they conclude that even a slight increase in the percentage of higher-level questions yields a large increase in the student level of production. When teachers ask questions that require students to process information and to make inferences, conclusions, or generalizations, the students learn and practice these cognitive operations.

PRINCIPLES OF QUESTIONING

Based on the literature, research, personal experience, and taped classroom discussions, Schiever (in preparation) developed ten principles of questioning. These generic principles can be applied to all content areas, classroom and playground problems or situations, and informal interactions between teachers and students. Questions that incorporate these principles require students to think, and strategies or techniques based on these principles can aid the development of thinking processes and strategies. The principles are as follow:

1. Questions are focused.
2. Questions are open-ended.
3. Questions require the use of information.
4. Proof or reasoning questions are asked.
5. Wait-time is allowed.
6. Discussion is appropriately paced.
7. Individual student responses are accepted without teacher comment.
8. Student responses are not repeated by the teacher.
9. A variety of ideas and student interaction are sought.
10. Clarification and extension questions are asked as needed.

Written or Oral Questions

The first four principles apply to both written and oral questions; the last six apply to oral questions, especially in the context of discussions. The following principles can be used as a guide when developing questions that require the use of information to formulate a response.

Questions are focused. The focus sets in motion a particular type of thinking operation (Taba, Levine, and Elzey 1964) and establishes the content parameters for responses. During a discussion, a *refocus* question may be required to bring the attention of the group back to the original focus. The following example from a taped discussion led by a trained teacher (T) illustrates the use of an initial focusing question and a refocus after a somewhat lengthy student (S) response to a clarification question:

T: All right, from the research we've done, and what you know already, what are some elements of architecture?

S: Arches

S: Lintels

S: Columns

S: Design

S: Site

T: How is the site an element of architecture?

S: Well, that's where something sits, I mean you can't build anything . . . you have to have a place to put the building.

T: OK, and what are some other elements of architecture?

By contrast, an untrained teacher may not set a clear focus for the discussion, as in the following example:

T: OK. Today we're going to talk about values and the value things that you made the other day, the steps to happiness and the keys to happiness, OK? Uh, what is a value first of all? Let's just kinda review that.

S: We didn't make them yesterday.

T: We didn't make what yesterday?

(Several students make comments.)

T: Anyway, what is a value? Yes.

S: Well, it's just like something that's important to you or something about you.

T: Something that's important to you or something about you. OK. Do all people have the same values?

Group: No! (Loudly)

T: OK. What things do you think affect people's values? What things, how do people, uh, get to have values, where do they get their values from?

S: Their personality and their situation.

T: Personality, situation, OK. That's true. If values are things that are important to people, and they get them from their situation, could somebody give me some more examples, or places, or—where do you get values from?

Notice how the untrained teacher has asked what is a value, how do people get values, and where do people get values from, all in a short period of time. The focus is not clear, and the scattered student responses reflect this. Identifying and keeping in mind the purpose of the question will help teachers formulate clear focus questions.

Questions are open-ended. Open questions have no predetermined right answer, and they cannot be answered by "Yes" or "No." Asking questions with one correct answer builds convergent minds—minds that look for simple, "right" answers and assume that "rightness" depends on authority rather than judgment. An open-ended question allows for spontaneity and responses in terms of individual perceptions (Taba, Levine, and Elzey 1964); students at a variety of cognitive levels may respond comfortably and appropriately to an open question. Examples from taped discussions follow.

T: If Peggy did decide to talk it over with her teacher, how do you think the teacher would react?

While this question asks students to infer behavior, even low-functioning students can respond. The openness of the question invites a variety of responses, all of which may be equally acceptable. Continuing with the tapescript of the untrained teacher, we hear the following:

T: All right, "having a good friend" is a value. Uh, is that something that you would say is universal? Universal means all, everywhere, whether you live in the United States or whether you live . . . what kind of value is that? Do you think it's universal?

Questions that require factual answers (one right answer) or that can be answered "Yes" or "No" are necessary when establishing the existence of a knowledge base or, at times, for clarification (Did you mean . . . ?). However, as illustrated by the preceding tapescript, responses to closed questions do not require thinking. As happened in this discussion, students frequently see a question like "Do all people have the same values?" as rhetorical and not worthy of individual responses. Frequently, yes/no questions set up a situation in which students merely try to guess what the teacher wants to hear. Obviously, they have a 50-percent chance of being right without thinking, which makes guessing easier—and learning and thinking minimal.

Questions require the use of information. If students are to develop complex thinking strategies, they must use the developmental processes regularly, at increasing levels of abstractness and complexity. Questions that elicit factual responses require only recall of information; higher-order questions call for higher-order thinking. The following excerpt from a taped discussion contains examples of questions that require the use of information.

T: What do you think might have caused them not to want him around?
S: 'Cause he was different.
T: What else might cause someone not to want someone else around, even in another situation?
S: If they didn't like him.
S: They think he's (unintelligible).
S: Or maybe they didn't want to get his opinion on something.
S: Or maybe they were jealous of him.

The teacher's questions ask students to make inferences about why the other animals did not want the Ugly Duckling around and to apply previously made generalizations about why people might not want other people around. Information must be processed to formulate appropriate responses to the questions.

Proof or reasoning questions are asked. When students make inferences, conclusions, or generalizations, they should be asked for support, which may take the form of factual support, examples, or the reasoning they engaged in. Many times people make and express an inference without examining their reasons for the inference. When asked to verbalize these reasons, they clarify their thinking, add to the group's body of knowledge, and build an awareness of the diversity of thinking in the group. In a group, several people may reach the same conclusion for different reasons; support responses illustrate this, and thus develop cognitive flexibility and openness among students. The following discussion contains examples of support questions and responses:

T: I would like to look at a couple of these solutions that you suggested. What do you think would happen if Travis did try to sell the dog?

S: I think that little Arliss would be a crybaby and everything and his mom would also, his mom would also be real mean to him, because it's little Arliss's dog.

T: Why do you think Arliss would cry?

S: Because he likes the dog, and he thought it was his, thinks it's his.

T: Why do you think Mom would be mean to him?

S: Because it's little Arliss's dog, and he didn't have a right to sell it.

T: What other possibilities are there if he sells it; what happens?

S: He could sell the dog to others and the dog would run away and come back to them.

T: So you think eventually the dog would come back. Why do you think so?

S: Well, Arliss might love the dog a lot and the dog would want to be with him.

T: Tim, what do you think would happen if he sells the dog?

S: (unintelligible)

T: Why do you think that would happen?

S: Well, uh, Travis (unintelligible).

T: What do you think would happen, Tracy, if he sells the dog?

S: Uh, Arliss will probably never speak to him again.

T: Why do you think Arliss would do that?

S: Because he'd be really mad that Travis sold Old Yeller. He loved the dog a lot.

The preceding support questions elicit a variety of viewpoints and types of reasoning. When teachers consistently ask for support of inferences, students begin to offer the support as part of the initial statement, without being asked. This offers another opportunity for teachers gradually to reduce their role in the discussion while developing autonomy in the students.

Many students have never been asked "Why" except when they were in trouble or "wrong." Therefore, the teacher must prepare them before beginning discussions in which "Why" will be asked as a matter of course. Something as simple as: "During our discussion you will find that many times when you respond to a question, I will ask you *why* you gave that answer. The reason I will ask is so all of us can understand how you figured out your answer or why you think that is a good response. When we share our thinking with each other, our discussions will not only be more interesting—we will all be getting smarter!"

The manner in which support is sought is critical. Asking "Why" in a deliberately low-key manner will usually lift the threat. However, if students seem apprehensive, the question could be worded as, "How did you decide to put those things together?" or "Tell us more about how you chose those things for the same group."

Discussions and Oral Questions

Wait-time should be allowed after asking questions and after student responses. As a student in one of the tapescripts pointed out to his teacher, "You ask a question, and I just start thinking about it, and you call on someone, and I stop thinking my idea. I still have ideas from way back there—I wish you would slow down!" An excellent way to ensure wait-time is to tell students, "In a minute, I am going to ask you (e.g., what the effects of the Chernobyl disaster were). Be thinking until I am ready to ask you." Or, if it works for you, take Dillon's (1988) suggestion, and sing "Baa, Baa, Black Sheep" in your mind every time you ask a question, to help develop the wait-time habit.

Some of the teachers whose tapescripts were used for examples in this chapter waited 15 or 20 seconds after questions or responses. Extended wait-time does not produce students who are squirming and being noisy; conversely, most students seem to be thinking, and the classrooms are relatively quiet.

When asking questions that require the processing of information, you must allow time for this processing to occur. Short- and long-term benefits in student learning and levels of thinking depend on waiting a minimum of 3 to 5 seconds after questions and student responses before refocusing or calling on another student.

Discussion is appropriately paced. The pace of a discussion is related to allowing wait-time, but also to "lifting" the discussion to a higher level when the current level has been explored sufficiently. A discussion that is too rapidly paced loses students by eliminating a satisfying level of exploration. Equally lethal, however, is the discussion that is too slow; attention will wander when a discussion lags or "over-explores" levels or issues. Pacing a discussion for maximum student interest, participation, and learning requires practice. Listening to and analyzing tape recorded discussions they have led help teachers develop a fine-tuned sense of pacing.

Individual student responses are accepted without comment by the teacher. This principle is directly opposed to the training many teachers received. As Rowe (1974b) observes, over one-fourth of some teachers' utterances are intended as positive reinforcement for their students.

However, evidence indicates that verbal praise is not conducive to thinking, a variety of responses, expanded or elaborated responses, or responses from a variety of students. Most students think that teachers are looking for *the* correct or best answer. When a teacher praises a response, the other students may stop thinking about the question, believing that the teacher has obtained the answer that was sought or that their response would not be as good as the praised one. As verbal rewards from the teacher increase, so do inflected, or questioning responses (Rowe 1974b). In their eagerness to give the answer the teacher wants, students try to guess at the response that will get praise. Praise for individual responses reinforces the idea that the teacher is the ultimate authority on the worth of ideas and information. It may prohibit or cut off other possible responses, and it becomes a mechanical, superficial, and meaningless habit.

Teachers can support students by listening, asking for expansion and clarification, and encouraging them to say more or to add to another's idea; by accepting ideas as neither good nor bad, but simply worth listening to (Trezise 1972). Accepting and *listening* to student responses is reinforcing. An analogy can be made between a teacher's verbal reinforcement of individuals and a cocktail party conversation, where one may chat with a person who pronounces one's every utterance as "super," "terrific," or "great." Most people far prefer conversing with someone who actually *listens* and accepts what one says, and shows interest by asking questions for clarification or elaboration. An interested audience is flattering and reinforcing.

Many teachers have trouble with the idea of accepting "wrong" ideas without correcting them. Teacher corrections of oral responses reaffirm that the teacher is the final authority on knowledge. A more student-centered approach is to record or accept the incorrect response and allow the students to find their own and each other's errors. Finding errors is a good way to learn, and students begin to realize their responsibility for their own learning.

If a response is so incorrect that the teacher feels uncomfortable accepting it, an explanation or reasoning may be solicited. If the response is very different from the discussion focus, it can be written in a different place if data are being recorded on the chalkboard (or jotted down if responses are not being recorded). The teacher can tell the student that this answer seems a bit different, so it's being written in a different spot, and it will be returned to later. At a later time, perhaps in a one-to-one situation, the teacher can ask the student for clarification, a source, or the line of reasoning related to the "incorrect" response, and help the student with any misconceptions that exist.

While praising an individual is not recommended, praising the entire group builds group rapport and allows the teacher to reinforce good thinking and extra (group) effort. When enough data have been listed or the time has come to "lift" the discussion to a higher level, stopping and commenting on the group's work can provide closure for this step and an emotional lift to take to the next one. Comments such as "Look at what a nice list of data we gathered" or "You all are doing super thinking today. I am impressed with the ideas you have mentioned!" make all the students feel good without labeling one idea or response better than others. Group praise or reinforcement also encourages group cooperation and supports the notion that ideas can be the result of the group working together.

Student responses should not be repeated by the teacher. While some questioning and discussion techniques include the component of teacher repetition of student responses for clarity and focus, this author does not recommend the practice. Generally speaking, when teachers repeat a response, they engage in (often unconscious) editing. Substituting even one word can make a difference in meaning; the teacher has reframed the idea in his or her terms. Accepting student responses implies that they are accepted *as is*; rephrasing changes the intent and may be seen as a putdown whereby the teacher's "better" word or idea is substituted for the student's.

If students know that everything their classmates say is going to be repeated by the teacher, they can become lazy listeners. They find it pointless to listen to each other when the "official" version, the truth according to the teacher, will soon be forthcoming. Repeating responses also takes time that could be used for student thinking and speaking. Dignify student responses by listening and by insisting that others listen to them.

Seek a variety of ideas and encourage student interaction. Many times serial responses are strikingly similar; "cow," "horse," "sheep," and barnyard animals will be named ad infinitum. When student responses fall into a pattern, variety should be sought by the question "What *completely different* (e.g., animals are found in North America)?" This question works wonders, and helps provide a variety of responses in discussions. The following tapescript contains an example of a variety question:

T: What would cause someone to hate you for your beauty?
S: Jealousy.
T: OK. Why would you say that would be true?
S: Because it's something you don't have and you want it.
T: What else would cause someone to hate you for your beauty?
S: If you don't have everything other people have, you might hate them for having all that stuff.
T: OK. We've mentioned jealousy several times here. What completely different idea do you have of why someone would hate you for your beauty?
S: Fear.
T: How would that work, that fear would cause them to hate you?
S: Well, like they might be afraid that because you were so beautiful you would have all the friends, or all the money, or, uh, even, like all the power.

Variety also is important for examining multiple aspects of an event, situation, or phenomenon. For example, if a group is discussing the effects of changes in China's communism, both negative and positive effects should be mentioned. At times the teacher may need to say, "So far we have mentioned only positive (or negative) things that would happen. What are some possible negative effects of these changes?" Frequently a group will tend to dwell on either negative or positive consequences or predictions, but even the most positive occurrences have negative aspects, and vice versa. Therefore teachers should always guide students to consider both.

Student interaction is important during discussions and other activities designed to develop thinking. As students become increasingly autonomous and realize they are somewhat responsible for their own learning, interaction is probable. Students can learn a great deal from each other; they can share their store of factual knowledge, their experiences, and their thinking processes.

Interaction is encouraged through seating arrangements that allow students to see each other during a discussion, by wait-time after student responses, and by teacher questions. Questions to encourage interaction include the following: "What similarities do you see between your answer and Jack's?", "Lupe, your comment is quite different from Susie's. How would you respond to her statement?", or "You placed yourself just to the right of Albert on the continuum. What made you decide that you were less in favor of keeping wild animals in zoos than he was?"

Clarification or extension questions should be asked as needed. When students use a word that others may not be familiar with or one that is open to differing interpretations, or when they do not express themselves clearly, they should be asked to clarify their response. Clarification questions include: "What is an example of . . . ?", "What do you mean when you say . . . ?", or "Please explain what you mean by . . . ." The following are examples of clarification questions from two tapescripts:

T: What do you notice happened to the Ugly Duckling when he got around other people or other animals? (focus question)

S: Well, they got mad at him and did things, that they kicked him and did some things.

S: They did some of the rejection things we were talking about last week, about hatred stuff.

T: What specific things? (clarification question)

S: Uh, ignoring him, or making him feel very uncomfortable.

T: What specific things did they do that made him feel uncomfortable?

S: Well, they told him how ugly he is and they, they just wouldn't notice what he *could* do.

T: Jason, what do you think will happen if he sells? (focus question)

S: If he sells it, he'll feel bad that he did it, and he might (unintelligible).

T: Travis will feel bad? Or Arliss will feel bad? (clarification question)

In the first example, the clarification questions are asked to elicit specific information, while in the second the student is asked to identify the person to whom he is referring. These teachers were alert to general and unclear statements and they asked questions to help the listeners understand the speaker's meaning.

Extension questions ask students to extend their own or other's responses, to build on ideas that have been mentioned. Predictions and inferences of causes and effects lend themselves to easy extension by the individual or by others. Questions such as "What else might happen?", "What do you predict would come about *after* this occurred?", or "What would cause . . . , that Josie mentioned?" encourage extension.

Clarification and extension of responses are two additional ways to dignify student responses. They require that teachers listen carefully and be mindful of the discussion purpose; responses chosen for expansion and extension should be those with the most potential for accomplishing this purpose.

QUESTIONING STRATEGIES AND THE CURRICULUM

Classroom questions prescribe the parameters for learning and determine whether students will learn content only, content and thinking skills separately, or content and process simultaneously. The use of higher-order questions in discussions, learning activities, and for evaluation offers a way to approach curriculum with the intent of integrating the teaching of curriculum content and process. Learning activities and evaluative measures are dealt with in the remainder of this chapter; Chapter 6 is devoted to discussions as part of the curriculum.

The United States Department of Education (1986) reviewed more than 61,000 questions in teacher guides, student workbooks, and tests for nine history textbooks and found that more than 95 percent asked for factual recall. If teachers want students to have repeated experience with answering high-level questions, they must not only master oral techniques, but also learn to modify textbook questions. Existing textbook learning activities and evaluative measures can be converted from low to higher levels by applying three of the principles of questioning: open-endedness, processing information, and examples or reasoning. Content, or factual information, can be learned and evaluated using activities and questions that incorporate these principles.

Learning Activities

The specific purpose or learning objective(s) of textbook activities frequently is not stated; therefore it must be inferred. For example, in *Our World* (Holt Social Studies, 1983), the following enrichment activity is suggested:

Have students make a chart with three headings: Tribal Traditions, British Traditions, and Influence of the Modern World. Have the students make entries concerning the development of Nigeria under each heading. (p. T229)

As presented, this exercise sets forth a classification task as a Type I problem. In other words, this task provides students with a format indicative of some adult's cognitive structure, which means that students will simply recall or look for the appropriate entries for each category. This is low-level cognition, and long-term retention of the information is not likely.

A modification can be developed, based on the inferred purpose. The content purpose seems to be for students to understand the effects of particular elements on the development of Nigeria. The process purpose may (or should) be the refinement of classification behaviors and developing concepts related to the content purpose (influence of elements).

The activity could begin with a concept development discussion (see Chapter 10) or a short discussion based on the focus question "What things we have learned about have influenced the development of Nigeria?" The data generated could be grouped, based on similarities, and labels generated for the groups. Students could be instructed to choose three of the labels to use as headings for a chart, and to use remembered information and source materials to complete the chart. This task presents a Type IV problem that not only requires classification, but also offers concept development and possible opportunities for drawing conclusions.

This activity is open-ended, because students can choose their labels and many "right" ways to complete the chart are possible. Information must be processed when labels are generated and when decisions are made regarding categorizing elements. If one or more of the elements related to the three designated headings is not mentioned and the missing element is seen as critical to student learning, the teacher could develop an interpretation of data discussion (see Chapter 11) on the effects of the element(s) not covered.

Proof or reasoning should be required when students create labels for group ("Why is that a good name for that group?") and can be asked for in support of the categorizations on the charts.

The following activity appears in *Physical Science—A Problem Solving Approach* (Ginn and Company, 1979).

The text has a photo of permanganate diffusing through a beaker of water. These questions appear next to the photo: How would you explain what you see here? What would be your hypothesis? (p. 312)

These questions are open, require the use of information, and require students to make generalizations. However, the activity has the potential of being more interesting and resulting in more learning with modifications.

The content purpose appears to be the development of concepts related to solubility and diffusion. The process purposes may be to apply existing generalizations ("How would you explain . . .") and to hypothesize. Additionally, students could explore cause-and-effect relationships, draw conclusions, and make (new) generalizations.

First of all, demonstrations are preferable to photographs; actual investigations should be conducted whenever possible. This activity could be expanded by demonstrating the dissolution and permeation of several powdered substances, possibly in water of varying temperatures. More experiences provide increased data on which students can base conclusions and generalizations. Whether students observe the permeation of one substance in water of varying temperature or several substances in water of similar temperature (Type III problems), an interpretation of data discussion (see Chapter 11) would lead them to examine causes or effects, draw conclusions, and make generalizations. The focus question could be "What specific things did you observe happening when we put permanganate in water?"

The activity is open-ended and requires the use of information as it appears. Examples or reasoning could and should be asked for ("Why do you think . . . ?", "Why do you hypothesize that . . . ?", "What is an example of . . . ?"), even if demonstrations and a discussion are not included. Including demonstrations and a directed discussion will increase the amount of higher-level thinking students must engage in, as compared to the original activity.

At this point, the reader may be thinking, "But I don't have time to do all of that for one activity; if I did, I would never finish the book!" This is true, and it supports the suggestion in Chapter 4 that teachers choose the most important concepts and principles and find ways for students to learn them by processing the content, rather than "covering" the book. Think about the many facts you memorized in school, such as the capitals of the fifty states, the counties of the state you resided in, or all of the U.S. presidents. How many of these do you remember? On the other hand, consider some investigation, field trip, speaker, simulation, or other experience that required you to process information *that you still remember today*. Students learn more from exploring a few concepts in breadth and depth than from memorizing the facts presented in a textbook.

Two examples of raising the level of textbook activities have been given; thousands more are possible. The examples were selected to illustrate that modifications can be made to activities that require only a low level of thinking or those that require moderate levels of information processing. To modify activities, the content and process purpose must be identified; these purposes indicate how best to incorporate or increase open-endedness, use of information, and examples or reasoning.

Evaluation

The infamous "End of Chapter (Unit) Review" or "Skill Check" typically is a list of questions asking for the recall of facts, frequently details (Type I problems). Glancing at the answers in the teacher's edition provides a clue as to the depth and comprehensiveness of the questions. For example, the following answers are provided in a teacher's manual: 1. Yes. 2. Yes. 3. Shallow water. 4. Shallow water. 5. Ahead of. 6. Ahead. 7. (Definitions and examples of (a) reflection, (b) refraction, and (c) Doppler effect) (*Holt Physical Science*, 1982, p. 92 TE). What (factual knowledge) students have learned can be determined and evaluated in other ways.

Selected questions from a *Moon Canyon* (Scott Foresman Reading, 1982), comprehension check (Type II problems) follow:

1. What was the "Grand Adventure"?
2. How did the adventure turn out?
4. Was more time spent getting ready for the La Salle II expedition or on the trip?
5. Did more of the La Salle II expedition take place in winter or in summer?
10. If you had been a member of the La Salle II expedition, which parts would you have liked best and least? (p. 475)

The correct answer for Question 2 is "Success," and the teacher's manual states that answering this question requires conclusions and interpretive and evaluative skills. The author finds it difficult to believe that these processes or skills are required to term the expedition a success. This example of information in a teacher's manual is included as a caveat; rarely does providing a one-word or short-phrase answer to this type of question require higher levels of thinking. Suggestions for modifying these questions follow.

The purpose of the quiz on the La Salle II expedition apparently is to check on reading comprehension. Question 10 is open-ended and requires some evaluative components; however, it should include asking for reasoning ("Why would you like those parts best and least?"). The following task presents a less detailed but comprehensive check of student knowledge as well as a requirement for the use of evaluative strategies.

Develop three to five criteria to evaluate the success of the La Salle II expedition. Based on these criteria, evaluate the expedition. Include the reasons you chose the criteria and specific examples to support your evaluation. (Type III problem)

Once again, students are asked to create their own cognitive structure for specified information. The content purpose of a comprehension check and the process purpose of evaluative strategies are accomplished through an open-ended task that requires the use of information and examples or reasoning. Requiring students to support responses with specific examples offers an opportunity to check on knowledge and the appropriate use of knowledge in evaluation. Additionally, students are able to demonstrate what they have learned without having either to memorize all the facts or try to guess which facts the teacher finds most important.

At the high school level, literature texts include questions that require more than rote memory, but room for improvement still exists. The text *English Literature* (Ginn and Company, 1979) contains the following questions about a sonnet by William Shakespeare and "Song" by John Donne. (The questions are numbered here for the convenience of the reader in the discussion that follows.)

1. With what words does he refer to his poetry in this sonnet?
2. With what kind of "monuments" is his poetry contrasted? Why are these monuments impermanent? (p. 152)
3. What, therefore is the foundation of the poet's assurance that he and his wife can never really be parted? How does he express it in the last two lines of the poem? (p. 154)

The purpose of these questions, which pose Type II problems, appears to be to assess the students' understanding of the poetry, especially specific phrases. This purpose could be served and other process purposes included by asking questions such as the following.

1. (Support question to follow the response to Question 1) Why do you think he uses these particular words? (Type III problem) or How effective are the words he uses? Why do you think that? (Type III problem)
2. (Extension question) How permanent is poetry? Why do you think that is so? (Type III problem)
3. (Evaluative question) How effective do you find the final two lines of the poem? Why is that? (Type III problem)

Generally speaking, texts seem to "spoon feed" students, breaking information down into small pieces and asking narrowly focused questions that direct them toward one correct answer. Adding open-endedness and the use of information and requiring examples or reasoning widen the scope and increase learning and thinking.

Many texts offer matching exercises or multiple-choice questions as evaluative exercises. In *Understanding Our Country* (Laidlaw Brothers Publishers, 1979), students are provided eight causes and effects of the French and Indian War and asked to match them. In *Gateways to Science* (McGraw-Hill Book Company, 1983), students are to match parts of plants with descriptions of the appearance or function of the parts (Type I problems). In *City, Town, and Country* (Scott, Foresman and Company, 1983), multiple-choice questions are offered to assess learning about rules, as follow:

1. Rules help people a. gather food b. make laws c. get along together.
2. The laws in a community are the rules that a. people don't like b. everyone must follow c. can be broken (p. 124) [Type II problem]

Matching exercises frequently become little more than guessing and process-of-elimination games, and the answers to multiple-choice questions can be terribly obvious, or arguable. A different approach to learning activities and assessment and evaluation exercises is needed. As detailed previously, the purposes of the activity or exercise should be identified, and these purposes should dictate the structure. In the preceding examples, changing the type of problem presented through discussions of causes and/or effects (see Chapter 11), researching one event and tracing its causes or effects, discussions of causes and/or effects of rules, a classroom simulation, or labeling the parts and functions of real plants would add at least two dimensions to the evaluation of student learning: interest and thinking processes.

As with any skill or practice, modifying the questions and activities provided by texts takes time and effort, and teachers have a multitude of demands on their time and energy. However, the excitement with learning and student growth that result make it worthwhile. And, as with anything, practice adds speed, and soon the task will not seem, nor be, unmanageable.

Student Questions

The mark of intelligent people is not what they know, but the questions they ask to find out about what they do not know. The thoughtful, thought-provoking question is a forgotten entity until someone asks one. Then those who hear the question marvel at its depth and perceptiveness and wonder why *they* did not think of it.

A student's question is the perfect opening for teaching (Dillon 1988), and what is learned in most instructional situations depends on the activities and *the questions* of the student; the question may be the primary tool by which individuals process information (Hunkins 1976). Learning to ask discerning questions should be a planned part of an education, yet Dillon (1988) found that of 721 students in twenty-seven classrooms, a *total* of 8 students asked a question. Further, teachers asked eighty questions per hour, while all students combined asked two per hour.

If student questions provide openings for teaching and determine the learning that occurs, teachers need to encourage students to ask questions and to nurture effective questioning skills. Some suggestions of ways to help students become more proficient at questioning follow.

First, students must know their questions are welcomed and valued. One good way to welcome student questions is to listen and attend to them (Dillon 1988). An interested audience is reinforcing for child, adolescent, or adult. In classrooms where teachers respect and value student questions, such questions proliferate and demonstrate increasing sophistication.

Modeling is an important teaching technique; behaviors we model are assumed by our students. Asking questions that require them to think, that have a clear purpose, and that visibly get results is an effective way to develop student questioning skills. The consistent use of such questions in academic, social, formal, and informal interactions with students is essential. The teacher needs to demonstrate that such questions are effective in all realms, and are not merely an academic behavior.

To encourage and dignify student questions, on the first day of school or during the first class, ask students for three questions they have about the topic, class, or school year (written, if they are old enough). List or collect these questions; distribute a copy of the list to the class. If possible, base recitations, discussions, learning activities, or tests on these or other student questions (Dillon 1988).

Before beginning a unit of study, viewing a film, hearing a guest speaker, reading an article, taking a field trip, or hearing a lecture, brainstorm questions students have. After filling the chalkboard, as a group decide which questions are most likely to produce the most helpful or greatest amount of information. Analyze a few to determine what makes them valuable questions. List these characteristics of helpful questions in a prominent location.

For a change of pace in evaluating learning, provide complex and comprehensive "answers" on a topic and require students to make up questions that match the answer (Type III problem). Formulating questions for one-word or short-phrase answers requires only memory; comprehensive and/or complex answers require more thinking. An example of such an activity follows.

Answer: Geothermal heat is a factor, as is the thickness of the Earth's crust in the specified area. Additionally, the underlying structure of the Earth plays a part.
Possible Question: What geologic conditions are related to the presence of volcanoes, hot springs, and geysers? (Based on *Science Reader Skill Builder,* Book 5, 1982, Readers Digest Educational Division)

The task for students is to formulate a question that fits the answer and to provide the connection between the question and the answer. If students disagree with information in the answer, they can find evidence that the answer provided is incorrect.

Students should be encouraged to ask questions to secure needed data or elicit inferences that can be compared with their own (Taba et al. 1971). The game "Twenty Questions" can be used to develop related skills. When five or ten minutes are left before the end of class, play a quick game. Think of an animal, vegetable, or mineral, and instruct students to ask questions that can be answered "Yes" or "No" to obtain information that will enable them to figure out what "it" is. After the twenty questions are used or when "it" is identified, ask students to determine questions that were particularly helpful in gaining information, how the questions could have been improved in general, and what questions could have been asked to provide salient data.

When students are relating a problem from their social or personal lives, ask them (individually or in a group) what questions they need to have answered to reach a decision. Or, in conflict situations, ask for and list the questions that must be answered before an equitable solution can be devised.

In short, if we want students to ask good questions, we must focus on questions in curricular and extracurricular contexts. This can be accomplished by modeling and incorporating the concept of asking useful questions in academic, social, and personal situations.

CHAPTER SUMMARY

Questions are important to learning, and teachers can learn to be more effective question askers. Principles of good questioning can be applied to oral and written questions, learning activities, and student assessment and evaluation. With practice and guidance, teachers can learn to adapt textbook questions and activities so they require students to process information rather than relying on rote memory. As teachers internalize the principles of good questioning, they naturally will model good questioning behavior for students.

The students not only will ask the teacher questions that require processing information, but they will ask each other this type of question, and the resulting thinking and learning are exponential.

6

Classroom Discussions

For many years a poster displayed in the college of education of a large western university carried the message: "Knowledge dispensed daily. Bring your own container." While the poster was intended as a joke, many teachers approach teaching as an "open up their heads and pour in the knowledge" task. This attitude reflects their own experiences as students and their teacher education and training. Teachers have been conditioned to consider themselves the conveyors of information and the answer givers (Taba, Levine, and Elzey 1964). However, some people believe an inverse relationship exists between how much teachers talk and how much students learn (Barnes 1989).

If students are to make meaning of their world through developing their own cognitive structures and are to become autonomous, lifelong learners, they must become information seekers, askers of questions, active participants in their learning. Classroom discussions can be the catalyst for and the learning ground wherein students develop such attitudes and skills. The term *classroom discussion* usually is interpreted as meaning a discussion in which the entire class is expected to participate. However, classroom discussions, planned and impromptu, can and should occur between two students, within cooperative learning circles or other small groups, and in larger and whole-group settings. Discussions should be tailored to fit teaching style, learning needs, and the concepts to be learned. Just as students learn to accomplish other learning tasks within small groups, so can they learn to participate in meaningful, structured, semistructured, or free discussions in such groups.

The purpose of this chapter is to assist teachers in planning and implementing classroom discussions that empower students to be the creators of their own knowledge systems. The purpose, planning, implementation, and evaluation of such empowering classroom discussions will be presented.

THE PURPOSE OF CLASSROOM DISCUSSIONS

When we talk about what we have done and observed and argue about what we make of our experiences, our ideas multiply, are refined, and finally lead to new questions and experiments (Rowe 1974b). If students are denied opportunities to talk about experiences and observations and to argue about meanings, they are deprived of significant cognitive development and meaningful learning. Discussions should assist students in understanding and lead to forming new questions and trying new ideas.

The general goal or purpose of classroom discussions is to facilitate the interaction of students in a way that contributes to the acquisition of knowledge, the development of thinking processes, or both. Subordinate purposes, or discussion objectives, may include the following:

- Motivate students or spark interest in new topics.
- Establish (or list) the existing pool of knowledge.
- Share perceptions or interpretations of intake experiences.
- Expand or build on the knowledge base.
- Develop thinking processes.
- Emphasize important points or aspects of ideas.
- Synthesize information (as in a culminating activity).
- Resolve conflicts.
- Develop solutions for problems.
- Assess the development of thinking process development in a group setting, which requires less time than assessing each individual separately.

TYPES OF DISCUSSIONS

Classroom discussions can be categorized according to their purpose or by the amount of teacher control necessary to achieve the purpose. Discussions may be loosely structured and free-wheeling, requiring little teacher direction; moderately controlled; or highly structured, with the teacher monitoring and guiding the direction and progress. Taba and colleagues (1971) identified three types of discussions, based on teacher control; these will be examined.

Free Discussions

Free discussions are used for opening a new topic and require little direction except for the initial focus. These discussions may involve listing problems, ideas, or facts. Personal spontaneity should be encouraged, with no evaluation of responses (Taba et al. 1971). The teacher may want to list ideas from free discussions on butcher paper for future reference, either during the unit of study or on its completion. The list can be used as an indicator of strengths and weaknesses to guide teaching, as a profile of student interests, or as a baseline for comparison. Saving and using a list generated during a discussion demonstrate a student-centered attitude and will not go unnoticed by students.

After students list related ideas, problems, and knowledge, they can generate a list of questions. This list can help motivate students and give direction to the unit of study. A format of "known, unknown, ideas, and problems" can be used if structure is desired or if students seem to need some prompting.

A free discussion should be short. The list and questions can be developed and recorded, and a promise made to return to the topic at a later date. Nothing is accomplished by dwelling too long on this task.

Brainstorming is a type of free discussion that encourages creative and flexible thinking. The purpose of brainstorming is to generate a large number of ideas on a topic, record them, and allow for and encourage "hitch-hiking" on the ideas of others. A critical aspect of brainstorming is withholding evaluation. Students should be reminded that during a brainstorming session, no idea is too wild or crazy—evaluation comes later, but for now all ideas are worth mentioning.

Semi-Controlled Discussions

As indicated by the name, a semi-controlled discussion is loosely structured. Its purpose is the exchange of ideas after a period of information intake. Students may have read, visited, or explored something and the teacher may want to establish the existence of a common knowledge base or want the students to integrate the new information. If small groups of students have gathered information independently, the sharing should be loosely structured; that is, the teacher can ask a focus question such as "What did your group learn about the threat of extinction to giant panda bears?" The purpose of the discussion is merely to share information, so clarification and extension questions may be asked as needed, but no preestablished sequence of questions will be used.

The teacher might develop a chart for comparing and contrasting information from a free discussion on the chalkboard or, for older students, provide a format and have them record the information to be compared and contrasted (Taba et al. 1971). At the close of this type of discussion, the students can be asked for a synthesis, summary, or tentative conclusion based on the information reported.

Controlled Discussions

Controlled or structured discussions have three phases, each with a different function. *Initiation* is the first phase, and its function is to arouse students' interest and get them involved in the discussion. An opening question that is clearly phrased and open-ended sets the tone for the initiation phase (Cornbleth 1977).

The *development* is the body of the discussion. During this phase, ideas are elaborated, refined, compared, evaluated (Cornbleth 1977), classified, and developed, or pertinent principles are derived. In a successful discussion, the body is a logical extension of the initiation.

The final phase of a discussion is a phase of *conclusion*, synthesis, or generalization (Cornbleth 1977). The first two phases form the basis for the third; when plans are made, conclusions reached, or generalizations drawn, they will be only as sound as the development allows them to be. From first phase to third, a structured discussion must proceed in a logical and developmentally sound manner if discussion purposes are to be realized.

In controlled discussions the students' cognitive processes are directed by a carefully planned sequence of questions. The purpose of a sequence of questions is to establish a particular sequence of steps in processing data or developing ideas. If the data or ideas are related to curriculum content and objectives, the discussion combines curriculum content with thinking processes. In controlled discussions, students supply the data and then process them in response to questions posed by the teacher (Taba et al. 1971). Such discussions need a structure such as that of the Hilda Taba Teaching Strategies, or other models such as Bloom's Taxonomy of Cognitive Objectives (Bloom 1956), Kohlberg's Moral Dilemmas (Kohlberg 1971), Krathwohl's Taxonomy of Affective Objectives (Krathwohl, Bloom, and Masia 1964), Taylor's Multiple Talents (Taylor 1986), or Williams's Strategies for Thinking and Feeling (Williams 1986). The use of a model provides a sequential or, as in the case of Taylor's and Williams's models, a systematic structure for a discussion.

The objective of classroom discussions is to encourage students to become more autonomous in their thinking and less dependent

on the teacher. A curriculum that stresses active learning and thinking processes and strategies includes a significant number of discussions. If student autonomy is to be developed, questions, or the
"seeking" functions of teaching, are vastly more important than the
"giving" (Taba et al. 1971), or telling, functions.

PLANNING CLASSROOM DISCUSSIONS

Detailed information on planning discussions based on the Hilda
Taba Teaching Strategies can be found in chapters 10 through 13 of
this text. The guidelines discussed here are general considerations
for planning controlled discussions.

Discussions are valuable following virtually any student intake
of significant information. Field trips, films, speakers, reading, experiments, or demonstrations are intake experiences on which discussions may be based. Before planning the discussion the teacher
needs to consider the amount and type of intake information, materials (such as reading matter or writing materials) that will be used
immediately preceding or during the discussion, and physical arrangements for the discussion.

The discussion structure or model should be selected based on
content and process objectives. For example, to develop the concept
of the seasonal and annual changes on Earth (*Concepts in Science,*
Harcourt Brace Jovanovich, 1980, Concept Level III), the Taba concept development strategy would serve to develop the concept and
the classification behaviors of the students. To teach toward the
objective of knowing the characteristics of forest regions (*The World
and Its People,* Silver Burdett Company, 1984) and their effect on
surrounding regions, the Taba interpretation of data strategy could
be used. Bloom's Taxonomy (Bloom 1956) could be used as a structure to evaluate issues implicit in content areas, such as the relationship of the greenhouse effect to world famine. Krathwohl's
Taxonomy (Krathwohl, Bloom, and Masia 1964) provides a structure
for exploring the affective component of content, such as the use of
animals for medical research. And discussions based on Kohlberg's
Moral Dilemmas (Kohlberg 1971) provide a way to examine moral
issues related to content, such as the allocation of resources for ex-
traordinary medical intervention. To reiterate, discussion structure
is determined by the content and process objectives of the curriculum.

A clear statement of the discussion purpose is critical to planning an effective discussion. The teacher needs to *write* a statement
of the discussion purpose, based on desired learning outcomes. Writ-

ing the purpose and objectives for any learning activity forces one to clarify and think through the possible directions it may take and how best to achieve desired learning. Developing written focus questions for each step or part of a discussion also is advisable; critically examining written questions helps one select those most likely to accomplish the goals of the lesson.

The focus questions at each step of the discussion should be related to the purpose of the step and to the overall discussion purpose. For example, in a discussion designed to compare, contrast, and evaluate events, the initial focus question should not be "What did you see in the film?", but "What happened in the film?" The initial focus on events eliminates the likelihood of superfluous data being offered and provides a mindset for the discussion. From the first to the last focus question ("Which of the events we have discussed do you believe was most important?"), the questions center on events.

The type and content of focus questions affect learning outcomes, making their formulation critical to learning and to good discussions. Focus questions set the ceiling for the level of responses, circumscribe the mental operations students will perform, determine which points are explored, and prescribe which cognitive processes are used (Taba, Levine, and Elzey 1964).

The sequence of questions is critical to achieving learning objectives. The use of a model to structure discussions helps to ensure a developmentally sound sequence or pattern of questions.

Implementing Classroom Discussions

A well-planned discussion, like any other teaching activity, can fail miserably when plan meets students, if classroom management and atmosphere are not conducive to this type of learning. The teacher's attitude sets the classroom climate and may be *the* most important factor in any discussion (Taba et al. 1971). This attitude must convey respect for individual students, the group, and learning in the abstract and as it occurs in this classroom. An openness and willingness to accept people and ideas are important, as are more mundane considerations, such as student manners and classroom management concerns.

At the beginning of the school year and before every discussion until desirable habits are formed, students should be instructed in and reminded of discussion etiquette. This includes actively listening to others, not interrupting others, and *never* ridiculing or laughing at an idea. A reminder of how good and important ideas may seem outrageous when new is the Wright brothers' experience. A reminder to students can be as simple as "Remember, people laughed at the Wright brothers because they *knew* that flying machines was a crazy idea." Even very young children can learn and feel good about respecting each other's ideas, saying very smugly, "We respect each other's ideas in this classroom." This is a foundation for the realization that people can disagree with each other's ideas without denigrating or attacking each other; that good ideas can take many difference guises.

The size of the group affects student participation in discussions. The larger a group, the more likely that several or many students will not participate. This can be handled in several ways. At times dividing a class in half may be feasible, with one half working on independent seatwork and the other half engaged in a discussion. The situation is reversed at a later time, so that all students have both completed the seatwork and discussed the topic.

If dividing the group for the entire discussion is not practical, at certain steps of the discussion, groups of four or five students can be instructed to discuss, record, and perhaps come to consensus on points, issues, or reasons for recommended actions. These groups should fluctuate, so that students do not always work with the same people, and their composition should allow for a balance of the assertive and the quiet. Before working in small groups, students always should have instruction and practice in assuming the various group roles.

Cooperative learning groups can be used to generate lists of data and/or to work through discussion steps. This approach is especially effective when students are familiar with the discussion steps and with working within a small, cooperative group.

The question of raised hands is always asked when discussions are the topic. Whether to require students to raise their hands and be called on before answering is a teacher decision determined by student behavior, teacher comfort, and perhaps philosophy. Most teachers find that calling on students with raised hands prevents the more talkative, opinionated students from dominating a discussion and losing the thoughts of the quieter students. An intrapersonal philosophical conflict sometimes develops between wanting to encourage free expression, yet being concerned about quieter, less confident students expressing their views. Each teacher has to find what works best in this regard for the students and his or her own comfort.

Planning Discussions for Assessment

Sometimes a teacher is unsure of the amount of information students may have, or the level of their expertise with developmental thinking processes. In such cases, discussions can be used to assess the level of either content acquisition or process development. Assessment discussions should be controlled discussions; the structure makes a systematic check on content and/or process level feasible. As with all controlled discussions, the content and process objectives will determine which model is used.

Assessment discussions usually are shorter than other structured discussions, because the knowledge base is not extensive. Depending on the model or strategy used, all or only part of the steps may be used for assessment. For example, the recycling step of Taba's concept development may be difficult for students before they have studied a topic, and conclusions, generalizations, and evaluation may not be feasible if students do not have a sufficient knowledge base.

During discussions used for assessment, teachers should make a record of data and observations that can be kept and examined carefully at a later time. Assessment discussions provide helpful information for determining how much and what emphasis should be planned for skill development or a unit of study.

Discussions as Evaluation

Discussions are effective (nontraditional) evaluation instruments. They can be used as pre- and post-measures or as a series of measurements of student growth. Taping discussions that are used for evaluation is critical; analysis of a taped discussion is more informative than an on-the-spot analysis during the discussion.

Whether the purpose of a discussion is to expand or to evaluate the student knowledge base, the teacher may want to check on the breadth and/or depth of individual knowledge. This can be accomplished by asking each student to jot down pertinent data or information before the discussion begins. Such an activity may serve a dual purpose of focusing student thought and providing information on students who did not read or could not understand the assignment. The written information can be collected or merely shared; either way the teacher is apprised of the student knowledge base.

STUDENT SELF-EVALUATION

Students of all ages can be taught to rate the level of their responses and evaluate their participation in discussions. They can listen to taped discussions, evaluating their contributions and charting their improvement. Additionally, peer evaluation is beneficial. Students within cooperative learning groups can evaluate each other's performance and the performance of their group as a whole.

Jan Bodnar (1980) developed forms to evaluate student performance in discussions. The first, "Evaluation of Discussion Skills," Figure 6-1, may be reproduced for use in rating student discussion behaviors related to eleven skills. Evaluation forms can be completed for several students while listening to a taped discussion. Specific feedback is helpful; examples of very good or weak responses, or suggestions for improvement should be provided under the criteria when possible.

A "Student Self-Evaluation" form based on the work of Bodnar appears in Figure 6-2. The generic form may be duplicated and used for any structured discussion; the steps or stages can be written at the top of the columns across the grid. The steps of any strategy or discussion type can be entered. Similar forms can be devised, listing fewer or other skills on which students are being focused.

The first seven behaviors listed on the Student Self-Evaluation form are positive; the last three are negative. Students need to be instructed in what the listed behaviors consist of so they can become aware of their own level of participation. When teaching students self-evaluation, start with one to three skills, depending on the age of the students. Explain what the skill consists of and provide several examples and nonexamples. If the focus skill is "Gives relevant response to question," an explanation is that the response is related to the topic under discussion and makes sense in context. To a question such as "What do you predict will happen if next year we have a four-day school week?" the following answers would be relevant: "We'd have to stay in school longer each day," "Families would spend more on baby-sitters," and "We'd have more homework." Responses such as "I like three-day weekends" or "Would teachers get to stay home on Fridays?" would not be relevant to the focus question. As skills or criteria are taught, students should be expected to evaluate themselves, until they are aware of all the skills on which the teacher wants to focus.

Evaluation of taped discussions is time-consuming and requires instructing and monitoring students as they learn to look for and evaluate specific behaviors. However, students can become expert at questioning and thinking skills through self-evaluation. A rotation can be established, so that four students are evaluated on each discussion. The identity of the four can be announced following the discussion, so that students do not "coast" in a discussion because they will not be evaluated. Bodnar developed forms for use with high school students; others have used her form, modified or as is,

FIGURE 6–1 Evaluation of Discussion Skills

Name: _____

Discussion Topic: _____ Date: _____

CRITERIA/COMMENTS	RATING
1. Gives relevant responses that are informative and follow the focus of the discussion	1 2 3 4 5
2. Provides adequate support for statements	1 2 3 4 5
3. Provides concise clarification and extension	1 2 3 4 5
4. Demonstrates the ability to view situations from various perspectives	1 2 3 4 5
5. Willing to listen to others and modify position when presented with evidence	1 2 3 4 5
6. Listens to and builds on the ideas of others	1 2 3 4 5
7. Suggests possible limitations of statements and avoids overgeneralizations	1 2 3 4 5
8. Questions other students, asking them to support, explain, or extend their thinking	1 2 3 4 5
9. Avoids interrupting others	1 2 3 4 5
10. Shows respect for ideas, opinions, and values of others	1 2 3 4 5
11. Submits an accurate self-evaluation	1 2 3 4 5

General comments:

FIGURE 6–2 Student Self-Evaluation

Name _____

Date _____

Topic _____

STUDENT BEHAVIOR								
1. Gives relevant response to question								
2. Provides support for statements								
3. Provides concise extension and clarification								
4. Views situation from various perspectives								
5. Suggests limitations of statements; avoids overgeneralization								
6. Builds on the ideas of other students								
7. Questions other students; asks them to support, clarify, or extend ideas								
8. Gives inappropriate response								
9. Interrupts another student								
10. Critical of the ideas and/or values of others								

From Jan Bodnar, 1980.

with elementary-age students. Younger students can begin learning to analyze discussions, look for specific skills, and complete (perhaps simplified) self-evaluation forms.

Self-evaluation should be presented to students as a way to improve their thinking and speaking skills and should be treated as an important part of the curriculum. After the initial fascination with, and embarrassment by, recordings of themselves, students can become very serious and involved in self-improvement. Listening critically to oneself and others is an effective way to learn to think and express thoughts logically and clearly.

CHAPTER SUMMARY

Classroom discussions offer a way for students to interact with curriculum content, using selected thinking processes and strategies. Through examining, reforming, and expanding ideas in discussions, students master both content and processes. Discussion types range from unstructured to highly structured, and discussions can be used to assess, augment, or evaluate student knowledge. Those who are masters at leading discussions may be master teachers. Teachers can evaluate student participation in discussions and they can evaluate their own performance in relation to specific criteria. Using a discussion for multiple purposes (group interaction, processing of information, and self-evaluation of discussion participation) exemplifies efficiency in the classroom.

7

Self-Evaluation to Improve Teaching Skills

The good news is that with instruction, practice, and feedback, one can become very good at asking questions and leading discussions. The bad news is that the perfect discussion does not exist. No matter how proficient, how smooth, how polished the questioning and the timing, *something* always could have been done better. However, through continuing self-evaluation, discussion leaders can come closer to perfection.

The case has been made in this book for questions as a critical element of curriculum and, indeed, learning. Ongoing self-evaluation offers a way to improve questioning skills continually. This chapter includes a consideration of discussion leader self-evaluation in general and in relation to the four Hilda Taba Teaching Strategies.

Teachers who are participating in peer coaching or other staff-development models may be able to supplement self-evaluation with the elements of such a model. In cases such as this, combination of professional development techniques may be very effective. However, many teachers are in schools where administrative and/or financial support for staff development is minimal. The information in this chapter is offered to educators who want to improve their skills but who have little official support for their efforts.

METHODS OF SELF-EVALUATION

Teachers, like other human beings, are creatures of habit, and habits are hard to change or break. Additionally, while teaching, a teacher has hundreds of things to think about and numerous decisions to make, as well as instructional concerns and decisions. Therefore, only two or three behaviors should be targeted for change or eradication at one time. When those behaviors are learned (or unlearned) to criterion, others can be selected. Teaching is too intricate a task to alter rapidly; small, manageable changes are realistic and provide reinforcement to the learner.

Teacher self-evaluation and change can result from the use of tape recorded discussions and a form for discussion leader evaluation. These two methods are discussed in the following sections.

Tape Recording Discussions

The easiest, cheapest, least obtrusive way to evaluate one's discourse is through tape recording classroom interactions and discussions. Videotaping is wonderful, because one can see facial expressions and body language as well as hearing interchanges, but it is not as easily manageable as an audio tape. Therefore, this discussion will center on tape recordings.

Once a particular strategy or technique is learned, listening to and analyzing every discussion in its entirety may be too time-consuming. However, entire discussions can be taped, but only fifteen minutes listened to and analyzed. The fifteen minutes should vary systematically among the initiation, development, and conclusion of discussions. Even if only a fifteen-minute segment has been analyzed, the entire discussion can be listened to either in a cassette deck or using a small portable tape player while driving. Concentration will be less intense when driving than during a formal tape analysis, but errors can be caught and possibilities for improvement identified.

A form that lists teacher behaviors and the steps or phases of the planned discussion should be used when analyzing discussions. Using a form to analyze audio tapes helps one identify patterns of behavior, such as refocusing too frequently, or errors such as asking closed questions or neglecting to request support if needed. Saving completed analysis forms over a period of time offers the opportunity to document growth and improvement in questioning skills. The generic form shown in Figure 7–1 can be duplicated for use, or a form can be developed to suit individual preferences and needs. The teacher behaviors are the same on the generic form as on the Discussion Leader Profile forms for the Taba Strategies; the reader is referred to the next section for instructions for analyzing discussions.

Using the Discussion Leader Profile

The Discussion Leader Profile (Figure 7–2 through Figure 7–7) is designed to facilitate recording the frequency of particular teaching behaviors. Some of these behaviors make possible the successful

FIGURE 7-1 Discussion Leader Profile

Leader _____

Grade & Topic _____

Number of Students _____

Date _____

DISCUSSION LEADER BEHAVIOR						
1. Asks focus or refocus question						
2. Asks for reasons						
3. Seeks variety						
4. Seeks clarification or extension						
5. Asks closed or rhetorical question						
6. Gives opinion or value judgment						
7. Does task students were asked to do						
8. Edits or changes a student's idea						
9. Rejects, ignores, or cuts off student response						
10. Repeats student response						

Adapted from Institute for Staff Development 1971a, b, c, d.

FIGURE 7–2 Discussion Leader Profile—Concept Development

Leader _____

Grade & Topic _____

Tryout Number _____

Number of Students _____

Key

✓ —when you did

X —when you should have but did not

Ⓓ —when you did but should not have

DISCUSSION LEADER BEHAVIOR	LISTING	GROUPING		LABELING		SUBSUMING	
	1	2	5	3	5	4	5
1. Asks focus or refocus question							
2. Asks for reasons							
3. Seeks variety							
4. Seeks clarification or extension							
5. Asks closed or rhetorical question							
6. Gives opinion or value judgment							
7. Does task students were asked to do							
8. Edits or changes a student's idea							
9. Rejects, ignores, or cuts off student response							
10. Repeats student response							

Adapted from Institute for Staff Development 1971a, p. 135.

FIGURE 7-3 Discussion Leader Profile—Interpretation of Data

Leader _____

Grade & Topic _____

Tryout Number _____

Number of Students _____

Key

✓ —when you did

X —when you should have but did not

ⓥ —when you did but should not have

DISCUSSION LEADER BEHAVIOR	STEP 1 Data	STEP 2 Causes or Effects	STEP 3 Prior Causes or Subsequent Effects	STEP 4 Conclusions	STEP 5 Generalizations
1. Asks focus or refocus question					
2. Asks for reasons					
3. Seeks variety					
4. Seeks clarification or extension					
5. Asks closed or rhetorical question					
6. Gives opinion or value judgment					
7. Does task students were asked to do					
8. Edits or changes a student's idea					
9. Rejects, ignores, or cuts off student response					
10. Repeats student response					

Adapted from Institute for Staff Development 1971b, p. 171.

Copyright by Allyn and Bacon. Reproduction of this material is restricted to use with *A Comprehensive Approach to Teaching Thinking* by Shirley W. Schiever.

FIGURE 7–4 Discussion Leader Profile—Application of Generalizations

Leader _____

Grade & Topic _____

Tryout Number _____

Number of Students _____

Key

✓ —when you did

X —when you should have but did not

Ⓥ —when you did but should not have

DISCUSSION LEADER BEHAVIOR	STEP 1 Predictions	STEP 1 Reasons	STEP 2 Conditions	STEP 3 Consequences	STEP 3 Reasons	STEP 3 Conditions	STEP 4 Conclusions	STEP 5 Generalizations
1. Asks focus or refocus question		—		—	—	—		
2. Asks for reasons		—		—	—	—		
3. Seeks variety		—						
4. Seeks clarification or extension		—		—	—	—		
5. Asks closed or rhetorical question		—		—	—	—		
6. Gives opinion or value judgment		—		—	—	—		
7. Does task students were asked to do		—		—	—	—		
8. Edits or changes a student's idea		—		—	—	—		
9. Rejects, ignores, or cuts off student response		—		—	—	—		
10. Repeats student response		—						

Adapted from Institute for Staff Development 1971c, p. 121.

FIGURE 7–5 Discussion Leader Profile—Resolution of Conflict

Leader _____

Grade & Topic _____

Tryout Number _____

Number of Students _____

Key
✓ —when you did
X —when you should have but did not
(✓) —when you did but should not have

DISCUSSION LEADER BEHAVIOR	DATA 1	REASONS & FEELINGS 2	POSSIBLE SOLUTIONS 3a	REACTIONS 3b	SELECTED SOLUTIONS 4a	SHORT & LONG-RANGE CONSEQUENCES (4c–4e)
1. Asks focus or refocus question						
2. Asks for reasons						
3. Seeks variety						
4. Seeks clarification or extension						
5. Asks closed or rhetorical question						
6. Gives opinion or value judgment						
7. Does task students were asked to do						
8. Edits or changes a student's idea						
9. Rejects, ignores, or cuts off student response						
10. Repeats student response						

Adapted from Institute for Staff Development 1971d, p. 133.

(FIGURE 7–5–Continued)

DISCUSSION LEADER BEHAVIOR	DATA 5	REASONS & FEELINGS 6	EVALUATION OF SOLUTION 7	ALTERNATIVE SOLUTIONS 8	GENERAL STATEMENTS 9
1. Asks focus or refocus question					
2. Asks for reasons					
3. Seeks variety					
4. Seeks clarification or extension					
5. Asks closed or rhetorical question					
6. Gives opinion or value judgment					
7. Does task students were asked to do					
8. Edits or changes a student's idea					
9. Rejects, ignores, or cuts off student response					
10. Repeats student response					

Adapted from Institute for Staff Development 1971d, p. 134.

FIGURE 7–6 Discussion Analysis Form (for general, concept development, interpretation of data, or application of generalization discussions)

Do not listen to your taped discussion a second time, but, based on your recollection and impression of the discussion, respond to the following questions:

A. In what ways could you have improved

   1. your preparation for the discussion (intake experience[s], motivation, lead-in, introduction)?

   2. management of the discussion (seating, materials, etc.)?

   3. your arrangement for making data readily visible and available to students?

   4. transitions between steps of the discussion and discussion pace?

   5. participation by the students?

   6. classroom climate and the general tone of the discussion?

B. In what ways, if any, could you have reworded your focusing question to improve the discussion

   1. at Step 1?

   2. at Step 2?

   3. at Step 3?

   4. at Step 4?

   5. at Step 5?

C. What improvements would you like to make in your questioning techniques or discussion strategies?

D. In what other ways could you have conducted the discussion differently?

Adapted from Institute for Staff Development 1971a, p. 136.

implementation of discussions, while others restrict or prohibit student cognitive development. This section is designed to guide the novice in listening to a taped discussion and recording pertinent information on the Discussion Leader Profile.

The Discussion Leader Profile forms may be duplicated for discussion analysis. A form is provided for each of the four Hilda Taba Teaching Strategies. Ten teacher behaviors are listed on the left side of the form, and the steps of the discussion are listed across the top.

FIGURE 7–7 Discussion Analysis Form—Resolution of Conflict

Do not listen to your taped discussion a second time, but, based on your recollection and impression of the discussion, respond to the following questions:

A. In what ways could you have improved

1. your preparation for the discussion (intake experience[s], motivation, lead-in, introduction)?

2. management of the discussion (seating, materials, etc.)?

3. your arrangement for making data readily visible and available to students?

4. transitions between steps of the discussion and discussion pace?

5. participation by the students?

6. classroom climate and the general tone of the discussion?

B. In what ways, if any, could you have reworded your focusing question to improve the discussion

1. at Step 1?

2. at Step 2?

3. at Step 3?

4. at Step 4?

5. at Steps 5 through 8?

6. at Step 9?

C. What improvements would you like to make in your questioning techniques or discussion strategies?

D. In what other ways could you have conducted the discussion differently?

Adapted from Institute for Staff Development 1971a, p. 136.

Copyright by Allyn and Bacon. Reproduction of this material is restricted to use with *A Comprehensive Approach to Teaching Thinking* by Shirley W. Schiever.

As you listen to the taped discussion, mark the form in the following way:

Put a mark in the appropriate box for the behaviors indicated. Make a check (✔) for each time the behavior occurred appropriately, an X each time the behavior did not occur *but should have*, and a circled check (⊘) each time the behavior occurred *but should not have*. A ✔, X, or ⊘ should be recorded for *every* behavior of the teacher. Specific instructions for recording each of the ten behaviors follow.

1. *"Asks focus or refocus question."* When the discussion leader asks the focusing question for each step, a check should be put in this box under the appropriate step of the strategy. If more than three to five checks appear in a focus/refocus box, the teacher is not allowing enough wait-time; questions are being asked repeatedly and needlessly, without allowing students the opportunity to think. In most cases, checks made after the fifth check for focus/refocus questions at a step should be circled checks.

2. *"Asks for reasons."* These support questions should be asked in steps that require proof or reasoning as evidence or support. They should be asked for every response at these steps, unless the student volunteers the support. Sample support questions include: "Why did you put these items together?", "Why do you think that . . . would cause . . .?", or "What makes you say that he was feeling angry?"

3. *"Seeks variety."* Teachers may need to ask either of two types of variety questions at every step, or only once or twice. When student responses are very similar to each other, the first type of variety question should be asked: "What *completely different* (e.g., things do people do to people against whom they are prejudiced)?" If only positive or negative phenomena are being mentioned, the second type of variety question should be asked: "What (negative) (positive) effects would come about?"

4. *"Seeks clarification or extension."* Clarification questions ask for an example of what the student has mentioned or for an explanation of a word or term that is unusual or unclear. These questions may be needed at any step. Additionally, questions that seek to extend responses should be marked in this row. Discussion leader statements such as "What else might belong with the group Joan just made?" or "Tell us more about that idea" ask for extension.

Discussion leader behaviors 5 through 10 are negative behaviors that limit student cognitive development. The goal for discussion leaders is to avoid these behaviors.

5. *"Asks closed or rhetorical question."* Closed questions can be answered by "Yes" or "No" or have a predetermined right answer. Questions such as "Can you think of anything else?", "Can you make a general statement about how people react to strangers?", and "When did World War II begin?" are closed questions. Rhetorical

questions require no answer; "We all know that anger is necessary for this to happen, don't we?" is a rhetorical question.

6. *"Gives opinion or value judgment."* All student responses should be accepted without negative or positive comments, such as "What a good idea!" or "I don't think that would work, Kim." Praising the entire group at the end of each step is an appropriate way to reward students, build group rapport, and satisfy the teacher's desire to give positive reinforcement.

7. *"Does task students were asked to do."* The teacher should *lead* the discussion and *not* contribute ideas to it. The cognitive development of students depends on their engaging in the processes of thinking; listening to the discussion leader's groups, labels, predictions, reasons, consequences, conclusions, or general statements does not result in thinking or learning.

8. *"Edits or changes a student's idea."* Responses should be accepted and recorded at appropriate steps without change. If necessary, *the student* should provide a shortened version of the idea suitable for recording. If one or more students did not hear the response, the student who made it should be asked to repeat it.

9. *"Rejects, ignores, or cuts off student response."* The teacher's role is discussion leader and facilitator. Ignoring, rejecting, or cutting off responses does not lead to successful discussions.

10. *"Repeats student response."* No positive benefits result from repeating student responses, and it may lead to editing. The teacher should encourage students to focus on each other's remarks and to expand or question them as they see fit.

The discussion analysis forms given in Figures 7–6 and 7–7 are an important part of self-evaluation. The taped discussion is not to be listened to an additional time to complete this part; the questions should be given thoughtful consideration, then answered, based on what the discussion leader remembers about the discussion.

CHAPTER SUMMARY

Listening to and analyzing tape recorded class discussions are aids to becoming a more effective discussion leader. The author suggests that all class discussions be tape recorded and analyzed and evaluated. Teaching skills can be improved through critical self-examination, which can be facilitated through use of the Discussion Leader Profile and the discussion analysis forms provided.

8

Models for Improving Teaching Skills

Teachers in general are concerned about how they teach and what their students learn, and most teachers believe students should learn and apply the higher levels of thinking. Yet even a cursory review of the literature on teaching and contemporary education reveals that, while students are acquiring factual knowledge, they are not learning to process information, to think. The critical question becomes "How can teachers transfer what they know/learn about teaching thinking into classroom practice?" The purpose of this chapter is to answer that question.

Changing teaching habits is difficult; Galloway and Seltzer (1980) believe that no more difficult task faces a teacher. Graduate courses, workshops, or the development of a skill do not ensure competence and transfer (Galloway and Seltzer 1980; Joyce and Showers 1980). However, nearly all teachers can be successful in learning new teaching strategies if certain conditions are met (Joyce and Showers 1980). A major focus of Joyce and Showers's (1980) review of over 200 research studies on teacher training was an analysis of inservice components that contribute to learning. Five important components were identified:

1. Presentation of theory or description of skill or strategy
2. Modeling or demonstration of skills or models of teaching
3. Practice in simulated and classroom settings
4. Structured and open-ended feedback about performance
5. Coaching for application or transfer of skills to the classroom

Further, Joyce and Showers (1980) identify four outcomes, or levels of impact, of teacher training. These outcomes are:

1. Awareness of the new area or skill
2. Concepts and organized knowledge related to the skill

3. Understanding of principles and acquisition of necessary skills
4. Application and problem solving

Only after teachers reach the fourth level is their use of new skills likely to have an impact on students.

In a later work, Joyce and Showers (1982) present the concept of *executive control,* the understanding of the set of principles that govern the approach or skill that is learned. This understanding includes knowing why the approach works, what it is good for, and what are its major elements. This level of comprehension is similar to metacognition, wherein one is able to think about and analyze one's own thought processes. Executive control of a teaching strategy allows for analysis, modification, and transformation of the strategy while teaching, for maximum effectiveness. Therefore, possessing executive control of a strategy implies the attainment of a fifth level of impact that is the most powerful.

The author sees parallels between the components of teacher training and outcomes identified by Joyce and Showers (1980, 1982). These parallels, which are illustrated in Figure 8–1, are not identified by Joyce and Showers. However, matching the two sets may serve as an aid when estimating the possible effects of inservice or teacher training programs. In Figure 8–1, the components of teacher training are listed in the left column and the outcomes on the right. The first component, the presentation of theory, could be assumed to result in awareness, as modeling or demonstration of a technique could be presumed to lead to the formation of concepts and organizing knowledge, and so on with the rest of the components and outcomes.

A variety of options exists by which teachers may attempt to upgrade existing strategies or learn new ones. They make take college or university coursework, develop an individual plan for improvement, participate in traditional inservice programs, or become involved in peer coaching (Joyce and Showers 1980). The author of this text believes that developing executive control is necessary for the effective use of new teaching strategies. In this chapter the concept of executive control will be used to examine models for teacher development. Coursework, an individual plan for improvement, peer coaching, and school district inservice will be discussed in terms of the five important components of inservice identified by Joyce and Showers (1980) and their levels of impact.

As used in this chapter, *coaching* is the process whereby teaching skills are observed and critiqued between or among peers, in an effort to learn new skills or polish old ones. The term *peer coaching*

FIGURE 8–1 Parallels Between Joyce and Showers's (1980, 1983) Components and Outcomes of Teacher Training Programs

COMPONENTS OF TEACHER TRAINING	OUTCOMES
Presentation of theory	Awareness
Modeling or demonstration	Concepts and organized knowledge
Practice	Principles
Feedback	Application, problem solving
Coaching	Executive control

is used to refer to the training model developed by Joyce and Showers (1980, 1982).

UNIVERSITY OR COLLEGE COURSEWORK

Most courses at the college level use lecture as the primary mode of instruction and tend to be long on theory and short on application. A typical class therefore does not include four of the five important components for changing teacher behavior: modeling, practice, feedback, or coaching. However, modification of class structure makes the inclusion of four of the five components possible. An example of a teaching methods course modified in this way follows.

Presentation of Theory or Description of Skill or Strategy

The subject of the hypothetical class used to exemplify coursework modification is the inductive or discovery approach to teaching processes and strategies of the Spiral Model. During the early part of the semester the instructor will present the model and relevant learning theory and research, such as the work and writing of Bruner, Dewey, Kohler, Piaget, Taba, and Wertheimer. This theory and research will be in the context of a rationale for and explanation of the Spiral Model and the discovery method of teaching and learning. These presentations will focus on how inductive reasoning and the Spiral Model fit with the content of all disciplines.

Students also need knowledge of how inductive processes relate to the Spiral Model and information on developmental levels of reasoning and the model. They need to learn the skills of inductive teaching: how to help students collect and classify data, develop concepts, derive principles, draw conclusions, and make generalizations. Before they can transfer the concepts, principles, and strategies they have learned to the classroom, they need to acquire skills in using the model and inductive techniques in a variety of content areas and for varying levels of students (Joyce and Showers 1980).

Demonstration

After students have basic information on the Spiral Model and inductive reasoning, they need to experience inductive learning based on the model. For example, students could list specific learning activities they commonly use and form groups of activities based on perceived similarities. After generating labels for the groups, the students could identify which processes or strategies of the Spiral Model are required for individual or groups of activities. Further, they should identify which activities require inductive reasoning and/or which can be modified to require such cognition.

Next, students could determine what seems to be necessary for concepts or activities to be taught inductively. Based on this, each student could make a statement regarding the best content area or activity with which to begin inductive learning. After students share these statements, each can make a general statement about inductive learning based on the Spiral Model.

The experiences detailed above provide for inductive learning based on the Spiral Model:

- *Classification*—grouping learning activities
- *Concept development*—labeling categories and determining which processes or strategies of the Spiral Model each requires
- *Deriving principles*—determining which characteristics of concepts and activities make them suitable for inductive learning
- *Making generalizations*—the general statement

An important part of this activity is debriefing. That is, the instructor should use a grid or some other format to show the class which of the activities they engaged in relate to which components of the Spiral Model.

Practice in Simulated and Classroom Settings

Course requirements should require the use of inductive teaching based on the Spiral Model with each other and students or other young people. If the university students are not teaching, they may prevail on friends for audiences of students, or use Scout, YMCA, YWCA, church, or other groups. The practice sessions should be tape or video recorded and self-evaluated according to criteria provided by the instructor of the class.

Structured and Open-Ended Feedback

The instructor also should listen to or view at least portions of the taped lessons, evaluating the performance by the criteria provided to students (structured feedback). In addition to this evaluation, comments related to the lesson and teaching performance should be made to highlight strengths and weaknesses demonstrated during the lesson (open-ended feedback). Students should be allowed to reteach lessons and resubmit self-evaluated tapes until they achieve the level of mastery they desire. The practice and feedback bring students to the principle and skill level of impact.

Coaching

The coaching component cannot be ensured beyond the duration of the class. However, if two or more students who are taking the course have the desire and teaching assignment proximity to set up a continuing "coaching" agreement, they should be encouraged to do so. Lacking this, students can be encouraged to continue to tape record and self-critique lessons, and to look for a coach among colleagues. Self-analysis is not as effective as the coaching model, but it does help teachers to continue improving their skills.

Acting as a coach is an extremely valuable experience; observing someone else attempting to master a skill results in insights, understanding, and smoother application of the skill. Combined with the other four components, coaching brings teachers to the application and problem-solving level of impact.

The previous discussion points out that college or university courses can provide most, but not all, of the components necessary for teachers to develop executive control of new teaching strategies. Instructors at this level are encouraged to incorporate the four components that lend themselves to this type of class, and to inform students of the value of coaching and encourage them to seek a colleague who is amenable to this concept. For maximum effectiveness, coaching must have the support of school administrators, so that teachers have time to observe and coach peers. However, lacking this, determined teachers can combine classes and use planning or preparation time for observation, demonstration, and other coaching activities.

INDIVIDUAL PLANS FOR IMPROVEMENT

Many school districts require teachers to select or develop personal plans for professional growth each year, either as part of a career ladder structure or as an evaluative tool. This offers an opportunity for teachers who want to learn a new technique or improve teaching skills to accomplish two goals simultaneously. With any approach to improving teacher skills or effectiveness, the most important ingredient is the individual's commitment to learn. The person who engages in an individual plan for improvement faces a more challenging task than one who takes part in other types of programs; an individual effort requires high degrees of personal motivation and self-discipline, as well as the effort required to learn and practice a new skill.

A description of the steps in a hypothetical personal plan that includes the five components follows.

Presentation of Theory or Description of Skill or Strategy

An individual must find descriptions of the theoretical base and practical applications that are relatively self-explanatory and easily understood. Access to a comprehensive library or professional collection is desirable; reading from a variety of sources may be necessary to develop understanding. The readings must include examples of application of the theory or strategy, since examples help develop awareness, organize new knowledge, and form related concepts.

Modeling or Demonstration

Before undertaking to learn independently, the individual should locate another teacher who possesses the target skills and is willing to demonstrate (be observed while teaching) the strategies. After such an observation, the demonstrator should spend time with the observer, making explanations, highlighting fine points, and answering questions. Continued demonstrations help the trainee organize the theoretical knowledge and develop related concepts.

Practice in Simulated and Classroom Settings

Initial practice of new skills is best accomplished with less-than-classroom-size groups. A teacher may be able to use a reading group or some other subset of the entire class to practice a new technique. A smaller group makes trying out new behaviors more comfortable; the fewer the students, the more the teacher can think about what she or he is doing or needs to be doing. Continued practice in a classroom (and feedback) will bring the teacher to the principles and skills level of impact; the new strategy or skill is nearly familiar enough to become part of the teaching repertoire.

Structured and Open-Ended Feedback

This step may be difficult for individuals to arrange. The person who has mastered the strategy needs to observe the teacher who is learning to use it. When this can be arranged, the observer should provide informal feedback following the observation, as well as a critique based on theoretical tenets or predetermined criteria (structured feedback). The time required to observe, critique, and discuss another teacher's lessons is significant and perhaps overwhelming in light of other demands. However, if this can be accomplished, the learning teacher should be able to internalize the principles and skills of the target strategy through this step.

Coaching

Coaching for application involves helping teachers analyze the content to be taught and the approach to be taken and making plans to help the person being coached adapt the new teaching approach to students and/or personal teaching style. Coaching can be provided by peers, supervisors, professors, curriculum consultants, or others who possess expertise in the strategy being applied (Joyce and Showers 1980).

As with securing feedback, coaching may be difficult for individuals to arrange. However, its importance makes the effort worthwhile. If at all possible, the coaching component should be written into individual plans for improvement, using a supportive administrator or colleague. Two aspects of coaching contribute to its value. Being coached offers obvious advantages such as feedback and support. However, *acting* as a coach also will help the novice; observing someone else helps clarify steps that should be taken or points that should be made. Seeing weaknesses or shortcomings in a colleague's approach can serve to highlight similar discrepancies in one's own techniques.

As noted above, under ideal conditions an individual plan for improvement may be designed to contain the five components that promise the possibility of executive control of a teaching approach. Being aware of the ideal, concerned teachers can incorporate those elements possible into plans for improvement as they work toward refinement and modification of their teaching approaches.

INSERVICE

Inservice training is a school district response to the need of teachers to increase their proficiency. Typically it consists of activities designed to advance the knowledge, skills, and understanding of teachers in ways that lead to changes in their thinking and behavior (Fenstermacher and Berliner 1983). Appropriate inservice training forms a vital link between student learning needs and the adoption by teachers of educational practices that will serve those needs (Dettmer 1986).

Critical ingredients for successful school improvement programs include (a) a well-defined, "classroom-friendly," effective innovation; (b) ample, appropriate, and continuous help for teachers; (c) clear direction from administrators; and (d) attention to institutionalization (permanent incorporation of the change) (Loucks and Zacchei 1983). Factors that contribute further to the successful implementation of a program include central office initiative; stable leadership (Huberman 1983); teacher commitment; training and follow-up by credible people; and budgetary, curricular, and administrative support (Loucks 1983).

The following example of a plan for change is based on the decision by a school governing board to make higher levels of thinking one of the basic skills in their school district curricula.

Preparation

A committee composed of parents, teachers, and administrators should be formed to establish goals and objectives for the teaching of thinking in the district. This committee also should search the literature and make recommendations regarding a needs assessment and the steps of effective inservice; teacher input and involvement in decisions about inservice are critical to the success of such programs. District staff who will be charged with incorporating recommendations and implementing the inservice plan also must be consulted during the needs assessment.

Presentation of Theory or Description of Skill or Strategy

Several approaches to teaching thinking should be selected, and a brief description of the underlying theory and rationale and teaching methods for each should be circulated. Teachers should be allowed to select an approach that fits with their personal philosophy of teaching and teaching style. Participation in inservice training should be encouraged and rewarded.

Early workshops should concentrate on building awareness of the nature of the approach, how it can be used, and how it fits into district curricula. These sessions should balance the theoretical with the practical and establish the connection between them.

Modeling or Demonstration

Demonstration lessons should be provided and should be analyzed by participants, with the workshop leader ensuring that key points are made. The connection between aspects of the theory and related teaching behaviors or steps should be made clear. Repeated demonstrations will help participants develop important concepts about the technique and organize related knowledge.

Practice in Simulated and Classroom Settings

Workshop participants can develop lesson plans together or individually and use these with small groups of students and with each other. As teachers feel more proficient and comfortable with the new skills, they can use them in their classes. As they use the approach, they will begin to derive the principles of the strategy as well as mastering skills.

Structured and Open-Ended Feedback

If participating teachers tape record their practice sessions, the workshop leader can give them feedback. Based on lesson plans and tape recordings, the leader can make a reasonably accurate judgment of participants' level of knowledge and skill. Through pertinent feedback, teachers will begin to acquire the skills for adapting the new behaviors to specific groups of students.

Coaching

The coaching component should be built into an effective inservice plan. Teachers who take the workshop can act as coaches for each other, or other teachers who have mastered the methods can coach those who are learning. Through coaching, participants learn to apply the new strategy effectively and integrate it into their teaching repertoire.

As illustrated here, school district inservice can be designed to develop executive control of new teaching strategies. However, if the change is to be district-wide and permanent, the factors identified earlier must be incorporated.

School-wide commitment to the concept of peer coaching is critical to its success. Such commitment is demonstrated by strong support from the principal and by funds allocated to the implementation of peer coaching.

PEER COACHING

Based on its perceived effectiveness, Joyce and Showers (1982) recommend that school faculties be divided into coaching teams who
regularly observe and provide helpful feedback on each other's teaching. For the purposes of this discussion, coaching will be considered
only as one of the components necessary for teachers to integrate a
new teaching method or approach into their repertoire. The example
used in Joyce and Showers's article, "The Coaching of Teaching"
(1982) also is used here. This example follows the steps taken by
members of the English department of Lazarus High School in Sac-
ramento, CA as they learned a new teaching strategy, Synectics (Gordon 1961).

Presentation of Theory or Description of Skill or Strategy

To acquire the necessary background, the teachers read William Gordon's book *Synectics* and saw a videotape of Gordon explaining the
underlying theory. They already had an awareness of the importance
of Synectics as a teaching tool to encourage creative thinking and in
studying fiction and poetry. By viewing the tape and reading the
book they established a foundation for understanding and using
Synectics.

Modeling or Demonstration

An expert on Synectics came to the school, demonstrated it several
times, and held discussions with the teachers. Additionally, the
teachers visited another school where the teachers had used Synectics for several years. These experiences enabled the Lazarus teachers
to organize the knowledge they had gathered on Synectics and helped
them form and develop related concepts.

Practice in Simulated and Classroom Settings

Next, the Lazarus teachers planned minilessons in creative writing,
poetry analysis, and the use of metaphor. Each teacher practiced the
strategy several times with other teachers before trying it out, in
teams of two, with able students. They were learning the principles
and skills necessary to teach Synectics.

Feedback and Coaching

When the teachers were ready to try the strategy with larger groups,
one team member taught while the other observed and provided

constructive criticism; then they changed places. Sometimes they taught together. Each person practiced several times with the coaching partner present to reflect on progress and to offer suggestions for improvement. In teams they began to use Synectics in the classes in which they thought the strategy would be most likely to be productive and successful.

As they used the strategy, questions arose that sent them back to Gordon's book, and they revisited the teachers who were experienced in using Synectics. Additionally, they engaged a Synectics consultant who reviewed the theory and provided tips for practicing and coaching each other.

Through these experiences the teachers derived and continued to refine the principles and skills that made them able to apply the strategy and problem-solve to make it more effective. These teachers may be presumed to have developed executive control of strategies for teaching Synectics.

As is obvious, in this real-life application the practice, feedback, and coaching for application steps are not separate entities; rather they merge with each other. The important factor is that all steps are included and the essentials of the process remain intact. Peers have engaged in coaching each other to reach a high level of proficiency with a new and useful teaching strategy.

CHAPTER SUMMARY AND CONCLUSION

The purpose of this chapter is to examine several ways that teachers can learn new teaching approaches or techniques. Believing Joyce and Showers's (1982) concept of executive control to be useful, the author used that as a criterion for evaluating each of four models: college or university coursework, individual plan for improvement, school district inservice, and peer coaching. Peer coaching develops executive control without modification of the model. The other three models, however, must be modified and expanded to include important components so that they are more likely to develop executive control of new teaching strategies.

The parallels between the coaching process for teachers as described here and the athletic model are obvious. The main difference is that the model is used consistently in athletics and is seldom used in teacher training. Rather than discarding the model as too expensive, too lengthy, or too difficult, those who educate and train teachers need to recognize the soundness of the approach for learning complex behaviors. We recognize that Olympic medalists must have expert instruction, an understanding of how the body works, continual and extended practice, and coaching—expert feedback on progress and areas for improvement. Why are we so reluctant to acknowledge that teaching is at least as complex as swimming or throwing a discus?

Perhaps the time has come for educators to recognize publicly that gaining executive control over such a complex set of behaviors as teaching requires an information base, observation, practice, feedback, and coaching. With this recognition will come a willingness to approach learning new strategies as a complex task that cannot be accomplished quickly or without extended effort. Certainly if teachers aspire to developing complex thinking strategies in their students, they must gain executive control of the appropriate teaching methods. The time to recognize the complexity of teaching and to act accordingly has arrived.

PART THREE

THE HILDA TABA TEACHING STRATEGIES

9

Overview of the Strategies

The Hilda Taba Teaching Strategies are included in this book for two reasons. First, their inclusion provides an updated, better organized text for those instructors who are teaching the strategies and using photocopies of the 1971 Staff Development materials (or pieces of them) as a text. Second, the strategies have a sound research base and exemplify one effective way to teach complex thinking strategies.

The teaching strategies program developed by Hilda Taba consists of four sequential questioning techniques that provide specific means for accomplishing curriculum goals at all grade levels and in all content areas (Trezise 1972). These techniques were developed on the basis of almost fifteen years of research on children's thinking and how it could be developed (Taba, Levine, and Elzey 1964; Taba 1966; Wallen et al. 1969). Basic cognitive strategies were identified from theory and research, and sequences of questions were designed to promote the acquisition of each strategy (Taba et al. 1971). Taba is best known for her work on social studies curriculum, but the techniques she developed are generic.

The purpose of this chapter is to put the Hilda Taba Teaching Strategies into a context for the reader. A brief discussion of the philosophical, theoretical, and research base underlying the strategies, reports of research on the effectiveness of the strategies, and an overview of the strategies will provide understanding of this widely applicable example of a way to teach thinking.

PHILOSOPHICAL, THEORETICAL, AND RESEARCH BASE

Taba incorporated many of John Dewey's ideas in her work, along with the research and writing of Piaget, Bruner, and Vygotsky (Maker 1982b). Taba believed that learning by discovery brings process (thinking) and content into a transactional relationship. The essence of this relationship is that the learner establishes a relation between existing schemata and new phenomena and remakes or extends schemata to accommodate new facts and events. This is closely related to Piaget's concepts of assimilation and accommodation, wherein new information received by a learner either is fitted into existing cognitive structures (assimilation) or the existing structures are reorganized to fit the new information (accommodation). In other words, the process of knowledge acquisition is seen as a successive development of structures that are tested, modified, or replaced in ways that facilitate learning and thinking (Glaser 1984).

Taba (1964) agreed with the Piagetian invariant sequence of cognitive growth postulate but disagreed with the notion that only age and maturation affect this growth. She proposed that conceptualizing the development of thought as a continuous stream or a series of transformations rather than an additive assertion of specific skills would be more accurate. Further, Taba believed that school experiences can and should be designed to trigger and enhance cognitive development.

The Hilda Taba Teaching Strategies were developed through three studies of a large number of elementary school children in a wide variety of classrooms. These strategies are based on the following assumptions (Taba, Levine, and Elzey 1964; Trezise 1972):

1. Thinking is learned and can be learned developmentally; therefore it can be taught.
2. Thinking involves an active transaction between the individual and data. Data become meaningful only when an individual performs certain cognitive operations on them.
3. The ability to think cannot be "given" by teachers.
4. Precise teaching strategies can be developed and used to encourage and improve student thinking.
5. The quality of individual thinking differs, but all normal students are capable of thinking at abstract levels.
6. All subjects offer an appropriate context for thinking.
7. Precise teaching strategies will improve and encourage student thinking.
8. Thinking takes many forms; the specific thinking processes to be developed should be clear in the teacher's mind.
9. Teaching students to think is the basic goal of all education.
10. A great deal of accumulated knowledge is not necessary before beginning to think on a topic.
11. Learning to think is not a byproduct of memorizing the thoughts of others.

12. The effectiveness of people's thinking depends largely on their thinking experiences.

Teachers find that use of the strategies makes significant cognitive growth possible as students master content. Observers are amazed at the responses of students, even those who customarily are taciturn, during a well-planned (Taba) discussion led by a nonjudgmental teacher (Trezise 1972). Students enjoy and recognize the value of such discussions, as evidenced by the following comments of fourth-grade students, written after their first interpretation of data discussion.

It was educational, I couldn't say things write (sic) off of my head. I had to think.
I thought it was very fun because I got to open up and say what I felt.
I felt this activity was educational and interesting. It demonstrates how the blacks had to live.
I thought it was educational and we had to dig deep inside our thoughts and use our brains. (M. O. Fleming, personal communication, February 1988)

RESEARCH ON EFFECTIVENESS OF THE STRATEGIES

The studies that resulted in the existing Hilda Taba Teaching Strategies used an achievement test, *Sequential Tests of Educational Progress* (STEP); an objective test developed for the studies, *The Social Studies Inference Test*; and data from the analysis of taped classroom discussions and interactions. Some of the general conclusions of the studies are listed below.

- Formal operational thinking appears much earlier than Piaget assumed, but follows the sequence he identified. Formal thinking begins in grade two and continues through grade six, with about one-sixth of all thought units in grade six (trained classrooms) being at the formal operational level (Taba, Levine, and Elzey 1964).
- The most marked single influence on cognitive performance was the teaching strategies, including (a) the nature of questions asked (questions requesting low-level thinking drew low-level responses; higher-level questions resulted in higher-level responses); (b) what the teacher gives to and seeks from students; (c) timing, including pacing of questions and "lifting" questions; and (d) the selection of items for elaboration by students. The nature of questions asked was the critical element in students' cognitive development (Taba, Levine, and Elzey 1964).

- *Reiteration* (repetition) of student responses constitutes 46 percent of teacher function but *has little impact* on the course of the discussion (Taba, Levine, and Elzey 1964).
- Students in the experimental groups performed better on the tests and in discussions than did students in the control groups (Taba 1966).
- Trained teachers sought more high-level thinking and received more high-level responses than untrained teachers.
- Teacher training is more effective when directed toward specific strategies rather than overall improvement in teaching (Taba, Levine, and Elzey 1964).

Further studies of the effectiveness of the Taba strategies have been conducted since the original research. Ahn (1973) studied 244 children in grades kindergarten through five for a period of three years. The experimental group in the primary grades made significant improvement in flexibility and ability to make inferences, and the intermediate students became significantly better at making inferences. The Michigan Department of Education surveyed over 200 teachers trained in the Taba techniques. Virtually all of these teachers reported that the strategies were highly useful in their classrooms, in all subject areas. Large numbers of these teachers named the strategies as the most valuable teaching technique they had ever acquired (Trezise 1972). Hanninen (1983) studied a small group of gifted seventh-grade students and found certain higher-level thinking skills such as divergent thinking to be significantly improved following consistent use of the Taba strategies. In a study of gifted fifth- through seventh-grade students, Schiever (1986) found that regular use of the strategies positively affected the growth of higher-level thinking. Hanninen (1989) compared the students of teachers with training in the Hilda Taba Teaching Strategies with students of untrained teachers. She found that trained teachers had an impact on the creative and critical thinking behaviors of their students. Student thinking reflected increased fluency and flexibility, as well as significantly increased inferencing skills and recognition of the assumptions of arguments, as measured by the *Watson-Glaser Critical Thinking Appraisal.*

THE STRATEGIES

The Hilda Taba Teaching Strategies are highly structured teaching methods that lead students through a series of sequential intellectual tasks by asking them open-ended but focused questions. The four strategies—concept development, interpretation of data, application of generalizations, and resolution of conflict—were not designed to be hierarchical, but they may be learned and used sequentially because they build on each other.

Three of the four strategies are in the cognitive domain, the fourth in the affective. The cognitive strategies contain affective elements and the affective strategy has a strong cognitive component. The strategies provide for a mixture of cognition and feeling, valuative, and attitudinal elements (Trezise 1972).

Use of the Taba strategies stresses the individual interpretation of meaning, a very important aspect of reading and thinking skills. This characteristic makes the strategies useful in any reading program as well as in all content areas. Additionally, teachers have discovered the Taba approach is effective with elementary, junior high, and high school students (Trezise 1972).

Within each strategy the prescribed sequence of questions is critical, as it is based on the development of cognitive processes. Through thinking about and responding to questions, students process information, develop concepts, and formulate generalizations for themselves. The use of the strategies redirects students from memorizing information preprocessed by others to mastering the systematic intellectual skills of productive, autonomous thinkers (Taba 1966).

The *concept development strategy* provides a structure for students to form, clarify, and extend concepts. This is accomplished through responding to open-ended questions that require them to enumerate items related to an idea and/or experience, classify (group) the items based on some similarity or relationship, label the groups, subsume items under (other) labels and labels under (more inclusive) labels, and reorganize the data and recycle the steps.

The *interpretation of data strategy* requires students to make inferences about short- and long-term cause and effect relationships. They also must support their inferences, draw conclusions, and make generalizations about the relationships.

In the *application of generalizations strategy*, students are asked to make short- and long-term predictions about a hypothetical situation, based on their own knowledge of similar situations. They limit their predictions by specifying necessary prior and/or attendant conditions and establish the causal link between the prediction and the conditions (applying generalizations). They must support predictions and inferences, draw and support conclusions, respond to a provided generalization, and support the response.

The emphasis of the *resolution of conflict strategy* is on helping students see the complexity of human interactions, especially in conflict situations. Further, they interpret attitudes, values, and feelings of the individuals involved in the focus situation to generate a variety of possible solutions and to analyze these alternatives in relation to their consequences and effects on the people involved. Students then are asked to volunteer similar situations in their lives or the lives of people they know. These situations are analyzed through basically the same procedures as the focus situation, and students are asked to generalize about human behavior in this type of situation.

Taba (1966) realized that good teaching consists of more than asking good questions. She believed that a good sense of timing and a particular, logical sequence for questions also are critical to encouraging students to think through ideas for themselves. In the strategies, teaching youngsters to think means helping them to formulate data into conceptual patterns, verbalize relationships between discrete segments of data, make inferences from data, make generalizations on the basis of data and test these generalizations, and become sensitive to relationships such as cause and effect and similarities and differences (Trezise 1972).

In addition to Taba's strong belief that students individually *must* think through data if the data are to be meaningful, she also believed that separating process from content is impossible. She saw the richness and significance of the content with which students work as affecting the quality of their thinking (Taba 1966). The selection and organization of content that is rich and significant enough for developing thinking skills are important aspects of learning the teaching strategies.

CHAPTER SUMMARY AND CONCLUSION

The Hilda Taba Teaching Strategies are basic cognitive strategies for developing students' complex thinking abilities. They are based on the research and writing of Piaget, Bruner, Vygotsky, and Taba and her associates. The four strategies are concept development, interpretation of data, application of generalizations, and resolution of conflict. Research conducted since the development of the strategies reaffirms their effectiveness. Taba (1966) believed that the combination of developmental thought modules into strategies offers a useful compromise between the science and the art of teaching. The experience of educators continues to validate her belief.

10

Concept Development

Concepts are the building blocks of cognition—the attainment and development of concepts in content areas are the goals of education. Children entering kindergarten usually understand the concept of counting, that numbers symbolize objects and can be used and manipulated. Through schooling, life experiences, and maturation, number concepts are expanded and developed until students are able to use them in abstract and sophisticated applications. Educators seek ways to introduce and develop a multitude of concepts effectively throughout the school years.

Often educators and authors of textbooks assume that having students read about concepts will bring understanding and reach educational goals. However, students must form their own cognitive structures through processing related information. Through this processing comes the understanding necessary for application of concepts to complex thinking tasks. Taba's concept development strategy provides a way such understanding can be reached. In this chapter the author presents a synthesis of existing information on the strategy, and clarifies and expands this information. (Unless otherwise noted, the information in this chapter is drawn primarily from three sources: Institute for Staff Development 1971a and n.d.; and Maker 1982b.)

THE CONCEPT DEVELOPMENT TASK

The concept development strategy provides a way to examine and organize different relationships between data. As do all the Hilda Taba Teaching Strategies, the concept development task combines content (*what* is taught or learned) with process (*how* it is taught or learned). The demonstration lesson in Figure 10–1 illustrates the combining of process and content in a concept development discussion plan. Through identifying and naming a variety of relationships between behaviors that reflect prejudicial thinking (process

FIGURE 10–1 Demonstration Discussion Plan—Concept Development

STRATEGY: Concept Development
Lesson plan by Shirley Schiever

Topic ___Prejudice___
Level ___Demonstration—All___

DISCUSSION PURPOSES

Content: To clarify and extend students' concept of prejudice.

Process: To identify and name a variety of relationships between behaviors that reflect prejudiced thinking.

PREDISCUSSION PROCEDURES
Dependent on age level—be sure students understand what the word "prejudice" means

MATERIALS

BEHAVIORAL OBJECTIVES	FOCUSING QUESTIONS	TEACHER'S ROLE	SUPPORT PROCEDURES
STEP ONE—DATA Students will enumerate specific human behaviors that reflect prejudice.	Based on what you know & have observed (learned), what specific things do people do that show prejudice against someone else? (Or . . . what specific things do people do to those against whom they are prejudiced?)	1. Focus on specific, relevant data. 2. Record data. 3. Limit list length, time spent on step. 4. Seek variety.	List data on chalkboard. Seek clarification & variety as necessary. Review (read over) list of data before beginning next step.
STEP TWO—GROUPS AND SUPPORT a. Students will group items based on common attributes or other relationships. b. Students will provide reasons for their groupings.	a. Which of these behaviors on our list go together because they are alike in some way? b. Why do you think ⟶, and ⟶ go together?	1. Mark groups that students form. 2. Seek support.	Listen to responses to determine types of groups being made, relationships seen.
STEP THREE—LABELS AND SUPPORT a. Students will suggest appropriate labels for grouped items. b. Students will state reasons labels are (or are not) appropriate.	a. Remembering the reasons we grouped these behaviors together, what is a good name for this group? b. Why is that a good name for this group? a. What is another good name for this group? b. Why . . . ?	1. Seek at least three labels for each group. 2. Record labels. 3. Seek support.	Listen to responses, watch for opportunities for student interaction.

Form adapted from Institute for Staff Development 1971a pp. 27 & 28.

(FIGURE 10–1–Continued)

BEHAVIORAL OBJECTIVES	FOCUSING QUESTIONS	TEACHER'S ROLE	SUPPORT PROCEDURES
STEP FOUR—SUBSUMING & SUPPORT a. Students will subsume listed behaviors under more than one label and labels under more inclusive labels. b. Students will give reasons for subsumptions.	a. Which of the items now under one label would fit under a different label? b. Why does __ belong under __? a. Which items not under any label would fit under one of the labels? b. Why . . . ? a. Which of these labels could go under another label? b. Why . . . ?	1. Delineate task clearly. 2. Encourage flexibility.	Write subsumed labels in outlined form. Allow time for thinking. Model variety in question stems.
STEP FIVE—REGROUPING (RECYCLE 2, 3, & 4) a. Students will form new groups for different reasons, label the new groups, and subsume items and labels under labels. b. Students will give support for new groups, new labels, & new subsumptions.	a. Looking at our list again, what completely different groups can you make, putting behaviors together because they are alike in some way? b. Why . . . ? Etc.	1. Same as in steps 2, 3, and 4. 2. Encourage discovery of _new_ relationships.	Erase previous groups and labels (leave data.). Be alert for groups that were made previously. Same as for steps 2, 3, & 4.

Form adapted from Institute for Staff Development 1971a p. 29.

(FIGURE 10–1–Continued)

COGNITIVE MAP
STRATEGY: Concept Development

Topic: Prejudice

STEP 1 Possible Data	STEPS 2 & 3 Possible Groups and Labels	STEP 4 Possible Subsumptions
imprison	snub	**Items under Labels**
snub	exclude	
exclude from group	deny privileges	Emotional Weapons
deny privileges (e.g., club membership)	deny rights	imprison
deny rights (e.g., voting, jobs, decent houses)	ignore	bully
call names	→ Emotional Weapons / Hurt Feelings / Psychological War / Covert Abuse	scare
make fun of/denigrate	make fun of	segregate
look down on	look down on	
pick fights	pick fights	Racial/Ethnic Supremacy
bully	bully	convince others of less worth
assault (hit, chase)	assault	
burn their house	try to scare	**Labels under Labels**
try to scare	→ Kid Stuff / Physical War / Overt Abuse	
believe stereotypes	segregate	Racial/Ethnic Supremacy
spend less money on (school, houses)	ignore	Psychological War
kill	less money	Covert Abuse
segregate	lower salary	Overt Abuse
enslave	snub	
ignore	→ Society with Classes / Ways to Stay "On Top" / WASP Reign	Covert Abuse
joke about	STEP 5—Possible New Groups & New Labels	Emotional Weapons
provide poor education	kill	Psychological War
pay lower salary	enslave	Maintain Status Quo
convince others of less worth	imprison	
	ignore	
	snub	
	make fun of	
	→ Killer Actions / Destruction / Wipe Out	
	lower salary	
	less money for school, houses	
	deny rights	
	→ Economic Warfare / Poor Get Poorer / Lower Class	

Form adapted from Institute for Staff Development 1971a, p. 30.

objective), students clarify and extend their concept of prejudice (content objective).

Concepts are formed, clarified, and extended through the following steps of a concept development discussion:

1. Enumerate items related to the focus idea.
2. Group the listed items in a variety of ways according to perceived similarity or some type of relationship.
3. Develop several labels for each group, based on the rationale for grouping.
4. Subsume items under different labels and labels under other labels by relative inclusiveness.
5. Recycle steps 2 through 4, making completely different groups and labels.

The sequence of the steps in the concept development strategy is important, as it is based on research and moves the students from low to higher levels of thinking. The strategy provides a structure for students to move from data that are concrete or relatively concrete to the manipulation of ideas (labels) that are abstract.

Purpose

The purpose of the concept development task is to assess the level of concept development and to encourage students to discover new relationships (expand and develop concepts they hold) as they organize a mass of information. Students need to understand the various components of ideas and to realize that relationships exist between elements of the ideas or the data. The steps of the concept development strategy assist students in discovering and understanding these relationships.

The cognitive map for the lesson plan on prejudiced behavior (Figure 10–1, page 146), illustrates how students may discover new relationships through a concept development discussion. The behavior "snub" is related to other actions it is grouped with, such as "deny rights" and "segregate," to the labels for the groups it is in, such as "Psychological War" and "Society with Classes," and, in the recycling phase, to "imprison," "enslave," and "Destruction." Through exploring such relations, students begin to understand the concept of actions that reflect prejudice.

By facilitating assimilation of new information and accommodation of existing cognitive structures, use of the concept development strategy makes possible the organization of data or information into meaningful, student-determined units or groups. The strategy provides for not only the development but also the organization and reorganization of concepts. In general, the strategy helps students develop (a) more openness and flexibility in their thought processes, (b) a cognitive structure for organizing data, and (c) a process for organizing and reorganizing new data in the future.

Rationale for Individual Steps

Step 1—Listing
The purpose of listing is to get data in front of students in a form that is meaningful to them. Listing a variety of data related to a specific topic helps develop the skill of determining relevancy and gives students a base of information that includes many new ideas, since the group pools its thinking. Additionally, this pooling of knowledge provides all the students with a common base of data.

Step 2—Grouping
When grouping data on the basis of similarities or relationships, students engage in the task of noticing differences as well as common attributes and relationships between and among items. They see groups made by others, which expands each student's view of how items are similar and different (assimilation of ideas). This grouping process also promotes the identification of multiple attributes, stimulates a flexibility and openness to different thinking styles (accommodation), and creates a respect for the ideas of others.

Support for the formation of each group is a critical aspect of the grouping step. Verbalizing reasons for grouping (a) helps students clarify their reasoning for themselves and others, (b) allows other students to add to a group made by someone else, and (c) enables teachers to understand the students' cognitive structure (e.g., the basis for grouping, such as function, class, or mixed).

Step 3—Labeling
Finding a word or phrase to express the relationship or commonality among diverse items is an abstracting or synthesizing process. The student abstracts a few descriptive words or synthesizes these words into a label that conveys the essence of the basis for grouping. Labeling is efficient, as the label symbolizes all the items sharing that relationship or common attribute(s). The more accurate and inclusive the labels, the more capably the student can deal with diversity. A variety of labels gives students several from which to choose, and consistently asking for variety in labels will result in developing vocabulary and creativity.

Step 4—Subsuming

To *subsume* means to classify within a larger category or under a general principle. In the concept development task, the purpose of subsuming items under (different) labels is to establish or explore new relationships of the data and labels. The purpose of subsuming labels under other, more inclusive labels is to discover terms that are more encompassing, therefore more abstract and general. The cognitive task of subsuming requires and develops further an awareness of a hierarchical system of super- and subordination, in which lower-order items are subsumed under items of a higher order of generality (Taba 1966).

Subsuming items from one group (or items that have not been placed in a group) under a different label or putting labels under more inclusive labels enables students to become more efficient thinkers. The more inclusive the label, the more efficient it is in helping one deal with many specific details. "Society" includes more ideas than "social class," which includes more than "economic level," which includes more than "job." Learning to subsume helps students develop the concept of inclusiveness and helps them deal more competently with ideas.

Step 4 of the concept development strategy contains two separate and distinct subsumption tasks. The first asks students to subsume (a) items that are not under a label under existing labels or (b) items now under one label under a different label. The purpose of this task is to allow students to see new relationships among the data, in addition to those already noted, and interrelationships between data and between labels. The relationships drawn at this step may be more subtle, complex, or abstract than those first noted, since the first groupings tend to be based on obvious similarities or relationships. The subtleties, complexities, and abstractness are revealed to the group and the teacher through the responses to the support question "Why does, e.g., 'Psychological War' belong under 'Racial/ Ethnic Supremacy'?"

The second subsumption task is that of subsuming labels under other (more inclusive) labels. The purpose of this exercise is to demonstrate that some labels are more general and broader than others, and that relationships and interrelationships exist between labels as well as between data and labels. Finding the broader phrase (label) prepares students to learn outlining techniques, organize paragraphs, construct topic sentences, select main ideas, and make generalizations.

Step 5—Recycling

In the fifth step, steps 2 through 4 are completely recycled. This step is essential to the purposes of the concept development strategy.

Since data are grouped in *completely different* ways, additional cognitive benefits are derived. These benefits include (a) the opportunity to see new relationships among the data; (b) the opportunity to build on previous ideas, coming up with other ideas that are more abstract or less obvious; (c) the revelation that different ways of grouping data can help achieve different purposes; and (d) promoting the idea that new ways to look at the same data and new relationships always can be found, and that people bring to each experience a new viewpoint based on previous experiences. Recycling promotes openness and flexibility in thinking, since it illustrates the results of reexamining data.

Conceptualization of the Concept Development Task

Teachers should conceptualize the strategy before attempting to conduct a discussion. Conceptualization requires that the teacher understand the underlying rationale and purpose of the entire discussion and individual steps. The time spent conceptualizing is an investment in the efficiency and effectiveness of planning and leading discussions. Feeling comfortable with and understanding the rationale and steps of the strategy promote effective implementation.

Figure 10–2 is a graphic representation of the concept development strategy designed to help the reader conceptualize the strategy. The step numbers and main tasks appear across the top of the figure, and symbols portray the execution of the strategy. Note that in Step 2 the data are grouped according to perceived relationships, and the support for Step 2 comes from this relationship. At Step 4, items first are subsumed under labels and then labels are subsumed under other labels. Step 5 is the recycling of steps 2, 3, and 4. The author suggests that readers use Figure 10–2 in conjunction with the rationale for and descriptions of each step. While at a glance the figure may seem confusing, such graphic depictions have been found invaluable to those who are learning the strategies.

Planning a discussion can be done using a "cookbook" approach, modeling objectives, questions, and support procedures on an existing lesson. Such planning does not demonstrate understanding, nor does it necessarily lead to conceptualization, even with repeated use. To execute successfully any of the Hilda Taba Teaching Strategies, the teacher must internalize the underlying purpose and rationale. Without such an understanding, discussions will not develop the desired cognitive processes in students.

FIGURE 10–2 Graphic Representation—Concept Development

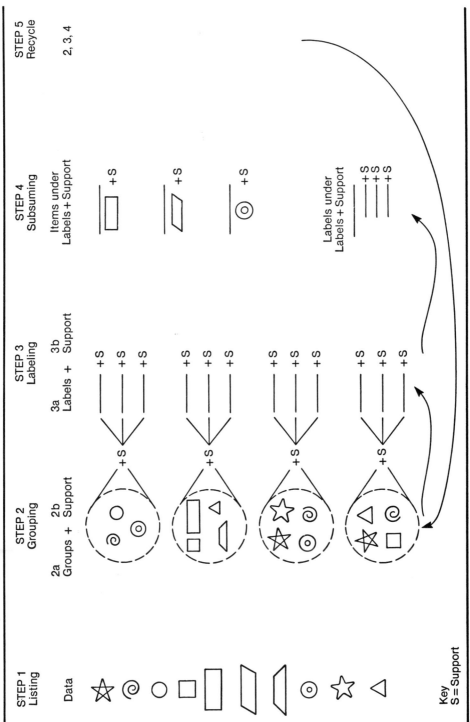

Overt and Covert Behaviors in Concept Development

Taba's 1966 study was designed to examine both the psychological processes of learners and the logical properties of their products (thoughts) to assess the effectiveness of the teaching strategies she had developed. This design reflects her belief that the processes of thought are psychological (covert), but the product and content of these processes are observable (overt) and can be assessed by logical criteria and evaluated by the rules of logic. Each cognitive task has two sets of operations: the overt activities of individuals and the covert mental operations required to perform the overt activities. The covert operations determine the sequence of the overt activities, representing the sequential skills necessary for a specific task (Taba 1966).

When planning a learning experience, teachers should consider the covert processes that underlie the overt steps necessary to reach the (cognitive) teaching goal. For example, if the task is enumeration, individuals must differentiate one item from another (e.g., dogs from snakes) as well as differentiating between classes (mammals and reptiles). Such differentiation requires analyzing global wholes (e.g., living creatures) and breaking them into specific elements with specific properties (Taba 1966).

The focusing question for each step of the concept development strategy must be designed with both the covert and overt objectives in mind. In Figure 10–3 the step purpose; the overt, or behavioral objectives; the covert, or thinking objectives; and general or possible focusing questions are listed for each step of the strategy. This chart can be used when planning concept development discussions or activities.

PLANNING A CONCEPT DEVELOPMENT DISCUSSION

Successful concept development discussions require careful and detailed planning. Discussion leaders must have a clear purpose in mind and outline the strategies to be used and the responses that can be anticipated. This careful planning is not to ensure that students will suggest certain data, groups, or labels. Rather, it enables the teacher to be an effective catalyst in a discussion that achieves its stated purpose.

FIGURE 10–3 Overt-Covert Behaviors—Concept Development

STEP	1	2	3	4	5
Purpose of Step	*Develop List of Relevant Data*	*Form Groups on Basis of Some Relationship*	*Generate Several Labels for Each Group*	*Establish New Relationships, Find More Inclusive Labels*	*Develop Flexibility, Raise Level of Thinking*
OVERT Behavioral objectives	Enumerate relevant data.	(a) Group items by common attributes or relationships. (b) Name relationship or commonality.	(a) Suggest appropriate labels for groups. (b) Support appropriateness of labels.	(a) Subsume items under (different) labels, labels under labels. (b) Support subsumptions.	(a) Suggest different groups and labels, subsumptions based on different relationships. (b) Support new groups, labels, subsumptions
COVERT Thinking objectives	Recall items from intake or experience. Differentiate relevant from irrelevant data.	(a) Notice relationships, attributes. (b) Identify commonalities or relationships.	(a) Synthesize commonality. Generalize with word or phrase. (b) Compare, evaluate.	(a) Notice hierarchies and "new" relationships. (b) Identify hierarchies or relationships.	(a) Notice different relationships & characteristics. (b) Identify different relationships & characteristics.
FOCUSING QUESTIONS (General)	What specific things did you see? Hear? Read? What do you notice about ____?	(a) Which of these belong together because they are alike in some way? (b) Why do you think ____ & ____ & ____ go together?	(a) Remembering the reasons we put these together, what would be a good name for this group? (b) Why is that a good name?	(a) Which of the items under one label also fit under another label? Which labels will fit under another label? (b) Why . . . ? etc.	(a) Which items go together for completely different reasons? etc. (b) Why . . . ? etc.

Adapted from Institute for Staff Development 1971a, p. xv.

Discussion Plan Form

The blank discussion plan form (Figure 10–4) may be duplicated for use when planning concept development discussions. Use of this form as suggested below will help ensure a well-planned discussion.

Determining Discussion Purposes

Teachers who are unfamiliar with the Hilda Taba Teaching Strategies may not be accustomed to formalizing three elements of the lesson: content purpose, process purpose, and a cognitive map. However, each is critical to an effective discussion.

A good discussion has two well-defined purposes: the content purpose and the process purpose. These purposes are the foundation of the discussion procedure and must be stated clearly for the execution of a meaningful and worthwhile discussion. The *content purpose* must include a clear statement of what the teacher wants the students to clarify or extend. For example, in the demonstration lesson plan the content purpose is "To clarify and extend students' concept of prejudice." Through naming, grouping, labeling, and recycling these three steps, students will develop further their concept of prejudice. The *process purpose* states what the teacher hopes students will achieve as a result of how they deal with the data. The process purpose for the demonstration lesson is "To identify and name a variety of relationships between behaviors that reflect prejudiced thinking." As the steps are completed, students will establish new, expanded views of the relationships between, for example, segregation and societal classes.

Cognitive Mapping

A critical aspect of planning a concept development discussion is developing a cognitive map. The page of the discussion plan entitled "Cognitive Map" should be used for this purpose. Completing the cognitive map aids in examining possible data, groups, and labels, increasing the effectiveness of the discussion leader. Developing a cognitive map helps provide the following:

- A structure for thorough exploration of the discussion topic through charting the directions a particular discussion might take. This exploration highlights ideas on which to build, as well as indicating the variety of ideas that may result from the data base.
- A way of checking the feasibility of the discussion plan. By developing the cognitive map, the teacher may find that the possible relationships she or he wants explored cannot be developed based on the given data.

FIGURE 10–4 Discussion Plan Form—Concept Development

STRATEGY: Concept Development

Topic _____
Level _____

DISCUSSION PURPOSES
Content:

PREDISCUSSION PROCEDURES

Process:

MATERIALS

BEHAVIORAL OBJECTIVES	FOCUSING QUESTIONS	TEACHER'S ROLE	SUPPORT PROCEDURES
STEP ONE—DATA		1. Focus on specific, relevant data. 2. Record data. 3. Limit list length, time spent on step. 4. Seek variety.	
STEP TWO—GROUPS AND SUPPORT		1. Mark groups that students form. 2. Seek support.	

(FIGURE 10–4–Continued)

BEHAVIORAL OBJECTIVES	FOCUSING QUESTIONS	TEACHER'S ROLE	SUPPORT PROCEDURES
STEP THREE—LABELS AND SUPPORT		1. Seek at least three labels for each group. 2. Record labels. 3. Seek support.	
STEP FOUR—SUBSUMING & SUPPORT		1. Delineate task clearly. 2. Encourage flexibility.	
STEP FIVE—REGROUPING (RECYCLE 2, 3, & 4)		1. Same as in steps 2, 3, and 4. 2. Encourage discovery of new re-lationships.	

Form adapted from Institute for Staff Development 1971a, pp. 28 & 29.

(FIGURE 10–4–Continued)

COGNITIVE MAP
STRATEGY: Concept Development

STEP 1	STEPS 2 & 3	STEP 4
Possible Data	*Possible Groups and Labels*	*Possible Subsumptions*
		Items under labels
		Labels under labels

• A basis for the development of a variety of focusing questions that maintain the planned direction of the discussion.

Prediscussion Procedures and Materials

1. *Decide what data are needed, how data will be gathered, and what materials will be needed.* On the planning form, record prerequisite experiences, necessary materials, and physical arrangements for the discussion.

Purposes of the Discussion

2. *Determine what concepts are to be clarified or expanded in this discussion.* Record this content purpose.

3. *Record the process purpose for the discussion.*

Behavioral Objectives, Focusing Questions, and Support Procedures

4. *Refer to Figure 10–3 for the general behavioral objective for Step 1 of the discussion.* Based on this general objective, write the specific objective for the step (e.g., "Students will enumerate specific human behaviors that reflect prejudice"). Record the objective on the planning form.

5. *Using the general focusing question from Figure 10–3 as a guide, formulate the focus question for Step 1* (e.g., "Based on what you know and have observed, what specific things do people do that show prejudice against someone else?"). Record the focus question on the planning form.

6. *On the cognitive map, list possible student responses under "possible data."* If these responses are not related to the content purpose of the discussion, reformulate the question and repeat this step again.

7. *List support procedures for Step 1 on the planning form.* These may include physical arrangements, reminders to yourself, and/or sample clarification, variety-seeking, or refocusing questions.

8. *Refer to Figure 10–3 for the general behavioral objective for Step 2.* Repeat planning steps 4 through 7 for each step of the discussion. Alternate between the overt-covert behavior chart, the cognitive map, and the discussion plan form to ensure the formulation of focus questions that are likely to accomplish the stated goals of the discussion.

IMPLEMENTING THE STRATEGY

The discussion plan form is designed to be used for planning *and* leading discussions. The completed form should be kept where it is easily visible and referred to during implementation of the concept development strategy.

Listing

At Step 1, listing a variety of *specific* data is critical. If in response to the focusing question "What specific things do people do that show prejudice against someone else?" the student response is "Be mean," the response is too broad. The clarification question here should be "What is an example of mean behavior?" The example should then be recorded as data. If the Step 1 responses are too inclusive, each response constitutes a group, and the task of making groups and assigning labels becomes very abstract or impossible, thus defeating the purpose of the discussion. For example, "mean" is a possible label for a group of behaviors; if it were included as data, other, equally broad terms would be needed to make groups, and labeling a group consisting of "mean," "hateful," and "horrid" becomes too abstract a task for the students.

Record the students' responses *in their own words.* If a response is too long, ask the student to give the same idea in fewer words so that it will fit on the chalkboard or flip chart, or abbreviate words as you write the response. When a student response does not seem to fit the focus of the discussion, the teacher may (a) ask, "What do you mean by . . .?", (b) ask, "How do you see . . . being related to our focus on (concept)?", or (c) accept and record the response as given.

Young children can draw data (pictures of items) or select pictures from an assortment. They should be able to handle the data—pictures, attribute blocks, containers, buttons, items from the teacher's desk—and physically move things from one group to another. Felt charts and sentence charts also can be used so data can be manipulated. Small groups of students each may have their own set of concrete items to manipulate, as when attribute blocks are used. If pictures are lined up on the chalkboard tray, at the grouping step children can come to the front of the room and move the pictures into groups. This allows the students to move around, an important consideration when working with younger children.

Data can be collected in advance of the discussion by the students. Students could collect examples (pictures, snapshots, signs, newspaper articles, tape recordings, records) of prejudice. These data are evidence of prejudiced behavior and are especially meaningful to students, since they collected them.

Student-generated data are valuable, and using butcher paper rather than the chalkboard allows the teacher to keep the list to add to as new data are gathered, scrutinize the list for errors when the knowledge level is more sophisticated, or use it later for an interpretation of data task. Such lists also can serve as records of student growth, not only in knowledge but in levels of thinking (labels and groups) as well. When students see that their responses are not only recorded but used and can chart the growth of the group in knowledge and skills, they become active partners in their own learning.

Many times, calling on slower or more reticent students first is a sound practice, as this may be the only level at which they are able (or willing) to respond. Further, a slow student who has raised his or her hand and not been called on may concentrate on remembering that item, should the chance to respond come again, and therefore not attend to the rest of the discussion. Another way to encourage the participation of all students is to give the focus question and allow a few minutes for students to jot down what comes to mind before calling on anyone.

If students begin a pattern of similar responses (e.g., "hit," "kick," "scratch," "bite"), after about three responses the teacher needs to break the pattern to obtain the desired variety of responses. An example of a question seeking variety is "What *completely different* things do people do when they are prejudiced?"

The discussion should be paced to allow for a variety of responses and flexibility of thinking, but it must move rapidly enough to keep as many students as possible interested and participating. Having a clear idea of where you want the discussion to go (as detailed on the cognitive map) helps achieve the balance necessary to reach both of these goals.

The most common error of the novice discussion leader is to spend too much time collecting data. Such an error makes the discussion too long, which loses student interest; makes the cognitive accomplishments of the later steps less precise; and frequently results in lack of time to engage in Step 5, which defeats a primary purpose of the strategy. The data list should be a representative sample of pertinent information, but it should not be exhaustive. A suggestion to the novice is to view Step 1 as the basis of the later steps, but not as a step in and of itself. Such a view may help prevent spending an excess amount of time on the step.

Another frequent error is accepting general rather than specific data, which causes problems at the labeling step. Finally, asking for "important" items at this step, which requires evaluation rather than merely determining what is relevant, is a mistake that is made occasionally.

The teacher's role at the listing step of the concept development task can be summarized as follows:

• To focus on data relevant to the purpose of the discussion
• To require specific data
• To seek clarification and examples of data when appropriate
• To record specific items
• To seek a variety of data
• To limit the length of the list and amount of time spent at this step

Many teachers find that commenting on the work of the group before moving to the next step encourages the students. Remarks such as "Look at what an interesting list of data we have generated! All of you seem to be ready to do some super thinking today" provide reinforcement to students without reaping the negative results of individual praise discussed in Chapter 5. Human beings enjoy praise, and group reinforcement goes a long way toward building the positive classroom climate necessary for the development of the higher levels of thinking.

Grouping

Before starting the grouping task, reviewing the data quickly is a good idea. Some students may not be able to see clearly, or certain words may be difficult to read. Hearing the list helps auditory learners and pulls the group together before starting a new task.

As students group the data listed during Step 1, they begin sorting out relationships as they see them. After a student has grouped items together, asking for the reason the group was formed is critical. The group should be made, then the reason given. Both parts of this step must be included, and the sequence is invariant. Never assume the reason for grouping was what seems obvious. If a student adds an item to an existing group and when queried as to the reason responds, "For the same reason that Sabrina made the group," ask the student to say it in his or her own words. A simple "How do you say it?" will suffice.

Students who are not able to make a new group may be able to contribute to the discussion if they are asked, "Which item(s) might be added to (e.g., group number six)?" Students who think more slowly or who lack self-confidence may participate in this way. Additionally, giving a few minutes to think about the task after the focus question before anyone is called on may aid students.

The simplest way to denote groups for students who are old enough to understand the system is to put numbers or symbols by the items. Start with group number one, marking a "1" or the symbol for the group (e.g., a star) next to each item named to the group, and continue with group "2," and so on. When one item has four or five numbers next to it, the variety of relationships shared by this item is apparent; if several items have many symbols by them, you can conclude that category boundaries (and therefore student reasoning) are not very precise or that your list of data is exhaustive and therefore precise reasoning is not required to make categories.

A common error at Step 2 is not including "because they are alike in some way" in the focus question. However, in their zeal to include this component, novices have been known to ask the support question "Why would you put those together because they are alike in some way?" Students are confused with this statement that seems to be a question with a built-in answer.

An error that may occur at Step 2, 3, or 4 is asking for two cognitive tasks at once. This is done when one asks a question similar to this: "What is a good label for this group, and why is it a good label?"

The role of the teacher at Step 2 of the concept development task includes the following:

• To seek groups formed for a variety of reasons
• To require support for the basis of grouping
• To listen to determine level and type of classification schema
• To designate the groups formed by marking in some way

Labeling

At Step 3, students are attempting to establish a hierarchy by finding a label that is inclusive enough to encompass the items in a group. Seeking a variety of labels helps ensure that some inclusive ones will be suggested.

Some labels are more abstract than others; some are abstractions of a reason, while others are summaries of key ideas. For example, in the cognitive map on page 146, labels such as "Emotional Weapons," "Covert Abuse," and "Racial/Ethnic Supremacy" are abstractions of reasons, while "Physical War," "Ways to Stay 'On Top'," and "Society with Classes" are summaries of key ideas. Teachers need to be aware of the level of labels as a means of assessing the depth of knowledge and level of sophistication of thinking on given topics.

Students must be asked why the label they have suggested is a "good name" (or label) for that group. The support question focuses students on the issue of evaluation, or judging the "goodness of fit," the accuracy, and/or inclusiveness of the label. Often two or more students will think of the same label, but for different reasons. Hearing the reasons of others gives students a broader perspective on the labeling process.

When students give support for labels, they should not use the label itself in the response. For example, if a group was labeled "Hurt Feelings," the support statement "Because all those things hurt people's feelings" is not acceptable. An acceptable support statement is "Because they all make people (or humans) feel bad." This requires students to stretch their thinking and helps expand their vocabularies.

Frequently, time constraints prohibit the labeling of every group that was formed. If choices must be made between groups to develop labels for, a variety of groups should be selected, and the decision should be made with the content purpose of the discussion in mind. In other words, those groups with the most potential for assessing, clarifying, or expanding the focus concept are the groups that should be labeled. Additionally, at least three varied labels should be sought for each group selected.

If not all the groups are going to be used for labeling, some explanation should be offered to students. Comments such as "You have done such a lot of thinking and we have so many good groups that I will have to choose just a few for the next step" will help to alleviate the feeling that some groups (and thus some students' thinking) are "better" than others.

At Step 3, a common error is asking for a "label" or "name" rather than a *good* label/name based on the reasons for putting the items together. Additionally, if students are told they cannot use the label in the support before they are asked for the label, they become confused. Sometimes teachers become confused, as well, and tell students they cannot use words on the data list in their support. The parameters for support (not using the label itself) should be given when the support is asked for, and an example provided if the technique is new to the students.

The teacher's role at Step 3 includes the following:

- To establish the link between the label and the relationship of items in a group through the focus question

- To require verbalization of this link through the support question
- To require support for labels that does not include the label itself
- To encourage group interaction regarding appropriateness or inappropriateness of labels
- To seek a variety of labels for each (selected) group
- To record the labels, noting with number or symbol to which group the labels belong

Subsuming

Step 4, subsuming, has two distinct parts: (a) the subsuming of items under labels and (b) the subsuming of labels under other, more inclusive labels. Separating the cognitive tasks is preferable; the first focus question can ask which items now under one label or not under any label will also fit under a (different) label. Some teachers prefer to break down this first part of the step further and ask (a) which items now under one label also would fit under another label, then (b) which items not under any label would fit under one of the labels. The first few times a group of students engages in subsuming this division of tasks may be necessary to avoid confusion.

Both parts of the subsuming step require the establishment of hierarchies of inclusiveness. While several labels are appropriate for a specific group, many times only one of those labels is inclusive enough to have items from other groups (or not in any group) subsumed under it. Similarly, when the task is to subsume labels under other, more inclusive labels, only a few of the labels are inclusive enough to have other labels subsumed under them.

Note: The purpose of Step 4 is *not* to have every datum in a group or under a label. Data that are not grouped with others or put under a label may have a more abstract relationship with other data or labels that will be discovered in Step 5. At no time should the discussion leader seek the placing of every piece of data in a group, just for the sake of "using up" the data.

When students are novices at the concept development task, their labels may be very similar to each other and not very inclusive, making the subsuming of labels under other labels more rare than that of items under other labels. Usually, however, one or two relatively more inclusive labels are developed, even if the cognitive task is a new one for the group. After even limited experience, more students develop the concept of inclusiveness, and labels become more encompassing.

If students do not understand the task after the initial focus question at Step 4, the teacher may give an example to illustrate what is being asked. An example outside of the focus topic is best, but if one does not come to mind, choose one of the items and say, "For example, which label, other than those for the 'star' group, would 'spinach' fit under?" A few students will grasp the idea from the example, and as they subsume items under labels, other students will begin to understand.

Most problems at Step 4 are caused by not dividing the sub-sumption task into three parts (items under [different] labels, items not under a label under a label, labels under other labels). Many teachers are unfamiliar with subsumption as a concept; they are able to outline, find main ideas, and so forth, but they are not accustomed to the task as it occurs in this strategy. Their lack of clarity and confidence is reflected in their focus question and in student responses.

The role of the teacher at Step 4 includes the following:

- To make the task clear through the initial focus question and/or an example if necessary
- To encourage flexibility of thinking
- To encourage student interaction regarding similar or very different subsumptions
- To note student ability/inability to grasp the concept of subsumption

Recycling

Recycling steps 2, 3, and 4 is critical to the accomplishment of the concept development task. Teachers who have spent too long on steps 1 and 2 may find that they and their classes are reluctant to "start all over again." However, the depth of thinking and the ex-pansion of the concept make the effort worthwhile. If a teacher re-alizes that too much time was spent at Step 1 and too much data recorded, using only part of the data for recycling makes the task more manageable and the thinking more challenging. After recycling, point out to the students how their groups, labels, and subsumptions were more sophisticated and required better thinking. The obvious ideas usually come out during steps 2, 3, and 4—Step 5 requires more thinking, and the results reflect this.

When using the concept development strategy to assess stu-dents' knowledge base, such as at the beginning of a unit of study, Step 5 may receive few responses. The dearth of responses may reflect the lack of information students have on the subject, which is what the teacher needs to know before beginning the unit.

The novice discussion leader may be tempted to omit the re-cycling of previous steps. The content purpose of clarifying and *extending* a concept and the process purpose of identifying and naming a *variety* of relationships among data require that the data be reprocessed. Grouping data for completely different reasons requires that students stretch their thinking and look beyond the obvious. Groups that are formed on the basis of more subtle and/or complex relationships and interrelationships require more abstract labels, which raises thinking levels. Subsumption acquires a new dimension when labels are more abstract; greater numbers of items will fit under labels, and the difference in degree of inclusiveness of labels becomes finer and dictates more discernment and precision.

Omitting or cutting short Step 5 is a mistake beginners make. Veteran discussion leaders recognize this step as important and pace the discussion so it can be included.

APPLICATIONS OF THE CONCEPT DEVELOPMENT STRATEGY

The concept development strategy was designed as a discussion strategy, but the steps also can be experienced or written. When students are planning a presentation, they group similar items or information and label the groups. Their understanding of the topic at hand will increase significantly if they are encouraged or required to develop more than one set of groups of data or information and corresponding labels.

The concept development task also is functional when students are arranging a bulletin board or other type of display, designing and making a chart to bring order to a mass of data, or organizing a notebook. The strategy is ideal for "pulling together" the experiences from field trips or other enrichment experiences, as well as information from units of study.

Concept development discussions can be used to assess the amount of information students have on a topic or how well they understand the information they have. The strategy enables the teacher to assess the level of concept development before beginning and after completing a unit of study. Tape recording both the pre- and the post-discussions provides evidence of the level of student concept development and growth during the time span of the unit.

Cooperative learning or other types of student groups can be used to involve actively all or most students in the concept development task. The author suggests that data be generated by the entire group. When students are familiar with the strategy, small groups can label, subsume, and recycle the steps. A recorder for each group should make note of data groupings, labels, and subsumptions and a spokesperson should share these with the entire class. The spokesperson should be instructed to share only one or two ideas not mentioned by other groups. Sharing information from the recycling should yield the best view of the level of understanding as well as the most interesting (complex and abstract) ideas.

A strength of the concept development strategy is that students can participate actively at their own level, but the responses of others may expose them to other, higher, or more abstract levels of thinking. An example of this is a student who groups items on the basis of physical characteristics, a low level of abstractness, while other students group them according to function, a higher level of abstraction, or class category, the most abstract attributes. The more abstract grouping provides a model for students functioning at the lower levels.

For a sample list of concepts that can be clarified or extended through a concept development discussion, see page 178. The sample lesson plans also can be used to spark ideas for application of the strategy.

CHAPTER SUMMARY

Concepts are essential to thinking, and developing concepts is the purpose of education. The concept development strategy developed by Hilda Taba and her colleagues provides a structure for students at all ages to establish relationships among the mass of data to which they are exposed. In this way individuals learn to order things in their lives and become able to confront problems more effectively. In this way, too, teachers can become more effective, education can become more relevant, and students can become "turned-on," competent thinkers.

SAMPLE CONCEPT DEVELOPMENT LESSON PLANS

DISCUSSION PLAN FORM

STRATEGY: Concept Development
(Institute for Staff Development 1971a)

Topic   Attributes of Concrete Objects

Level   Early Elementary (also suitable for educable mentally retarded, ages 6–14)

DISCUSSION PURPOSES

Content: To clarify and extend students' concepts of characteristics such as function, size, shape, texture, and color.

Process: To identify and name a variety of relationships among concrete objects.

PREDISCUSSION PROCEDURES

Children, in groups of five, examine and manipulate a variety of items from the teacher's desk. Items may be left in the drawers, taken out and put on a table, or children may draw items they saw and felt.

MATERIALS

A variety of items typically found in the teacher's desk drawers (tape, pencils, paste, glue, staples, chalk, crayons, rubber bands, etc.).

BEHAVIORAL OBJECTIVES	FOCUSING QUESTIONS	TEACHER'S ROLE	SUPPORT PROCEDURES
STEP ONE—DATA Students will enumerate items from the teacher's desk.	What were some of the things you saw and touched from my desk?	1. Focus on specific, relevant data. 2. Record data. 3. Limit list length, time spent on step. 4. Seek variety.	

Form adapted from Institute for Staff Development 1971a, p. 27.

BEHAVIORAL OBJECTIVES	FOCUSING QUESTIONS	TEACHER'S ROLE	SUPPORT PROCEDURES
STEP TWO—GROUPS AND SUPPORT a. Students will group items by similarity or other relationships. b. Students will explain why they think certain items belong together.	a. Which of these things you found in my desk should go together because they are alike in some way? b. Why did you put staples, paper clips, and tape together?	1. Mark groups that students form. 2. Seek support.	Grouping of items may be done by using the objects themselves, child-drawn pictures of the objects, or, if the children are able, printing the name of each item on sentence strips. (For the latter, more than one strip for each item is necessary so items can be put in more than one group.) Be alert to nonverbal cues that indicate need for further clarification. Encourage addition to groups for the same reasons and a variety of groupings.
STEP THREE—LABELS AND SUPPORT a. Students will suggest appropriate names for the groups that have been formed. b. Students will support their labels with evidence or reasoning.	a. Thinking about the reason we put these together, what would be a good name for this group? b. Why do you think, e.g., THINGS TO HOLD THINGS is a good name for this group?	1. Seek at least three labels for each group. 2. Record labels. 3. Seek support.	If children have a very short attention span, elicit labels as each group is made and subsume items (Step 4) after labels have been given and explained. Then go back and form a new group. Essentially this means cycling steps 2, 3, and 4, one group at a time, for as long as the attention holds. Elicit a variety of ideas for labels. What would be another good name for this group?

Form adapted from Institute for Staff Development 1971a, p. 28.

Copyright by Allyn and Bacon. Reproduction of this material is restricted to use with *A Comprehensive Approach to Teaching Thinking* by Shirley W. Schiever.

BEHAVIORAL OBJECTIVES	FOCUSING QUESTIONS	TEACHER'S ROLE	SUPPORT PROCEDURES
STEP FOUR—SUBSUMING & SUPPORT a. Students will suggest or physically move items under other different labels. Students also will put labels under other more inclusive labels. b. Students will explain why subsumed items and labels belong under other labels.	a. Which of these things that are now under one name also belong under one of the other names? For example, "glue" is under WHITE THINGS. What other labels could "glue" go under? b. Why do you think, e.g., "glue" also goes under WET THINGS? a. Which of these labels do you think belongs under one of the other labels? b. Why do you think, e.g., BOOKS goes under PAPER?	1. Delineate task clearly. 2. Encourage flexibility.	If one or more items is already under more than one label, direct children's attention to this as a model for further subsuming. Encourage children to build or add to another child's attempts at subsuming. John saw that "rulers" also can go under THINGS THAT CAN HURT YOU. Who else has an idea like John's? Subsuming labels may be too difficult for children who are not yet reading. You can facilitate the process by printing the labels on sentence strips and having these moved one under the other.
STEP 5—REGROUPING (RECYCLE 2, 3, & 4) a. Students will suggest new groupings of items, labels for new groups, and new ways to subsume items and labels under labels. b. Students will give reasons for new groups, labels, and subsumption of items and labels.	a. Suppose we were to start all over again. Which of these things could you put together to make a brand new group because they are alike in some way? Etc.	1. Same as in steps 2, 3, and 4. 2. Encourage discovery of <u>new</u> relationships.	This step may not be needed if you have already recycled steps 2, 3, and 4. Or, this step may be another lesson. Strive for different groupings than the first time. This may require an additional look at the desk contents.

Form adapted from Institute for Staff Development 1971a, p. 29.

COGNITIVE MAP
Concept Development

STEP 1 Possible Data	STEPS 2 & 3 Possible Groups and Labels	STEP 4 Possible Subsumptions
paper clips	–THINGS TO WRITE WITH	Items under Labels
chalk	chalk	"coloring book" also under TOYS
marbles	ballpoint pens	"pencils" also under THINGS TO ERASE WITH
ballpoint pens	pencils	"ruler" also under THINGS THAT CAN HURT YOU
blackboard eraser	magic marker	
brown square eraser	crayons	Labels under Labels
clay	–THINGS TO HOLD OTHER	BOOKS under PAPER THINGS
brown wooden ruler	THINGS TOGETHER	THINGS TO CUT WITH under METAL THINGS
staples	paper clips	METAL THINGS and WOOD THINGS under
pencils	staples	THINGS THAT CAN HURT YOU
short round scissors	scotch tape	
long pointed scissors	rubber bands	
coloring book	safety pins	
lesson plan book	straight pins	
attendance book	glue	
scotch tape	–TOYS	
rubber bands	squirt gun	
safety pins	truck	
straight pins	–BOOKS	
thumb tacks	lesson plan book	
glue	attendance book	
colored paper	coloring book	
paper cup	–THINGS TO ERASE WITH	
squirt gun	grey round eraser	
truck	blackboard eraser	
blocks	brown square eraser	
magic markers	–WOOD THINGS	
crayons	ruler	
	blocks	
	pencils	
	–THINGS THAT CAN HURT YOU	
	staples	
	scissors	
	safety pins	
	straight pins	
	rubber bands	
	thumb tacks	

Form adapted from Institute for Staff Development 1971a, p. 30.

DISCUSSION PLAN FORM
STRATEGY: Concept Development
Lesson plan by Mary K. Conrad & Sandi Sherman

Topic ___Leadership___
Level ___Middle School___

DISCUSSION PURPOSES
Content: To clarify and extend students' concept of characteristics of leaders.
Process: To identify and name a variety of relationships among data.

PREDISCUSSION PROCEDURES

MATERIALS

BEHAVIORAL OBJECTIVES	FOCUSING QUESTIONS	TEACHER'S ROLE	SUPPORT PROCEDURES
STEP ONE—DATA Students will enumerate data related to their knowledge of leaders and their characteristics.	Based on your research, what characteristics do leaders have that set them apart from others?	1. Focus on specific, relevant data. 2. Record data. 3. Limit list length, time spent on step. 4. Seek variety.	Probe for variety: What other characteristics do leaders have that set them apart?
STEP TWO—GROUPS AND SUPPORT a. Students will group listed characteristics based on similarities. b. Students will state reason(s) characteristics belong together.	a. Which characteristics can be grouped together because they are alike in some way? b. What are your reasons for grouping these characteristics together?	1. Mark groups that students form. 2. Seek support.	Add new characteristics to the list upon student request. Have students verbalize all reasons so everyone can learn from them. Probe to get reasons that are more than repetition of the grouping.
STEP THREE—LABELS AND SUPPORT a. Students will give appropriate labels for the groups, based on the relationships used to group the characteristics. b. Students will state reason(s) characteristics belong together.	a. Based on your reasons for grouping these characteristics together, what would be an appropriate label for them? b. Why do you think ___ would be a good label for this group?	1. Seek at least three labels for each group. 2. Record labels. 3. Seek support.	If necessary, have the group recall the reason the characteristics were grouped together. Ask for a variety of labels—What other names would be appropriate for this group? Ask the support question as each label is suggested.

Form adapted from Institute for Staff Development 1971a, pp. 27 & 28.

BEHAVIORAL OBJECTIVES	FOCUSING QUESTIONS	TEACHER'S ROLE	SUPPORT PROCEDURES
STEP FOUR—SUBSUMING & SUPPORT a. Students will subsume characteristics under one or more labels and labels under more general labels. b. Students will give reasons for thinking one or more characteristics belong under one or more labels, and their reasons for believing some labels belong under other labels.	a. Which of these characteristics that are now under this label can also be placed under another label? b. Why do you think — could also go under —? a. Which of these labels could go under another label? b. Why would — go under —?	1. Delineate task clearly. 2. Encourage flexibility.	If a characteristic is already under two or more labels, point this out to help students get started. Ask support question each time a characteristic or label is subsumed. Ask for as many ideas as time allows.
STEP FIVE—REGROUPING (RE-CYCLE 2, 3, & 4) a. Students will put characteristics together for different reasons, label them, and subsume characteristics and labels under labels. b. Students will give reasons for putting characteristics together, reasons labels are appropriate, and reasons for subsuming characteristics and labels.	a. Looking at the list of characteristics, what completely different ways could you group them, putting them together because they are alike in some way? b. Why . . . ? Etc.	1. Same as in steps 2, 3, and 4. 2. Encourage discovery of new relationships.	The primary focus of this part of the lesson is flexibility and increased abstractness in thinking. Recycle steps 2, 3, and 4. Continue to ask for clarification and support.

Form adapted from Institute for Staff Development 1971a, p. 29.

COGNITIVE MAP
Concept Development

STEP 1	STEPS 2 & 3	STEP 4
Possible Data	*Possible Groups and Labels*	*Possible Subsumptions*
energetic	Workers, Getting Ahead	Items under labels
smart	energetic	Getting Ahead
courageous	hard-working	smart
honest	helpful	loyal
hard-working		honest
sense of humor	Good People, Trustworthy	persuasive
persuasive	smart	Good People
friendly	honest	friendly
study a lot	patriotic	helpful
helpful	loyal	
patriotic	unselfish	
loyal		Labels under labels
kind	Likeable, Fun, Good Friends	Admirable
brave	persuasive	Trustworthy
unselfish	friendly	Mature
	loyal	Good People
	sense of humor	Good Friends
		Likeable
	Quality, Mature, Admirable	Fun
	courageous	Trustworthy
	patriotic	
	loyal	
	honest	
	smart	
	unselfish	

Form adapted from Institute for Staff Development 1971a, p. 30.

DISCUSSION PLAN FORM
STRATEGY: Concept Development
Lesson plan by Mike Osborn
DISCUSSION PURPOSES

Topic ___Bill of Rights___
Level ___Secondary___
PREDISCUSSION PROCEDURES

MATERIALS

Content: To clarify and extend students' concept of the Bill of Rights.
Process: To identify and name a variety of relationships among data.

BEHAVIORAL OBJECTIVES	FOCUSING QUESTIONS	TEACHER'S ROLE	SUPPORT PROCEDURES
STEP ONE—DATA Students will list factual information on the Bill of Rights.	What specific information have you learned about the Bill of Rights?	1. Focus on specific, relevant data. 2. Record data. 3. Limit list length, time spent on step. 4. Seek variety.	
STEP TWO—GROUPS AND SUPPORT Students will a. group data on the basis of some perceived relationship b. support the groupings by providing their reasons.	a. Which of the items on our list belong together because they are alike in some way? b. Why do you think —, —, and — go together?	1. Mark groups that students form. 2. Seek support.	
STEP THREE—LABELS AND SUPPORT Students will a. label groups based on perceived relationships b. support the labels with evidence or reasoning.	a. Remembering the reasons we put these together, what would be a good name for this group? b. Why is that a good label?	1. Seek at least three labels for each group. 2. Record labels. 3. Seek support.	If labels are very similar, ask, "What would be a completely different good label for this group?"

Form adapted from Institute for Staff Development 1971a, pp. 27 & 28.

BEHAVIORAL OBJECTIVES	FOCUSING QUESTIONS	TEACHER'S ROLE	SUPPORT PROCEDURES
STEP FOUR—SUBSUMING & SUPPORT Students will a. subsume items under different labels and labels under labels b. support subsumptions with evidence or reasoning	a. Which items not under a label would fit under one of the labels? b. Why . . . ? a. Which items now under one label also would fit under another label? b. Why . . . ? a. Which of these labels would fit under one of the other labels? b. Why . . . ?	1. Delineate task clearly. 2. Encourage flexibility.	Mark subsumptions.
STEP FIVE—REGROUPING (RE-CYCLE 2, 3, & 4) See steps 2, 3, & 4.	a. Now take a second look at our list. What completely different groups can you make, putting items together because they are alike in some way? Etc.	1. Same as in steps 2, 3, and 4. 2. Encourage discovery of new relationships.	Erase or hide old groups, labels, and subsumptions.

Form adapted from Institute for Staff Development 1971a, p. 29.

COGNITIVE MAP
Concept Development

STEP 1	STEPS 2 & 3	STEP 4
Possible Data	*Possible Groups and Labels*	*Possible Subsumptions*
passed in 1791	Rights, Protection	Items under labels
1st 10 constitutional amendments	speech	Time Period
guarantees certain freedoms	assembly	jury trial
Continental Congress passed for,	accused	People Involved
of, and by the people	jury trial	protects accused
written at same time as	People Involved	
Constitution	Continental Congress	Labels under labels
reaction to English abuse	English	Rights
free speech	For, of, by	People
freedom to assemble	Passage, Time, Period	People
trial by jury	1791	Rights
protects accused	Constitution	Patriotism
freedom of religion	after Revolutionary War	
petition for grievance		
after Revolutionary War in		
National Archives		

Form adapted from Institute for Staff Development 1971a, p. 30.

SAMPLE TOPICS FOR CONCEPT DEVELOPMENT DISCUSSIONS

To Clarify and Extend the Concept	*First Focusing Question*
characteristics of the Etruscan culture	What specific items, habits, and occurrences have you learned while researching the Etruscan culture?
culture and cultural universals	If you were to bury artifacts that reflect our culture, what items would you bury?
heroes and heroines	What do you think of when I say the word hero? Heroine?
freedom	What words come to mind when you think of the word "freedom"?
sounds	What sounds have you heard during the last week?
nourishing food	What are some foods you eat?
groups to which people belong	What are some groups to which people belong?
folk tales	What elements have you noticed in the stories we have read during the last two weeks?
transportation	Besides walking, how can people move from one place to another?
measurement	In what ways do people measure things?
art as communication	What comes to your mind as you look at these paintings?
machines	What are characteristics of machines?
fractions	What have you learned about fractions?
(specific) animal	What are some characteristics of (e.g., whales)?
government	What things in your life are affected by government?
the emphasis of a field trip	What did you observe in (e.g., the museum of natural history)?
buoyancy	What do you notice about these objects that floated when we put them in water? Those that sank?
organizing ideas	Now that you have written pertinent information on notecards, which of the notecards go together because they are alike in some way?
poetry	What characteristics have you noticed as we have read these poems?
animal homes	What animal homes can you name?
periodic table	What are some properties of atoms?
sonnets	What do you notice about the sonnets we have read?

11

Interpretation of Data

Events and phenomena are related and interrelated in a variety of ways. The ability to infer cause–effect relationships is invaluable in social, academic, and professional settings, as is skill in the developmental processes of drawing conclusions and making generalizations. Using Taba's interpretation of data strategy is one way to develop such capabilities in students. In this chapter a synthesis of existing information on the strategy is presented. (Unless otherwise noted, the information in this chapter is drawn from three sources: Institute for Staff Development 1971b and n.d.; and Maker 1982b.)

The interpretation of data strategy provides for guided cognitive discovery on the part of the student. This strategy is inductive, and students progress from the specific to the general; data are gathered, interpreted, and organized to become the basis for conclusions and generalizations. In the strategy the accumulation of information is followed by explanations, which requires transforming descriptive information to become explanatory. This change is an example of assimilation and accommodation on the part of the student (Taba, Levine, and Elzey 1964).

THE INTERPRETATION OF DATA TASK

The steps of the interpretation of data task are as follows:

1. List data related to the focus topic.
2. Infer cause–effect relationships based on the data, and provide support for the inference.
3. Extend previous inferences by providing prior causes or subsequent effects of selected relationships and furnish support for these further inferences.
4. Reach and support conclusions based on the discussion.
5. Develop and support generalizations based on the discussion.

The process requires that students select relevant data for listing, form conceptual linkages between data and inferred cause–effect relationships, develop sound conclusions based on the linkages established, and generalize concepts to broader applications. The cognitive maps for the demonstration lesson plans (Figure 11–1 and Figure 11–2) illustrate how the (separate) exploration of causes or effects of prejudiced behavior can provide a basis for conclusions and generalizations about prejudice.

Purpose

Understanding seems to entail (a) development of causal schemata that allow inferences or predictions of causes and consequences, (b) development of the ability to organize the results of these inferences, and (c) discovery of the relations that link episodes (Trabasso 1986). Causal coherence occurs within or across a set of statements related to a causal event. In this set of statements is found a *patient* (person or object) who undergoes change(s) as a result of the *agent*'s actions or processes. The relationships between the patient and the agent provide coherence to the individual's understanding (Trabasso and Sperry 1985).

Events may cause or be joined in time with events in kind. That is, initiating events may cause other initiating events, goals may motivate subordinate goals, actions may enable other actions, and outcomes cause other outcomes (Trabasso and Van Den Broek 1985).

In the interpretation of data strategy, students are asked to detect causal relationships between data and a variety of inferred events and to predict or infer events related to the first predictions or causal inferences. These steps help them develop causal schemata and discover new connections and relationships between patients and agents, thus reaching a higher level of understanding. Conclusions and generalizations, asked for in steps 4 and 5, offer a structure for organizing the results of (their own and the group's) inferences, bringing coherence to students' understanding.

Living successfully in a rapidly changing world requires the abilities to understand causal relationships and to process data in ways that lead to sound conclusions and valid generalizations. The interpretation of data strategy provides a structure for students to infer causes and/or effects, establish the causal linkages, and develop conclusions and generalizations based on their own observations and experiences; to process data in their own way as well as to observe how their peers process the same information.

Rationale for Individual Steps

Step 1—Listing

Listing data develops a common information base for a group and offers the benefits that come from sharing information. Students have

FIGURE 11–1 Demonstration Discussion Plan—Interpretation of Data (Causes)

STRATEGY: Interpretation of Data

Lesson Plan by
Shirley Schiever

Topic ___Prejudice (Causes)___

Level ___Demo___

DISCUSSION PURPOSES

Process: To make and support inferences concerning cause–effect relationships, to draw and support warranted conclusions, and to develop and support generalizations based on the discussion of these relationships.

MATERIALS

Content: To draw warranted conclusions and make generalizations based on the following relationships:

fear
power   prejudice   actions
stereotypes   reactions
conflict

BEHAVIORAL OBJECTIVES	FOCUSING QUESTIONS	TEACHER'S ROLE	SUPPORT PROCEDURES
STEP ONE—DATA a. Students will enumerate instances of behavior that reflect prejudice.	a. What do people do to people against whom they are prejudiced?	1. Focus on specific, relevant data. 2. Record data. 3. Seek variety. 4. Limit list length, time spent on step.	
STEP TWO—CAUSES OR EFFECTS AND SUPPORT a. Students will state inferences about causes of selected data. b. Students will support inferences with evidence or reasoning.	a. What would be a cause of, e.g., segregating a group of people? b. Why would ___ cause people to segregate others? a. What would be another cause . . . ? b. Why . . . ?	1. Select data related to content purpose of discussion. 2. Seek support that establishes link or connection. 3. Seek variety (positive & negative inferences). 4. Record causes or effects.	Vary question stems. Seek causes of three to four data.
STEP THREE—PRIOR CAUSES OR, SUBSEQUENT EFFECTS AND SUPPORT a. Students will infer prior causes of selected causes. b. Students will support inferences with evidence or reasoning.	a. What would cause, e.g., people to want to feel better than a particular group of people? b. Why would that cause . . . ? a. What else would cause . . . ? b. Explain how that would work.	1. Select inferences related to content purpose of discussion. 2. Seek support that establishes link between inferences. 3. Record new inferences. 4. Be sure inferences are removed from data in abstractness.	Seek prior causes of two to four causes.

Form adapted from Institute for Staff Development 1971b, pp. 39, 40, & 41.

(FIGURE 11–1–Continued)

BEHAVIORAL OBJECTIVES	FOCUSING QUESTIONS	TEACHER'S ROLE	SUPPORT PROCEDURES
STEP FOUR—CONCLUSIONS AND SUPPORT a. Students will state conclusions based on inferences. b. Students will support conclusions with evidence or reasoning.	a. Based on our discussion, what do you think is the most important cause of prejudice? b. Why is that most important? a. Who else will tell us what they think is the most important cause of prejudice? b. Why do you think . . . ?	1. Focus on discussion as basis for conclusions. 2. Seek support. 3. Seek responses from a variety of students.	Conclusions should not be summaries of the discussion. Rather, they should represent the sorting of supported and unsupported inferences and a synthesis that indicates arriving at an understanding of relationships.
STEP FIVE—GENERALIZATIONS AND SUPPORT a. Students will make a general statement about prejudice. b. Students will support their statements with evidence or reasoning.	a. Thinking about what you know and our discussion, what general statement can you make about human behavior? b. Why do you say . . . ?	1. Move students from specific data or situation to general statement by focus question. 2. Seek support. 3. Seek responses from a variety of students.	Step can be written if students are tired of discussing. If written, ask for volunteers to share statements and reasons.

Adapted from Institute for Staff Development 1971b, p. 42.

(FIGURE 11–1–Continued)

COGNITIVE MAP
Interpretation of Data (Causes)

STEP 3	STEP 2	STEP 1
Possible Prior Causes	Possible Causes	Possible Data

STEP 1
Possible Data

imprison
snub
exclude
deny privileges
deny rights
call names
make fun of/denigrate
look down on
pick fights
bully
assault
burn their house
try to scare
stereotype
kill
segregate
provide poor education
enslave
ignore
pay lower salary
joke about

STEP 2
Possible Causes

fear
ignorance
not liking someone who is different
have heard things about that group

to feel powerful
want to feel better than "them"
afraid they'll ruin neighborhood, school, etc.
to keep them "lower"
want to save money
keep power over them
keep status quo
greed
they can get away with it
jobs don't require skill

STEP 3
Possible Prior Causes

different look
different language
different customs

people like to feel better than others
desire for power
if I'm better than "them," I'm good
comfortable
like being in power
need laborers
need cheap labor
feelings of others
society's values
society's beliefs

STEP 4
Possible Conclusions

The most important cause of prejudice is the desire for power.

. . . the need to feel superior to others

. . . . exploitation

. . . . greed

STEP 5
Possible Generalizations

Prejudice does not really benefit anyone.
Prejudice is related to societal power and economics.
Prejudice is part of human nature.

Form adapted from Institute for Staff Development 1971b, p. 43.

FIGURE 11–2 Demonstration Discussion Plan—Interpretation of Data (Effects)

STRATEGY: Interpretation of Data

Lesson Plan by Shirley Schiever

Topic ___Prejudice (Effects)___

Level ___Demo___

DISCUSSION PURPOSES

PREDISCUSSION PROCEDURES

Content: To draw warranted conclusions and make generalizations based on the following relationships:

fear ↘ conflict

power → prejudice → actions

stereotypes ↗ reactions

MATERIALS

Process:

To make and support inferences concerning cause–effect relationships, to draw and support warranted conclusions, and to develop and support generalizations based on the discussion of these relationships.

BEHAVIORAL OBJECTIVES	FOCUSING QUESTIONS	TEACHER'S ROLE	SUPPORT PROCEDURES
STEP ONE—DATA Students will enumerate specific, relevant prejudiced behaviors.	1. In what specific ways do people treat others against whom they are prejudiced?	1. Focus on specific, relevant data. 2. Record data. 3. Seek variety. 4. Limit list length, time spent on step.	Use data from "Causes" discussion. Skip this step.
STEP TWO—CAUSES OR EFFECTS AND SUPPORT a. Students will state inferences about the effects of selected data. b. Students will support inferences with evidence or reasoning.	a. What would be an effect of, e.g., calling people names? b. Why would that be an effect? a. What would be another effect. . . . ? b. Why . . . . ?	1. Select data related to content purpose of discussion. 2. Seek support that establishes link or connection. 3. Seek variety (positive & negative inferences). 4. Record causes or effects.	Allow wait time. Vary stem of support question. (Why do you think . . . ?, etc.) Seek effects of three to four data.

Form adapted from Institute for Staff Development 1971b, pp. 39 & 40.

Copyright by Allyn and Bacon. Reproduction of this material is restricted to use with *A Comprehensive Approach to Teaching Thinking* by Shirley W. Schiever.

(FIGURE 11-2-Continued)

BEHAVIORAL OBJECTIVES	FOCUSING QUESTIONS	TEACHER'S ROLE	SUPPORT PROCEDURES
STEP THREE—PRIOR CAUSES OR SUBSEQUENT EFFECTS AND SUPPORT a. Students will state effects of previously inferred effects. b. Students will give evidence or reasoning to support new inferences.	a. What would be an effect of, e.g., the segregated group feeling angry? b. Why would — be an effect? a. What other effects would — have? b. Why . . . ?	1. Select inferences related to content purpose of discussion. 2. Seek support that establishes link between inferences. 3. Record new inferences. 4. Be sure inferences are removed from data in abstractness.	When inferences relate to teaching generalization, move to Step 4. Seek subsequent effects of three to four effects.
STEP 4—CONCLUSIONS AND SUPPORT a. Students will state conclusions based on inferences of effects. b. Students will support conclusions with evidence or reasoning.	a. Based on our discussion, what do you think is the most important effect of prejudice? b. Why is that the most important? a. What does someone else think is the most important effect? b. Why . . . ?	1. Focus on discussion as basis for conclusions. 2. Seek support. 3. Seek responses from a variety of students.	
STEP FIVE—GENERALIZATIONS AND SUPPORT a. Students will formulate a general statement about prejudice. b. Students will support the statement with evidence or reasoning.	a. Thinking about all we have said, what general statement can you make about human behavior? b. Why do you believe . . . ? a. Who else will make a general statement about prejudice? b. Why do you say . . . ?	1. Move students from specific data or situation to general statement by focus question. 2. Seek support. 3. Seek responses from a variety of students.	If students need change, ask them to write their general statement and three reasons that support it.

Form adapted from Institute for Staff Development 1971b, pp. 41 & 42.

(FIGURE 11–2–Continued)

COGNITIVE MAP
Interpretation of Data (Effects)

STEP 1
Possible Data

imprison
snub
exclude
deny privileges
deny rights
call names
make fun of/denigrate
look down on
pick fights
bully
assault
burn their house
try to scare
stereotype
kill
segregate
provide poor education
enslave
ignore
pay lower salary
joke about

STEP 2
Possible Effects

exclusive group feels superior
feel angry
form own groups
feel hurt
hate people in power
feel hurt
call names back
withdraw
become mean
fight
become strong
power for some
unequal opportunity
segregated group angry
power group fearful
suspicion
no positive changes for segregated group
poor jobs
act different from well-educated
better education for group in power

STEP 3
Possible Subsequent Effects

closeness within group
riots
murders
vandalism
war
plot against power group
sabotage power group
give up
more on welfare
fewer rights
work to keep segregation
separate selves further
blame everything on "them"
attempt to disenfranchise "them"
more in jail
poor health
stereotypes reinforced
feel helpless and hopeless

STEP 4
Possible Conclusions

The most important effect of prejudice is war.
. . . more prejudice
. . . more segregation

STEP 5
Possible Generalizations

Prejudice comes from and leads to more prejudice.
Society as a whole suffers from prejudice.
Segregation is harmful to everyone.

Form adapted from Institute for Staff Development 1971b, p. 43.

the benefit of their collective observations and experiences, and they must decide on the relevancy of individual data. Student-generated data gives ownership in a discussion, which makes the discussions more interesting to students and invites wider participation.

Step 2—Inferring Causes or Effects
When students infer causes or effects, they are applying their own reasoning, experience, and knowledge to the data to arrive at and support their inferences. For example, in the demonstration lesson plan on page 183 an inference that hearing derogatory things about a group might cause their exclusion would be based on the experience and reasoning of the person making the inference.

By listening to different interpretations that are often equally justifiable, students learn to attend to and seek out the basis for differing ideas. Providing support for inferences helps students clarify their reasons and develop the habit of identifying the justification for their ideas.

Step 3—Inferring Prior Causes or Subsequent Effects
The development of new inferences based on supported previous inferences encourages students to probe deeply into phenomena that influence their lives, rather than looking only at surface conditions. Making further inferences about cause–effect relationships emphasizes that these relationships are usually complex and interrelated, rather than simple and linear. This step also brings to attention the fact that many influences are far removed from the immediate data or situations, as illustrated in the demonstration lesson plan (page 186) by the inference of poor health as a long-term effect of poor education.

Step 4—Reaching Conclusions
The fourth step requires students to draw conclusions, and even though they may not have all the information they would like, they must make the soundest conclusion possible and provide support for it. Reaching a conclusion is an intermediate step in the abstracting process; it requires sifting through information, choosing and evaluating that which is relevant, and making a conclusion based on the evaluation. Step 4 is a synthesizing one; students are required to look at all the causes or effects and choose the most important. Further, they must be able to provide support as to why that one is the most important.

Step 5—Generalizing
Generalizing is an efficiency-building technique similar to labeling. This task gives students practice in transferring knowledge from one situation to other, similar situations where it might apply. The transfer is from the specific to the general, and provides students with a tool to answer questions they have not yet encountered.

Conceptualizing the Interpretation of Data Strategy

As with the concept development task and indeed all effective teaching, the teacher must understand and internalize the purpose of the entire interpretation of data strategy as well as the cognitive tasks of each step. Figure 11–3 provides a visual representation of the strategy. Components of the strategy are represented by letters (e.g., "D" represents "data"), and the steps for a discussion of causes are on the left side of the data and those for an effects discussion are on the right. Some novices make a chart similar to this figure on a large sheet of paper and put it in an easily visible spot when they are leading discussions. One advantage of using a visual aid is that the overall strategy can be kept in mind throughout each step.

Overt and Covert Behaviors in Interpretation of Data

Thinking, which is covert, is manifested in overt behaviors. When planning learning experiences, the teacher should identify both overt and covert aspects of the teaching goal. Figure 11–4 lists the purpose; overt, or behavioral objectives; covert, or thinking objectives; and general or possible focusing questions for each step of the interpretation of data strategy. This chart serves as a guide for the planning process and as an aid in formulating focusing questions for each step of the strategy.

PLANNING AN INTERPRETATION OF DATA DISCUSSION

Effectively using the interpretation of data strategy requires careful and detailed planning. The teacher must identify the purpose of the discussion, conceptualize the techniques to be used, and be aware of the range of possible responses. This preplanning does not imply that teachers are seeking specific responses, but rather that they are prepared to guide the discussion toward its stated purpose.

FIGURE 11-3 Graphic Representation—Interpretation of Data

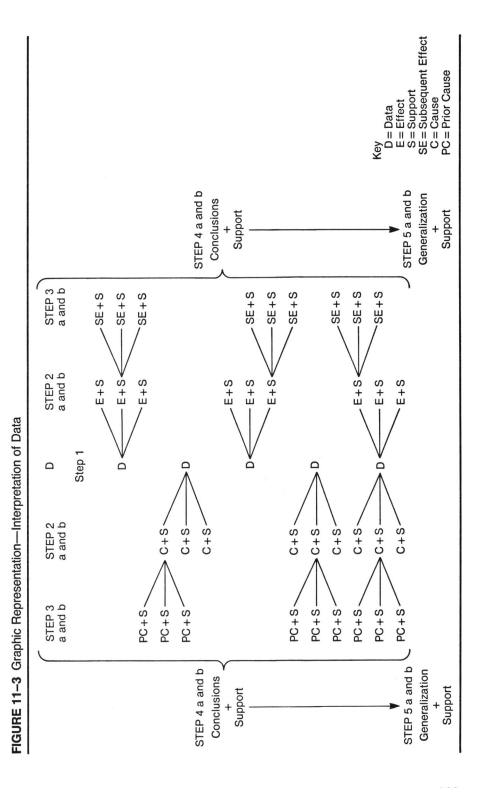

189

FIGURE 11–4 Over-Covert Behaviors—Interpretation of Data

STEP	1	2	3	4	5
Purpose of Step	Develop List of Relevant Data	To Establish Causal or Effectual Linkages for Selected Data	To Establish Complexity of Events or Phenomena	To Draw Conclusion Based on Inferences & Support	To Transfer Knowledge from One (Specific) Situation to Another, Similar One
OVERT Behavioral objectives	Enumerate relevant data.	a. State inferences about causes or effects. b. State evidence or reasoning to support inferences.	a. State inferences about prior causes or subsequent effects. b. Support new inferences.	a. State related conclusion.	State generalization based on conclusions.
COVERT Thinking objectives	Recall data.	a. Infer cause or effect. b. Identify supporting evidence.	a. Infer prior causes or subsequent effects. b. Identify evidence or reasoning.	a. Synthesize inferences. b. State evidence or reasoning in support.	a. Generalize about discussion to similar situations. b. Identify evidence or reasoning.
FOCUSING QUESTIONS (General)	What did you observe? Read? Hear?	a. What would cause __? What would be an effect of __? b. Why would __ cause __? Why would __ be an effect of __?	a. What would cause (cause)? What would be an effect of (effect)? b. Why do you think __ is a cause/effect of __?	a. What is the most important cause/effect of __? b. Why is that the most important?	a. What can you say in general about __? b. What from our discussion leads you to say that?

Adapted from Institute for Staff Development 1971b, p. 8.

Discussion Plan Form

Interpretation of data discussions can be complex. If they are to stay on focus and be productive in terms of the stated purposes, the dimensions of the discussion must be thought through carefully and recorded on the discussion plan form (Figure 11–5). This form is designed to aid in the planning and implementation of an interpretation of data discussion. Completing the form as suggested below facilitates the planning of a comprehensive, effective discussion.

Note that the forms for "cause" discussions and those for "effects" discussions are the same, except for the first page of the cognitive map. The column for possible data is on the right side for causes, on the left for effects. When planning an interpretation of data discussion, be sure to duplicate the correct page for the desired cognitive map.

Determining Discussion Purposes

The content and process purposes are the foundation of the discussion procedure and serve as reference points for evaluating every other part of the plan and the discussion itself. The content purposes should be a clear statement of the cause–effect relationships the teacher wants the students to recognize as *one* result of the discussion. In the demonstration lesson plan (Figure 11–1), the content purpose is to draw warranted conclusions and make generalizations based on the relationships between prejudice and fear, power, stereotypes, conflict, actions, and reactions. The content purpose helps the teacher make decisions regarding (a) what data will be needed, (b) ways to gather and organize data, and (c) what ideas to pursue in the discussion to provide ample opportunity for the stated relationship, along with valid conclusions and generalizations, to be discovered and stated.

Defining the content purpose relationships does not and should not dictate the number or kind of relationships students will make during the discussion. Neither does staying on focus imply restricting the discussion only to those aspects the teacher has determined in advance. The opportunity to explore a *number* of relationships and reach *many* warranted conclusions is the basic purpose for every interpretation of data discussion. Planning for the achievement of a particular content purpose simply makes it more likely that a particular purpose will be *one* of the outcomes of the discussion.

The process purpose states what the teacher plans for the students to achieve as a result of the manner in which they deal with the data. Generally, the intent is to have students arrive at warranted conclusions and generalizations through making and supporting

FIGURE 11–5 Discussion Plan Form

STRATEGY: Interpretation of Data

Topic _____

Level _____

DISCUSSION PURPOSES

PREDISCUSSION PROCEDURES

Content:

Process:

MATERIALS

BEHAVIORAL OBJECTIVES	FOCUSING QUESTIONS	TEACHER'S ROLE	SUPPORT PROCEDURES
STEP ONE—DATA		1. Focus on specific, relevant data. 2. Record data. 3. Seek variety. 4. Limit list length, time spent on step.	
STEP TWO—CAUSES OR EFFECTS AND SUPPORT		1. Select data related to content purpose of discussion. 2. Seek support that establishes link or connection. 3. Seek variety (positive & negative inferences). 4. Record causes or effects.	

Form adapted from Institute for Staff Development 1971b, pp. 39 & 40.

(FIGURE 11–5—Continued)

BEHAVIORAL OBJECTIVES	FOCUSING QUESTIONS	TEACHER'S ROLE	SUPPORT PROCEDURES
STEP THREE—PRIOR CAUSES OR SUBSEQUENT EFFECTS AND SUPPORT		1. Select inferences related to content purpose of discussion. 2. Seek support that establishes link between inferences. 3. Record new inferences. 4. Be sure inferences are re-moved from data in abstract-ness.	
STEP FOUR—CONCLUSIONS AND SUPPORT		1. Focus on discussion as basis for conclusions. 2. Seek support. 3. Seek responses from a variety of students.	
STEP FIVE—GENERALIZATIONS AND SUPPORT		1. Move students from specific data or situation to general statement by focus question. 2. Seek support. 3. Seek responses from a variety of students.	

Form adapted from Institute for Staff Development 1971b, pp. 41 & 42.

(FIGURE 11–5–Continued)

COGNITIVE MAP
Interpretation of Data (Causes)

STEP 3	STEP 2	STEP 1
Possible Prior Causes	*Possible Causes*	*Possible Data*

Form adapted from Institute for Staff Development 1971b, p. 43.
Copyright by Allyn and Bacon. Reproduction of this material is restricted to use with *A Comprehensive Approach to Teaching Thinking* by Shirley W. Schiever.

(FIGURE 11-5-Continued)

COGNITIVE MAP
Interpretation of Data (Effects)

STEP 1	STEP 2	STEP 3
Possible Data	*Possible Effects*	*Possible Subsequent Effects*

inferences regarding cause–effect relationships based on the data. The term *warranted* means that students are able to cite support, in the form of evidence or sound reasoning, to justify their conclusions. The general process purpose for the interpretation of data task is the following: Students will draw warranted conclusions and generalizations based on supported inferences of cause–effect relationships.

Planning Generalization

The planning generalization is a broad, abstract statement concerning the relationships in a focus situation or among phenomena. For example, the planning generalization for the demonstration lesson is "Prejudice is a self-perpetuating cycle." In this case, ideas related to the cyclical nature and self-perpetuity of prejudice would be selected for extension. The purpose of writing this statement is to define the scope of the discussion and focus on ideas that should be extended.

Planning the Discussion

The author recommends that only causes or effects be explored in a single discussion. Causes can be inferred one day and effects (of the same data) the next. Combining causes and effects in one discussion may confuse both students and teacher and make the discussion too long.

The following sections provide a step-by-step explanation of how to plan an interpretation of data discussion using the discussion plan form of Figure 11–5.

Prediscussion Procedures and Materials

1. *Decide what data are needed, how students will gather and organize the data, and what will be needed to conduct the discussion.* On the planning form, record materials students will use as references (films, magazines, people, textbooks), how students will work (individually, in pairs, in small groups, total class), how data will be recorded, prerequisite discussions (for example, a concept development discussion to organize the data), and physical arrangements for the discussion.

Purposes of the Discussion

2. *Determine what cause–effect relationships are to be explored in this discussion and record these on the form.* A helpful practice is to list a number of phenomena related to the focus topic and to "diagram" (by drawing lines or arrows) the cause–effect relationships for each phenomenon.

3. *On the discussion plan form, write a clear statement of the content and process purposes, using the relationships determined to be most productive.* The content purpose of the demonstration discussion plan is "To draw warranted conclusions and make generalizations based on the following relationships: (between) prejudice and fear, power, stereotypes, conflict, actions, and reactions." The process purpose is "To make and support inferences concerning cause–effect relationships, to draw and support warranted conclusions, and to develop and support generalizations based on the discussion of these relationships."

4. *Refer to Figure 11–4 for the general behavioral objective for Step 1.* Based on this general objective, write the specific objective for this step of your discussion, such as "Students will enumerate specific data related to prejudiced actions." If using data from a previous discussion or experience, this step of the planning and of the discussion can be omitted.

5. *Using the general focusing question from Figure 11–4 as a guide, formulate the focus question for Step 1.* For example, "What specific things do people do that show prejudice?" Record the focus question on the plan.

6. *Using the appropriate form (for causes or effects) of the cognitive map, record possible responses to your focus question or list previously recorded data.* Check the responses to see if these data are consistent with the content purpose of the discussion. If not, reformulate the focus question, record possible responses, and check again. Continue this process until the data given in response to the focus question will lead to inferences related to the content purpose.

7. List support procedures for Step 1 on the planning form. These procedures may include physical arrangements, reminders to yourself, and/or sample clarification, variety-seeking, or refocusing questions.

8. *Based on your planning generalization and the content purpose of the discussion (and the relationship diagram if you made one) determine which data will provide the richest opportunities for student inferences.* Mark these (three to five) items on the cognitive map.

9. *Using Figure 11–4, determine the general behavioral objectives for Step 2, and record the specific behavioral objective for this discussion, such as "Students will infer the causes (or effects) of specific prejudiced behaviors."* A second behavioral objective that deals with

support of inferences ("Students will support inferences about the causes (or effects) of prejudiced actions") also should be recorded.

10. *Using Figure 11–4, formulate your focusing question ("What would cause people to exclude other people from places or opportunities?").* Support question(s) ("Why would, e.g., fear cause . . .?") also should be recorded.

11. *Record possible effects (or causes) on the cognitive map.* If you plan to use the same data for both a cause and an effect discussion, complete the plan (and cognitive map) for one and then work through the other. That is, plan the entire "cause" discussion, then go through the same steps for the "effects" discussion, or vice versa.

12. *Continue using the overt/covert behavior chart, content and process purpose, cognitive map, and discussion plan form, making sure that each focus question will elicit responses related to the purposes of the individual step and the overall discussion.*
    The reader will note that there is no cognitive map for Steps 4 and 5 due to space considerations. The cognitive map for these steps can be completed on an additional sheet of paper.

IMPLEMENTING THE STRATEGY

Behaviors of the teacher as discussion leader will determine at what levels students think and to what extent they explore the desired relationships. Information in this section is included to help discussion leaders become more accomplished and successful at reaching discussion goals.
    The discussion plan form should be kept where it is easily visible and referred to during discussions. A successful discussion depends on the sequence and format of questions; referring to the plan helps ensure this.

Step 1—Listing

The purpose of Step 1 is to develop a list of data relevant to the focus of the discussion. The data listed must be specific and must include items related to the content purpose of the discussion. If student responses are too broad, an example or clarification must be sought. If the question "In what ways do people treat those who seem strange or different?" drew the response "Weird," clarification is needed. The clarification question would be "What do you mean when you say 'weird'?" or "What is an example of treating someone in a weird way?"

Using data recorded during a concept development discussion (as in the sample plans on prejudice) provides a number of benefits. By using previously generated data, students see that their earlier ideas and suggestions are valued and that this discussion relates to and builds on previous experiences and knowledge. Additionally, they are likely to see more abstract and complex relationships because the data are familiar to them.

The intake experience for an interpretation of data discussion should provide observable or factual, specific information. Articles such as editorials that contain opinions, conclusions, and generalizations are not appropriate.

The wording of the opening question should be related to the immediate purpose of enumerating data and to the overall purposes of the discussion. If the content purpose of the discussion is to build on events, the focus question at the first step must elicit data about specific events, so students will have pertinent data on which to base inferences.

The leader should keep the discussion at the enumerating step only long enough to generate a broad sampling of data. Whenever feasible, data should be listed on the chalkboard or butcher paper so the class can look at the data as a whole before moving to the next step. The first step usually can be accomplished in a short period of time if students have data from a common experience. When a broad and representative sample of data has been recorded, the teacher should move the discussion to the next step.

Novice discussion leaders may spend too much time at Step 1, listing more data than necessary, or they may list data that are not specific or are not related to the content purpose of the discussion. Thinking of this step as a prelude helps limit the time spent, and clear focus questions and an alert leader keep the data specific and relevant.

The teacher's role at Step 1 of an interpretation of data discussion can be summarized as follows:

- To focus on specific data that are relevant to the discussion purpose
- To seek a variety of data
- To seek clarification as necessary
- To record data accurately
- To limit the amount of data listed

After the data have been listed, the teacher will select several (three to five) data as those for which students will infer causes or effects in Step 2. Students may be sensitive to the fact that only a few data are selected. Before beginning Step 2, the teacher can re-assure them by saying, "All of these are interesting and pertinent; you all have a lot of information on this topic. We don't have time to discuss all of these; I have to choose only a few for the next step."

Steps 2 and 3

The purpose of the second and third steps of the interpretation of data task is to require that students make inferences about causes or effects of phenomena or events. Students should be looking for re-lationships among data and their inferences, and questions should be worded in a way that encourages the class to be tentative about knowledge and opinions. Questions such as "What would be some possible effects of this?" or "What do you think caused these people to do those things?" or "What do you think would be the effect of this?" rather than "What made these people do these things?" tend to elicit more qualified statements from students. Additionally, the model of an open-minded adult who states opinions with some de-gree of tentativeness helps develop this attitude in young people.

A variety of causes or effects should be inferred for each selected datum at Step 2 and for each selected inference at Step 3. Both positive and negative causes/effects should be sought actively by the teacher if both are not volunteered. Responses to the support ques-tions should establish for the individual and the group the connec-tions and the interlocking links. Step 3 inferences and support are more difficult for students to make because they are further away from the data and therefore more abstract.

Step 2—Inferring Causes or Effects

The purpose of Step 2 is to (a) elicit student inferences regarding causes or effects of selected data and (b) establish, through the sup-port statement, the linkage between the datum and the inference (cause or effect). In the demonstration lesson plan on page 183, if a student inferred that "fear" is a cause of excluding people, the sup-port question "Why would fear cause someone to exclude others?" is designed to identify the connection between fear and exclusion.

Students should be encouraged to make a variety of inferences (negative and positive) at this step, and they must establish the link between the data and the inference through support of their infer-ences. Seeking a variety of causes or effects for those data most closely related to the content purpose of the discussion illustrates to the students that events and phenomena have both positive and negative aspects and do not have single or simple causes or effects.

The most difficult task for the discussion leader at Step 2 is to ask support questions that lead students to verbalize the linkage between the data and their inferences (causes or effects). The support questions seem to be especially difficult in a discussion that explores causes. Suggested wording is "Why would . . . cause . . .?" or "How does . . . cause . . .?"

In a discussion exploring effects, some discussion leaders have a tendency to ask why the effect was *caused* by the datum, but the datum does *not* cause the effect. A possible support question at this step is "Why is . . . an effect of . . .?"

Another possible problem at Step 2 is using "might" or "could" in the focus question rather than "would." These words allow speculation, or a creative, brainstorming-type approach to making inferences, whereas the word *would* implies a reality base that sets the stage for establishing the linkage between inferences and data.

The teacher's role at Step 2 can be summarized as follows:

- To select data closely related to the discussion purpose
- To seek a variety of inferences for each selected (three to five) datum
- To record the inference
- To require the establishing of connections between inferences and data through support questions

The teacher again will select a few of the inferred causes or effects to explore further in Step 3. Reinforcement of the group's inferences before continuing may be reassuring to the students.

Step 3—Inferring Prior Causes or Subsequent Effects

Step 3 is an extension and expansion of Step 2, but the cognitive task is more abstract, since the inferences are made about inferences rather than data. At this step a few (three to five) inferences (causes or effects from Step 2) become the basis for further inferences. The purpose of this step is to (a) establish the complexity and interrelatedness of events or phenomena, (b) show long-term implications, and (c) illustrate multiple causes or effects of events or phenomena. Establishing conceptual links between the inferences of Step 2 and those of Step 3 and seeking a variety of inferences (negative and positive) is critical.

If a student should comment on or question further causes or effects, the teacher should pursue this line of thought, if only briefly. Inferring further causes or effects moves the discussion further away from the data and to a higher, more abstract level and helps to provide a basis for conclusions and generalizations. When student inferences relate to the teaching generalization, the discussion should be lifted to Step 4.

For variety, students can be put in small groups at this step with each group being assigned a cause or an effect from Step 2. Within the group, students infer and support prior causes or subsequent effects. A recorder records the inferences, and both inferences and support are shared with the entire group.

Common problems at Step 3 are similar to those at Step 2. Because of the abstractness of the task, establishing the cause or effect relationship between previous inferences and new ones is more difficult at this step. If students are to succeed in this task, the focus questions must be clear and the discussion leader must have the discussion purpose firmly in mind.

The teacher's role at Step 3 includes the following:

- To select inferences related to the content purpose and planning generalization of the discussion
- To record the new inferences
- To require the establishing of linkages between the new and previous inferences (between subsequent effects and effects or prior causes and causes) through support questions

Steps 4 and 5

The remaining steps in the task of inferring and generalizing involve combining and/or synthesizing relationships to draw conclusions and make generalizations. These skills are not an automatic result of maturation and experience; students need guided practice. Students can learn—and teachers can teach them—to make more thoughtful generalizations. When a teacher asks students to conclude and generalize, the cognitive task is to synthesize several relationships and make a statement about them. The task requires thinking and speaking in abstract terms as well as building on the ideas of others, giving reasons for opinions, and limiting statements to the data at hand.

Teachers should help students recognize the tentativeness of all conclusions and generalizations. This can be done by asking questions such as "In what kinds of situations would this not apply?"

Step 4—Drawing Conclusions

The purpose of Step 4 is for students to reach sound conclusions that are based on the inferences and the support aired during the discussion. Drawing a conclusion requires students to assimilate, synthesize, and evaluate the information from the discussion. Answering the question "Based on our discussion, what do you think is the most important effect of prejudiced actions?" requires the assimilation, synthesis, and evaluation of the discussion content to this point.

Most children and adults are not accustomed to being asked for conclusions, which makes Step 4 more important and more difficult to execute. Students need to realize that they are to synthesize the information they have on a specific topic and make a related conclusion. The question "Based on our discussion, what do you think is the most important cause of prejudiced actions?" tells students that they should draw together what was discussed as a basis for a conclusion. The support question should ask why the cause or effect mentioned is an important one (e.g., "Why is that the most important cause?").

When asking for a conclusion, "cause" or "effect" should be singular in the focus question. That is, do not ask for "most important causes" or "most important effects." Every student should be invited to respond, but students must understand that a variety of conclusions is not sought. Therefore, when seeking further responses, the question should be similar to this: "Who else will tell us what they think is the most important cause/effect of prejudiced behavior?"

The teacher's role at Step 4 can be summarized as follows:

- To focus on the inferences made during the discussion as the basis for the conclusions
- To seek responses from a variety of students
- To require evidence or reasoning that supports the conclusions

Step 5—Generalizing
The purpose of Step 5 is for students to transfer knowledge from one situation to other, similar situations. This is a process of moving from the specific to the more general. The focus question may require applying information about a city to a state, region, or other cities, or from an individual to a group of individuals or to people in general.

The scope of Step 5 depends on many factors, including the discussion purpose, the students, and the nature of the data. The narrowest scope would have students draw general conclusions closely related to the discussion focus. If the data for the discussion came from a story or novel, a narrow focusing question might ask students to generalize from those characters in the story that were discussed to those characters in the story who were not discussed. A broader scope would require students to generalize from the characters on which the discussion focused to people in similar situations or to people in general.

Two or three discussions in which students make general statements about particular situations that are similar or related may be desirable before asking for statements that apply to most situations of the same nature. For example, discussions of three different stories in which the characters are interacting with someone who is different in background, looks, or behavior might be held before asking students to generalize about this type of situation.

Whether the scope of Step 5 is narrow or wide, the focusing question must be clear. Generalizing is a difficult cognitive task; a confusing or vague question will make it more difficult. Focus questions asking for generalizations (Step 5) might include any of the following: "Based on our discussion, what would you say generally causes . . .?", "Thinking about all we have said here, what general statement can you make about the effects of . . .?", "Overall, what do you think generally could be considered to be true about . . .?", or "What general statement can you make about . . .?"

When students have had little or no experience in consciously generalizing, no true generalizations may be offered. If students make low-level generalizations or statements that are not generalizations, accept them and ask the support question just as you would for a generalization. Someone in the group will understand and make a general statement, and with practice many or most of the students will be able to make and support a warranted generalization.

In this step, as in Step 4, responses from a variety of students are desirable, but the refocus must indicate that different statements are not what is being sought. The refocus question might be worded like this: "Who else can make a general statement about prejudice?"

Students at the intermediate or higher grade levels can write their general statement and (two or three) supporting statements at Step 5. Writing the general statement allows shy, reticent, and slow students the opportunity to crystallize their thoughts privately. Often these students are more willing to share their thoughts when they have a chance to write them out first.

The most common error at Step 5 is in the focusing question rather than in delivery. The question at this step should move students from the specific to the general, and the tendency is to move from the specific to the less specific.

The teacher's role at Step 5 can be summarized as follows:

- To be sure the discussion has established a basis for student generalizations
- To move the students from specific events or phenomena to broader applications through the focus question

- To facilitate the sharing of general statements and support
- To require evidence or reasoning to support the general statements

APPLICATIONS OF THE INTERPRETATION OF DATA STRATEGY

The interpretation of data strategy can be used whenever the teacher wants students to make and support inferences, explore causal relationships, develop conclusions or generalizations, or discover underlying principles. By controlling the amount and type of content and materials, the strategy can be applied to any learning level; scientific, quantitative, literary, or symbolic data; and the different needs and learning styles of a variety of students.

Cooperative learning groups can be used at one, alternating, or all steps 2 through 5 of the interpretation of data strategy. If the teacher wants the causes or effects of many data explored, each group might be asked to make inferences based on different data. Assigning the same data to all groups can provide examples of the variety of possible causes or effects when the groups share their ideas. Even if the teacher has not organized the students into cooperative learning groups, alternating small- and large-group work can provide a way to check on individual students' skills. Additionally, change of format offers variety and recognition of different learning styles and needs.

After students are familiar with the process of interpreting data, they can be encouraged to use it to conceptualize and organize writing assignments (e.g., the causes or effects of feudalism, romantic literature). The strategy also is helpful when designing science projects, as for a science fair. A phenomenon of interest can be explored in terms of its causes and/or effects, conclusions drawn, and generalizations made.

Relationships suitable for an interpretation of data discussion can be found in the sample plans and discussion topics suggested for the concept development strategy. (An additional list is given on page 217.) The focusing question "What do you know about different racial and ethnic groups living in the United States?" was suggested for a concept development lesson. Given the resulting data, students also may explore a relationship such as the following:

| cultural differences of various ethnic and racial groups | ⟷ | assimilation rate and adjustment to the predominant culture |

As demonstrated by the preceding example, the difference between a concept development and an interpretation of data discussion is not in the topic, but in how the data are processed. The demonstration lessons here and in Chapter 10 illustrate the use of the same data for the two types of discussion. As is evident from examining these plans, the thinking processes used and discussion results are quite different, depending on the strategy used.

CHAPTER SUMMARY

The interpretation of data strategy provides a structure for exploring cause–effect relationships. Students infer and support causes or effects of data, infer and support prior causes or subsequent effects, draw conclusions, and make generalizations. The strategy has many and varied applications within curricula at any level. The planning and execution of an interpretation of data discussion has been detailed in an effort to provide the novice with ideas, guidance, and direction.

SAMPLE INTERPRETATION OF DATA
DISCUSSION PLANS

DISCUSSION PLAN
STRATEGY: Interpretation of Data
Institute for Staff Development 1971b
DISCUSSION PURPOSES
Content: To draw warranted conclusions about the following relationships:

amount and intensity of heat → rate and kind of change in forms of matter → what people do

Process:
To infer cause–effect relationships, to support inferences, to draw conclusions based on supported inferences, and to generalize from one instance to other such instances.

Topic   Effects of Heat on the Form of Matter
Level   Early Elementary
PREDISCUSSION PROCEDURES
Arrange children so all can observe the following demonstration. (Label pie tins.)

Tin #1—Put several ice cubes on pie tin, one under the others.
Tin #2—Put a single ice cube on pie tin.
Tin #3—Put a single ice cube on a pie tin and put this tin on a warming hot plate. (Children should see the reddened coils.)

Children should observe the experiment until the ice in Tin #3 is melted. (If you wish, you may extend the time until the water turns to steam and deal with this observation as well.)
MATERIALS: chalkboard or butcher paper, three aluminum pie tins, a bag of ice cubes, a hot plate.

BEHAVIORAL OBJECTIVES	FOCUSING QUESTIONS	TEACHER'S ROLE	SUPPORT PROCEDURES
STEP ONE—DATA Students will report what they observed.	Now that you've had a chance to watch the ice cubes on different tins, what did you see happening on Tin #1? Tin #2? Tin #3?	1. Focus on specific, relevant data. 2. Record data. 3. Seek variety. 4. Limit list length, time spent on step.	Record observations in the simplest words possible so all students can read the list and refer to it.

Form adapted from Institute for Staff Development 1971b, p. 39.

BEHAVIORAL OBJECTIVES	FOCUSING QUESTIONS	TEACHER'S ROLE	SUPPORT PROCEDURES
STEP TWO—CAUSES OR EFFECTS AND SUPPORT Causes a. Students will state inferences about the causes for: #1 not melting at the bottom, #2 melting a little, #3 melting fast, faster than the others. b. Students will cite evidence or give explanations in support of inferences.	a. What do you think caused the ice cube in #3 to melt fastest? b. Why do you think it was the hot plate that caused it? a. What do you think caused the ice cube in #2 to melt a little, but more than #1 and less than #3? b. What would the air in the room have to do with it? Etc.	1. Select data related to content purpose of discussion. 2. Seek support that establishes link or connection. 3. Seek variety (positive & negative inferences). 4. Record causes or effects.	
STEP THREE—PRIOR CAUSES OR SUBSEQUENT EFFECTS AND SUPPORT Prior Causes a. Students will state their inferences about what they think caused some of the conditions described in Step 2. b. Students will cite evidence or give explanations to support their inferences.	a. You say you think the warm air in the room made #2 melt a little. What do you think would cause the air in here to be warm? b. Why do you think people in the room causes it to be warm? a. What do you think caused the ice cube in #3 to get more heat than the others? b. How would the electricity cause it to get hot?	1. Select inferences related to content purpose of discussion. 2. Seek support that establishes link between inferences. 3. Record new inferences. 4. Be sure inferences are removed from data in abstractness.	

Form adapted from Institute for Staff Development 1971b, pp. 39, 40, & 41.

BEHAVIORAL OBJECTIVES	FOCUSING QUESTIONS	TEACHER'S ROLE	SUPPORT PROCEDURES
STEP FOUR—CONCLUSIONS AND SUPPORT a. Students will state their conclusion about the causes for the ice melting. b. Students will explain the reasoning behind their statements.	a. From what you observed and what we have said, what do you think is the most important cause of the ice melting? b. Why do you think more or less heat was the most important cause?	1. Focus on discussion as basis for conclusions. 2. Seek support. 3. Seek responses from a variety of students.	If summaries are offered rather than conclusions, say, "Yes, we did say all those things. Now what do _you_ think is the most important cause?"
STEP FIVE—GENERALIZATIONS AND SUPPORT a. Students will generalize about melting. b. Students will explain the reasoning behind their statements.	a. Thinking now of all we've said about this experiment and all you know about this, what could you say in one sentence about melting? b. Why do you think knowing about heat and melting helps us?	1. Move students from specific data or situation to general statement by focus question. 2. Seek support. 3. Seek responses from a variety of students.	

Form adapted from Institute for Staff Development 1971b, p. 42.

COGNITIVE MAP
Interpretation of Data (Causes)

STEP 3	STEP 2	STEP 1
Possible Prior Causes	*Possible Causes*	*Possible Data*

STEP 3 — Possible Prior Causes

Prior Causes

Other ice cubes kept room air away. ⟶

People are warm.
Sun makes room warm.
Children and teacher are warm.
Sun coming in windows warms room air.
Electricity in hot plate.
Electricity can make things hotter than
without it.

STEP 2 — Possible Causes

Immediate Causes

Ice cube on bottom coldest. ⟶

Air around top ice cubes warm. ⟶

Air around ice cubes warm. ⟶

Lots of heat.
Heat close to tin.

Room not as warm as hot plate. ⟶

STEP 1 — Possible Data

Observations

#1—ice cube on bottom didn't melt. Ones
on top melted a little.

#2—ice cube began to melt a little.

#3—ice cube melted fast. Tin got hot.

#3 melted much faster than #1 and #2.

STEP 5 — Possible Generalizations

Generalizations about Causes and Effects of Melting

If you know that heat melts things, you know how to keep things
the way you want them.

Keeping heat away from cold things keeps them cold longer.

STEP 4 — Possible Conclusions

Conclusions about Causes for the Ice Melting

The more heat there was, the faster the ice cube melted.

The ice cube that had the most heat closest to it melted fastest.

The warm air in the room made ice cube #2 and the outside ones
in #1 melt a little, but not as fast as the one in #3.

The cold from the other ice cubes kept the bottom one in #1 from
melting.

Conclusions about Effects of Knowing about Things Melting

When you know what heat does to things, you either put it on or
take it away.

People use a stove or something like that to put heat on things to
melt them, and they use a refrigerator to keep heat away so
things won't melt if they don't want them to.

Form adapted from Institute for Staff Development 1971b, p. 43.

DISCUSSION PLAN

STRATEGY: Interpretation of Data
Lesson plan by Roger Shanley

Topic _____ Stress _____

Level _____ Middle School _____

DISCUSSION PURPOSES

Content: To draw warranted conclusions about the causes of stress in everyday life.

PREDISCUSSION PROCEDURES

Arrange students in semicircle. Show film or provide article on stress.

```
                          Individuals
              Family          and
  Stress  →  School         Lives
              Assignments
              Sports
```

MATERIALS

chalkboard
tape recorder

Process:
To make and support inferences concerning causal relationships, to draw conclusions based on well-supported inferences, and to generalize from few instances to many.

BEHAVIORAL OBJECTIVES	FOCUSING QUESTIONS	TEACHER'S ROLE	SUPPORT PROCEDURES
STEP ONE—DATA Students will state data obtained from the material presented in class.	a. From (the film, article), what are some specific sources of stress?	1. Focus on specific, relevant data. 2. Record data. 3. Seek variety. 4. Limit list length, time spent on step.	Clarify vague responses.
STEP TWO—CAUSES OR EFFECTS AND SUPPORT a. Students will state their inferences about the causes of selected data. b. Students will give their reasons or an explanation in support of their inferences.	a. What would cause school to be stressful? b. Why would ___ make school stressful?	1. Select data related to content purpose of discussion. 2. Seek support that establishes link or connection. 3. Seek variety (positive & negative inferences). 4. Record causes or effects.	Encourage a variety of causes and support for inferences where not given. Make sure the major emphasis is on the cause of stress. Record answers on my own sheet as well as on the chalkboard.

Form adapted from Institute for Staff Development 1971b, pp. 39 & 40.

Copyright by Allyn and Bacon. Reproduction of this material is restricted to use with *A Comprehensive Approach to Teaching Thinking* by Shirley W. Schiever.

211

BEHAVIORAL OBJECTIVES	FOCUSING QUESTIONS	TEACHER'S ROLE	SUPPORT PROCEDURES
STEP THREE—PRIOR CAUSES OR SUBSEQUENT EFFECTS AND SUPPORT a. Students will state inferences regarding prior causes of selected causes. b. Students will state data or provide explanation in support of their inferences.	a. What would cause poor teachers? b. Why does __ cause people to be poor teachers?	1. Select inferences related to content purpose of discussion. 2. Seek support that establishes link between inferences. 3. Record new inferences. 4. Be sure inferences are removed from data in abstractness.	Remain open to new areas mentioned. Vary questions to avoid monotony. Avoid value judgments.
STEP FOUR—CONCLUSIONS AND SUPPORT a. Students will draw conclusions regarding the causes of stress in everyday life. b. Students will support their conclusions by evidence or the reasoning behind their statement.	a. From our discussion, what would you say is the most important cause of stress in everyday life? b. Why do you feel or what led you to believe this is a major cause of stress?	1. Focus on discussion as basis for conclusions. 2. Seek support. 3. Seek responses from a variety of students.	Make sure causes are concluded upon, not the original data.
STEP FIVE—GENERALIZATIONS AND SUPPORT a. Students will state generalizations about stress. b. Students will support these generalizations.	a. What general statement can you make about stress? b. Why do you feel this generalization is true?	1. Move students from specific data or situation to general statement by focus question. 2. Seek support. 3. Seek responses from a variety of students.	Students must write generalizations. Make sure support is given.

Form adapted from Institute for Staff Development 1971b, pp. 41 & 42.

COGNITIVE MAP
Interpretation of Data (Causes)

STEP 3	STEP 2	STEP 1
Possible Prior Causes	*Possible Causes*	*Possible Data*

STEP 3
Possible Prior Causes

age
maturity
inexperience
bad pay
poor training
bad reputation
want you to succeed
unrealistic
want you to show off
too busy
don't care
tired

STEP 2
Possible Immediate Causes

not enough pay
too many hours
lack of responsibility
too much work
bad grades
poor teachers
hurt ears
cause adrenalin
make nervous
too many hopes
fight themselves
don't listen

STEP 1
Possible Data

Data
work
school
friends
acne
weight problems
music
noise
lack of sleep
drugs
parents
spouses
movies

STEP 5
Possible Generalizations

Stress may be caused by family, occupation, or parental pressures.

STEP 4
Possible Conclusions

The most important cause of stress:

school

work

parents

Form adapted from Institute for Staff Development 1971b, p. 43.

DISCUSSION PLAN
STRATEGY: Interpretation of Data
Lesson plan by Roger Shanley
DISCUSSION PURPOSES

Content: To draw warranted conclusions about the trends or causes that resulted in Rome's decline and downfall.

Trend — "Decadent moral practices" ⟶ Decline/Fall
Cause ⟶ Poor money management   of Rome
         Strengthening global powers
         Weakened borders

Process:

Topic ___Downfall of Rome___
Level ___Secondary___
PREDISCUSSION PROCEDURES

Arrange seats to hear all responses.
Have students organize notes that relate to the later years of the Roman Empire.
Urge students to present material on later stages of Rome.

MATERIALS
Tape recorder
Overhead projector

BEHAVIORAL OBJECTIVES	FOCUSING QUESTIONS	TEACHER'S ROLE	SUPPORT PROCEDURES
STEP ONE—DATA a. Students will state data obtained from the specific research and investigation of Rome's later stages.	a. From the research and investigation of the later period in Rome, what are some specific observations you can make about the decline and downfall of Rome?	1. Focus on specific, relevant data. 2. Record data. 3. Seek variety. 4. Limit list length, time spent on step.	Ask for clarification of obscure language.
STEP TWO—CAUSES OR EFFECTS AND SUPPORT a. Students will state inferences about selected data. b. Students will give reasons or explanations in support of their inferences.	a. What would cause Rome's monetary system to become distorted or inflated? b. Why would ___ cause ___?	1. Select data related to content purpose of discussion. 2. Seek support that establishes link or connection. 3. Seek variety (positive & negative inferences). 4. Record causes or effects.	Encourage a variety of causes and get support for inferences where not given. Make sure the major emphasis is on causes vs. effects. Record answers on a sheet for later reference.

Form adapted from Institute for Staff Development 1971b, pp. 39 & 40.

BEHAVIORAL OBJECTIVES	FOCUSING QUESTIONS	TEACHER'S ROLE	SUPPORT PROCEDURES
STEP THREE—PRIOR CAUSES OR SUBSEQUENT EFFECTS AND SUPPORT a. Students will state inferences about prior causes of selected causes. b. Students will provide explanation or evidence in support of their inferences.	a. What are some of the causes for Rome to mint more money than they had backed by capital? b. What caused Rome's plunder to be lost or stolen? a. Why would Romans believing that no one would doubt their capital cause Rome's monetary imbalance? b. Why do you feel poor supervision caused Rome's plunder to be stolen?	1. Select inferences related to content purpose of discussion. 2. Seek support that establishes link between inferences. 3. Record new inferences. 4. Be sure inferences are removed from data in abstractness.	Remain open to new approaches or paths from students. Avoid monotonous questions by using a variety of question stems. Accept all responses. Avoid teacher value statements and judgments.
STEP FOUR—CONCLUSIONS AND SUPPORT a. Students will draw warranted conclusions regarding the decline/fall of the Roman Empire. b. Students will support their conclusions by citing the evidence or the reasoning behind the statement.	a. From our discussion, what would you say was the most important cause of the decline/fall of Rome? b. Why do you feel overexpansion was a major cause of the decline or fall in Rome? a. What led you to believe this to be true? b. Who else will tell us what they believe was the major cause of the decline or fall of the Roman Empire?	1. Focus on discussion as basis for conclusions. 2. Seek support. 3. Seek responses from a variety of students.	Accept student conclusions. Make sure to ask students to conclude about <u>causes</u> given and not the data.
STEP FIVE—GENERALIZATIONS AND SUPPORT a. Students will state generalizations about cycles of civilization. 1. Students will write the generalization. b. Students will support these generalizations.	a. What general statement can you make about civilizations? b. Why do you feel this statement is generally true?	1. Move students from specific data or situation to general statement by focus question. 2. Seek support. 3. Seek responses from a variety of students.	Make sure students write generalizations in full sentences. Make sure generalizations are supported.

Form adapted from Institute for Staff Development 1971b, pp. 41 & 42.

COGNITIVE MAP
Interpretation of Data (Causes)

STEP 3	STEP 2	STEP 1
Possible Prior Causes	*Possible Causes*	*Possible Data*
No actual goods or items	Not enough capital backup	Monetary system degenerated
Poor training		
	Poor management	Borders expanded beyond its limits
Improper accounting	Unstructured balance	
		Invaders infiltrated colonies
Expanded borders	Long distances	Poor rule from military/emperor
Who knows?	Bad weather	Communication problems
Need for money	Hijackings	

STEP 4	STEP 5
Possible Conclusions	*Possible Generalizations*
The most important cause of Rome's decline and fall was:	Countries decline and fall when they are weakened by various factors and events.
Poor leadership	
Greedy rulers expanding borders	
Aggressive invaders	

Form adapted from Institute for Staff Development 1971b, p. 43.

SAMPLE TOPICS FOR INTERPRETATION OF DATA DISCUSSIONS

To Draw Warranted Conclusions about the Relationships Between or Among	Step 2 Focusing Question
change—development of individuals in the Middle Ages	What would cause feudalism to develop?
world events—stock market fluctuations	What events led to the rise of IT&T stock? What would cause the rise of IT&T stock?
properties of atoms—periodic repetition—predictability of chemical and physical properties—chemical reactions	What properties cause relative reactivity among atoms?
intent to persuade—specific techniques—reaction of listener(s)	What do you think prompted Antony to repeat the phrase "honorable men" and refer to Brutus each time?
degree of difference in skills and customs of immigrants from receiving country residents—rate of assimilation—contribution of immigrant group	Why do you think Asian immigrants become successful more quickly than Mexican immigrants?
characteristics of number system—usefulness	What operations are possible because our system uses nine numerals and zero? What effect does zero have on our number system?
intent of cartoonist—political cartoons—understanding of issues—reactions of subject of cartoon	How do you think readers react to this cartoon? What effects does this cartoon have?
birth order—perfectionism, achievement, stress, expectations of self and others	What effects do you think perfectionism has on a person?
properties of triangles—ability to calculate unknown dimensions	What are you able to do or figure out since you know these two triangles have right angles?
cliques—thoughts, feelings, behaviors, and social control	What are some effects of, e.g., cliques being powerful?
censorship—degree of knowledge, fear, and desire for power	What would cause a women's group to call for banning Dungeons and Dragons?

12

Application of Generalizations

Applying generalizations is an important life skill. When a necessity exists to keep an appointment on the far side of town at 5:30 PM, the generalization that heavy traffic will require extra traveling time at that time of day allows one to arrive on time. Taba's application of generalizations strategy provides a way to teach students to apply previously learned generalizations and facts to explain unfamiliar events and infer consequences from known conditions. In this chapter a synthesis of existing information on the strategy is presented. (Unless otherwise noted, the information in this chapter is drawn from three sources: Institute for Staff Development 1971c and n.d.; and Maker 1982b.)

THE APPLICATION OF GENERALIZATIONS TASK

The application of generalizations task is an extension of inference and generalization making. It differs from the concept development and interpretation of data tasks in that inferences in the form of predictions, rather than data (facts), are listed to begin the discussion. This strategy invites divergence at steps 1 and 3 and therefore offers opportunities for the creative use of knowledge.

The specific steps of the application of generalizations task follow:

1. Make predictions based on a hypothetical situation or event and provide support for (selected) predictions.
2. Infer and support necessary conditions for selected predictions.
3. Infer consequences and necessary conditions for the predictions and provide evidence or reasoning in support of the inferences.
4. Draw and support a warranted conclusion.
5. Examine a generalization and support the affirmation, modification, or extension of the generalization.

This strategy develops in students the ability to make predictions about the future and enables them to apply previous learning. The test of understanding a concept or generalization is in the application; internalized concepts and generalizations can be used to make further inferences.

Purpose

The application of previously learned facts, principles, or processes to new situations is important for the transfer of knowledge, and it enables students to gain a greater depth of knowledge from their experiences. While the application of generalizations strategy allows for and encourages divergent thinking in making predictions, it also requires establishing the parameters of logical relationships. Students must generate the chain of causal links connecting their predictions and the necessary conditions within these parameters, requiring that logic and critical thinking be applied to the (divergent) inferences.

Rationale for Individual Steps

Step 1—Making Predictions
At Step 1, students are encouraged to use their creativity to brainstorm the possible results of some hypothetical event or situation. This step stimulates divergent thinking as well as offering the opportunity to link the resulting creative idea to reality through logic. Students need to learn how to make logical speculations based on a given set of circumstances that represent a situation similar to one with which they are familiar. In the demonstration lesson plan (Figure 12–1), the prediction "The new people will be lonely" is a logical speculation, given student knowledge and experiences.

Step 2—Inferring Conditions
Inferring the necessary conditions for a prediction is essential to building a logical, justifiable chain of possible relationships. Asking students to identify prior and attendant factors needed for a prediction to occur provides opportunities for them to apply previously gained knowledge to a new but similar situation. In the preceding example, students would be asked what else must happen or be true for the new people to be lonely.

Step 3—Inferring Consequences and Conditions
The third step is primarily an extension and recycling of the preceding steps, the difference being that this step builds on selected

FIGURE 12-1 Discussion Plan Form—Application of Generalizations

STRATEGY: Application of Generalizations
Shirley Schiever

Topic ___Prejudice___
Level ___Demo___

DISCUSSION PURPOSES

PREDISCUSSION PROCEDURES

As appropriate for age/experience of students.

Content: To modify or extend the following generalization: Prejudice is harmful to personal development and societal structure.

Process: To predict the consequences of a light-skinned family moving into a small, isolated community of dark-complexioned people, to support predictions with evidence or reasoning, to limit predictions by stating and supporting necessary prior or attendant conditions, and to draw warranted conclusions and suggest modifications or extensions of a given generalization.

MATERIALS

BEHAVIORAL OBJECTIVES	FOCUSING QUESTIONS	TEACHER'S ROLE	SUPPORT PROCEDURES
STEP ONE—PREDICTIONS & REASONS a. Students will state predictions of events and situations if a light-skinned family were to move into an isolated community of dark-skinned people. b. Students will state reasons that selected predictions might be made.	a. What do you think might happen if a family of very blonde, blue-eyed, light-skinned people moved into a small, isolated, rural community where only dark-eyed, dark-haired, olive-skinned people lived? (for selected predictions) b. Why do you think — might happen? Why else . . . ? What are other reasons this might happen?	1. Seek a variety of predictions. 2. Seek clarification as needed. 3. Record predictions. 4. Select predictions for which to seek reasons.	List predictions as given. Ask for clarification as necessary. Seek diversity of predictions. Select promising predictions (related to content purpose) and seek a variety of support for these predictions.

Form adapted from Institute for Staff Development 1971c, p. 23.

BEHAVIORAL OBJECTIVES	FOCUSING QUESTIONS	TEACHER'S ROLE	SUPPORT PROCEDURES
STEP TWO—CONDITIONS & SUPPORT a. Students will state necessary prior and attendant conditions for, e.g., —blonde family to draw closer —teacher to try to make blondes welcome —a few dark people to be nice to blondes b. Students will state evidence and reasoning that supports their ideas of necessary conditions.	a. What else would have to happen or be true for, e.g, the blonde family to draw closer? b. Why would that be necessary? a. What else . . . ? b. Why . . . ?	1. Record conditions. 2. Seek support for all conditions.	Select predictions that would fall on the 2nd or 3rd level of cognitive map to pursue. Seek a variety of conditions and support for prediction, then move to Step 3 for that prediction. After extension of prediction through Step 3, return to Step 2 for another prediction. Extend three or more predictions—include positive and negative predictions.
STEP THREE—CONSEQUENCES, REASONS, CONDITIONS, SUPPORT (Recycle 1 & 2) a. Students will state consequences of predictions examined at Step 2. b. Students will state evidence and reasoning supporting new predictions. c. Students will state necessary prior and attendant conditions for consequences. d. Students will provide supporting statements for the necessary conditions.	a. If the members of the blonde family did become closer to each other, what might happen to them? What else? b. (for selected consequences) Why might . . . ? Why else might . . . ? c. What else would have to happen or be true for (e.g., the family to decide to "stick it out")? d. Why would that have to happen (be necessary)?	1. Record consequences. 2. Seek reasons for selected consequences. 3. Seek conditions and support.	List consequences (new predictions). Seek several consequences for selected prediction before asking for (a variety of) reasons.

Form adapted from Institute for Staff Development 1971c, p. 24.

(FIGURE 12–1–Continued)

BEHAVIORAL OBJECTIVES	FOCUSING QUESTIONS	TEACHER'S ROLE	SUPPORT PROCEDURES
STEP FOUR—CONCLUSIONS & SUPPORT a. Students will draw conclusions about the consequences of the way minority populations are treated. b. Students will support their conclusions with evidence or reasoning.	a. Based on our discussion, what do you think is the most important consequence of the way minority groups are treated? b. Why is that the most important consequence?	1. Seek support for each conclusion. 2. Seek conclusions from a variety of students.	Listen, ask for support.
STEP FIVE—AFFIRMATION, MODIFICATION, OR EXTENSION OF GENERALIZATION a. Students will affirm, modify, or extend a given generalization. b. Students will support their affirmation, modification, or extension.	a. What changes, if any, would you make in this statement? b. Why would you . . . ?	1. Seek support for each response. 2. Seek responses from a variety of students.	Write generalization on chalkboard. "People who are different from others cause trouble in a community."

Form adapted from Institute for Staff Development 1971c, p. 42.
Copyright by Allyn and Bacon. Reproduction of this material is restricted to use with *A Comprehensive Approach to Teaching Thinking* by Shirley W. Schiever.

(FIGURE 12–1–Continued)

COGNITIVE MAP

STRATEGY: Application of Generalizations

Generalization to be modified or validated: People who are different from others cause trouble in a community.

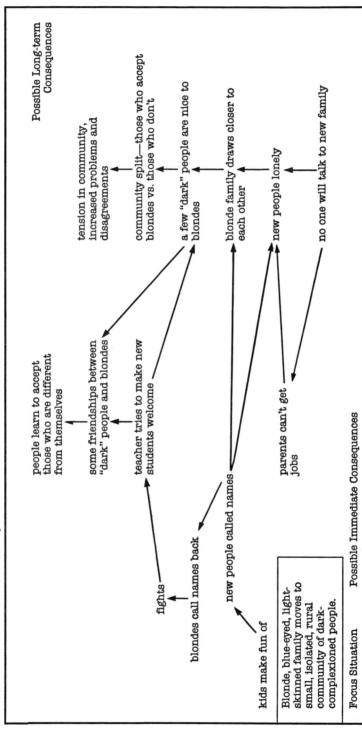

Possible Long-term Consequences

tension in community, increased problems and disagreements

community split—those who accept blondes vs. those who don't

a few "dark" people are nice to blondes

blonde family draws closer to each other

new people lonely

no one will talk to new family

people learn to accept those who are different from themselves

some friendships between "dark" people and blondes

teacher tries to make new students welcome

parents can't get jobs

fights

blondes call names back

new people called names

kids make fun of

Blonde, blue-eyed, light-skinned family moves to small, isolated, rural community of dark-complexioned people.

Focus Situation   Possible Immediate Consequences

consequences, which are the new predictions. As a recycling of the first two steps, Step 3 serves the same purpose as these steps, but additionally extends the predictions and conditions further from the original situation and thus provides more complex and abstract ideas than those at Step 2. In other words, predictions of long-term events are less certain and depend on more variables (including, in this case, the occurrence of the first prediction) than predictions of short-term events.

The processes in this step strengthen and expand the basic concept of multiple causality; the inferred conditions and support illustrate that no consequence is a direct outcome of a given proposition but that events and situations have multiple causes and effects. In the demonstration lesson (page 223), several conditions are necessary if the prediction about the new people being lonely is to occur.

Step 4—Drawing Conclusions

The fourth step offers the opportunity for students to draw and support conclusions based on ideas they have formalized in preceding steps. In making conclusions, they need to decide which of the predictions are most reasonable to expect, in terms of the conditions that are most likely to prevail. Therefore students must consider all the predictions, conditions, and reasons that were discussed and make a judgment based on this consideration.

Step 5—Examining a Generalization

Asking students to examine a generalization in light of the discussion strengthens their abilities to form their own general statements and to look critically at others' statements that may be too general, inaccurate, or unqualified. The teacher provides either the generalization the discussion was based on or a poor example of a generalization related to the topic and asks the students to modify or verify the statement.

While the Institute for Staff Development (1971c) authors suggest that Step 5 is optional, the author of this text sees it as an important step. Forming one's own general statements and looking critically at the statements of others are important skills for living productively in a complex society. Students cannot assimilate and retain all the factual knowledge available; generalized forms must be organized and adapted as new knowledge is encountered. Additionally, they need to be able to examine critically the generalized statements communicated through the media in order to make well-founded decisions and judgments.

Steps 1 Through 5—Providing Support

The procedure of asking students to support their statements at each step is basic to this strategy. In response to these questions, students *apply generalizations;* each time they give a reason, they are applying their knowledge in increasingly complex and abstract contexts. This strategy does not get its name from Step 5, but from the application of knowledge (generalizations) at the support phases of steps 1 through 4.

Conceptualization of the Application of Generalization Task

Teachers must have a clear understanding of the overall purpose of the strategy as well as the purpose and underlying rationale of individual steps if they are to lead an effective application of generalizations discussion. Figure 12–2 is a visual representation of the strategy that can be used as an aid in understanding the overall and individual cognitive tasks.

Overt and Covert Behaviors in Application of Generalizations

When planning and leading an application of generalizations discussion, the teacher needs to be mindful of the thinking objectives (covert behaviors) and the behavioral objectives (overt behaviors) for each step. These objectives determine the teacher's role and are critical to the formulation of clear focus questions. See Figure 12–3 for the overt-covert behaviors chart, which includes the purpose and general focusing questions for each step.

PLANNING AN APPLICATION OF GENERALIZATIONS DISCUSSION

Successful application of generalizations discussions require careful and detailed planning. The purposes of the discussion, strategies to be used, and possible responses must be considered carefully. Unless teachers are aware of the multiple possibilities of the topic, they may limit the discussion to the most obvious suggestions. Thoughtful preparation will ensure an appropriate depth of topic exploration and discussion.

Figure 12–2 Graphic Representation—Application of Generalizations

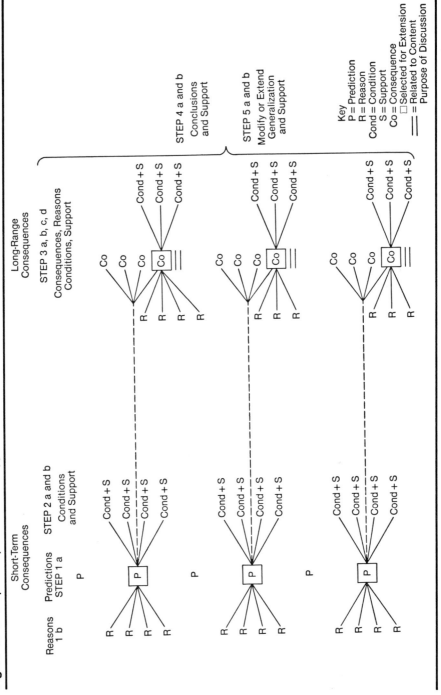

FIGURE 12–3 Overt-Covert Behaviors—Application of Generalizations

STEP	1	2	3	4	5
Purpose of Step	*Generate List of Logical Predictions*	*Determine the Limits and Necessary Conditions for Predictions*	*Extend Predictions and Conditions to More Abstract Level*	*Synthesize Discussion as Basis for Warranted Conclusion*	*Critically Examine a Provided Generalization*
OVERT Behavioral objectives	a. State prediction. b. Give reason for prediction.	a. Provide prior and/or attendant conditions for predictions. b. Give reason conditions are needed.	a. State possible consequences of predictions. b. Give reason for consequences. c. & d. Recycle Step 2.	a. State conclusion as to what is likely to happen.	a. Affirm or modify generalization.
COVERT Thinking objectives	a. Infer possible effects of hypothetical situation. b. Identify fact or generalization on which prediction is based.	a. Recall or infer necessary conditions. b. Identify facts or generalizations on which statement is based.	a. Infer possible effects of predictions. b. Identify facts or generalizations to support effects. c. & d. Same as Step 2a & b.	a. Synthesize inferred, supported predictions. b. Identify evidence or reasoning to support conclusions.	a. Differentiate, evaluate. b. Identify evidence or reasoning underlying evaluation.
FOCUSING QUESTIONS (General)	a. What might happen if __? b. Why do you think __ might happen?	a. What else would have to happen or be true for (prediction) to happen? b. Why would that be necessary?	a. If (condition) did happen and (prediction) what do you think would happen then? b. Why would that happen? c. & d. Recycle Step 2.	a. Based on our discussion, what do you think is most likely to happen if __? b. Why is that most likely?	a. What changes, if any, would you make in this statement? b. Why would you (make that change/leave it as is)?

Adapted from Institute for Staff Development 1971c, p. 9.

The Discussion Plan Form

The discussion plan form (Figure 12–4) is designed to facilitate the planning procedure. The form provides the format for planning and leading the discussion. Space is provided for basic information such as topic; content and process purposes for the discussion; prediscussion procedures; materials; behavioral objectives, focusing questions, teacher role, and support procedures for each step; and a cognitive map. Completing the discussion plan form as suggested below facilitates the development of a comprehensive, effective discussion.

Content Purpose

Two types of content purposes generally are appropriate for the application of generalizations strategy. One type is to test a generalization by applying the basic idea to a similar situation or by changing a variable in the situation that evoked the generalization. For example, students may have generalized that the overpopulation of a city may lead to a decreased quality of life. One way to test this generalization would be to ask, "What might happen if the population of our city were to double in the next year?" or "What might happen if the enrollment in this school were to double by next fall?" Both of these questions would be testing the generalization in a similar situation. Another approach is to change something in the original situation. The hypothetical situation posed by the question "What would happen in New York City if half the residents moved away?" requires the students to look at the reverse of a generalized situation. Either approach can be used for the purpose of testing a generalization.

Another type of content purpose requires predicting consequences of a given situation with no particular generalization in mind. Such a purpose would be appropriate when students have read a story up to a point and then are asked to predict what will happen next and to support the predictions. Students are applying generalizations every time they draw on their generalized knowledge to support their inferences.

In either case, the content purpose should define clearly what students are expected to know as the ultimate outcome of the discussion. The general content purpose for the application of generalizations is to modify or extend a specified generalization. Generalizations may come from textbooks, newspapers, curriculum guides, what "they" say, or from the students' previous discussions.

FIGURE 12–4 Discussion Plan Form—Application of Generalizations

STRATEGY: Application of Generalizations

Topic _____

Level _____

DISCUSSION PURPOSES

Content:

Process:

PREDISCUSSION PROCEDURES

MATERIALS

BEHAVIORAL OBJECTIVES	FOCUSING QUESTIONS	TEACHER'S ROLE	SUPPORT PROCEDURES
STEP ONE—PREDICTIONS & SUPPORT		1. Seek a variety of predictions. 2. Seek clarification as needed. 3. Record predictions. 4. Select predictions to be supported.	
STEP TWO—CONDITIONS & SUPPORT		1. Record conditions. 2. Seek support for all conditions.	

Form adapted from Institute for Staff Development 1971c, pp. 23 & 24.

(FIGURE 12–4–Continued)

BEHAVIORAL OBJECTIVES	FOCUSING QUESTIONS	TEACHER'S ROLE	SUPPORT PROCEDURES
STEP THREE—CONSE-QUENCES, REASONS, CONDI-TIONS, SUPPORT (Recycle 1 & 2)		1. Record consequences. 2. Seek reasons for selected consequences. 3. Seek conditions and support.	
STEP FOUR—CONCLUSIONS & SUPPORT		1. Seek support for each conclusion. 2. Seek conclusions from a variety of students.	
STEP FIVE—AFFIRMATION, MODIFICATION, OR EXTENSION OF GENERALIZATION		1. Seek support for each response. 2. Seek responses from a variety of students.	

Form adapted from Institute for Staff Development 1971c, pp. 24 & 25.

Copyright by Allyn and Bacon. Reproduction of this material is restricted to use with *A Comprehensive Approach to Teaching Thinking* by Shirley W. Schiever.

(FIGURE 12–4–Continued)

COGNITIVE MAP
STRATEGY: Application of Generalizations

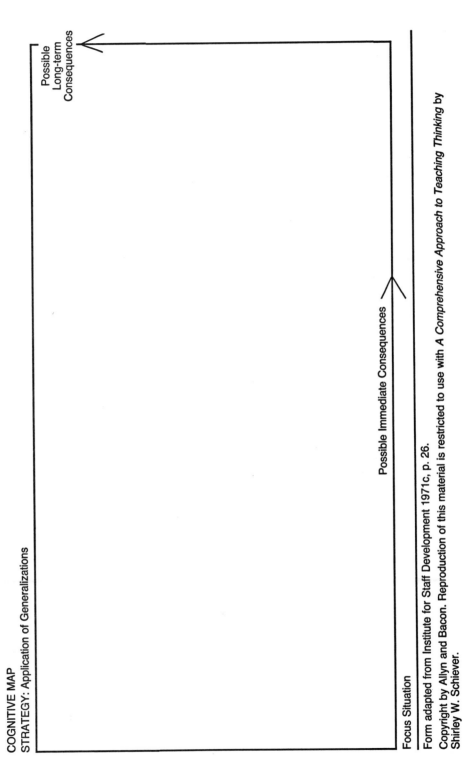

Focus Situation

Process Purpose

The process purpose of an application of generalizations discussion is stated as follows: "To predict consequences of a given set of circumstances, to support predictions with evidence or reasoning, to limit predictions by stating and supporting necessary prior or attendant conditions, and to draw warranted conclusions and suggest modification or extension of previously made generalizations on the basis of verified predictions."

The following steps should be taken when planning an application of generalizations discussion.

1. *Select or develop an appropriate generalization and record it under content purpose.* In the sample discussion plan on page 220, the content purpose is to modify or extend the following generalization: "Prejudice is harmful to personal development and societal structure."

2. *Record the process purpose for the discussion by adapting the general process purpose to the specific circumstances or events on which the discussion will be based.* The process purpose on page 220 is as follows: "To (a) predict the consequences of a light-skinned family moving into a small, isolated community of dark-complexioned people, (b) support these predictions with evidence or reasoning, (c) limit the predictions by stating and supporting necessary prior or attendant conditions, (d) draw warranted conclusions, and (e) suggest modification or extension of a generalization provided by the instructor."

Prediscussion Procedures

3. *Record on the planning form the experiences and material, if any, that are necessary for students prior to beginning the discussion.*

The Cognitive Map

4. *At the top of the cognitive map (page 231), record the teaching generalization for this discussion.*

5. *On the left side of the cognitive map, record the hypothetical situation on which the students will base their predictions.* The proposed situation in the demonstration plan is that a family of very blonde, blue-eyed, light-skinned people moves into a small, isolated, rural community where everyone who already lives there has dark hair, brown eyes, and olive skin.

Behavioral Objectives, Focusing Questions, and Support Procedures

6. *For one step at a time, use Figure 12–3 to determine what the covert behavior is for the step.* Refer to the general behavioral objective for the step, and, based on the content and process purposes of the discussion, develop a behavioral objective specific to this discussion. At Step 1 the general behavioral objective is "Students will state predictions." A specific objective for this step is "Students will predict what will happen when/if. . . ." As behavioral objectives are developed, record them on the form.

7. *Develop focusing questions for the step, using the general focusing question on the overt-covert behavior chart as a guide.*

8. *Record possible responses to the focus question on the cognitive map (page 231).* If responses will lead to the discussion purpose, record the focus question on the discussion plan form; if not, reformulate the question and check responses again.

9. *Note appropriate support procedures for the step on the form.*

10. *Continue planning the discussion by recycling steps 6 through 9 above.* Alternate between the (a) overt-covert behavior chart, (b) cognitive map, and (c) discussion plan form. This alternation will help even a novice to plan discussions that reach their stated goals.

IMPLEMENTING THE STRATEGY

To apply previous knowledge and make causal inferences, a context must be inferred. The context includes circumstances, which contain background conditions and presuppositions necessary for these inferences. Without circumstances, specific events lack meaning (Trabasso and Sperry 1985). In fact, the criterion of necessity is used to judge whether a causal relationship exists between two events (Mackie 1980). This criterion of necessity in the circumstances implies that the consequence is *dependent* on the cause or the event *determines* the consequence (Trabasso and Sperry 1985). That is, if I throw an egg at the wall and it breaks because it hits the wall, my action (throwing) determines the consequence (a broken egg). In this circumstance, throwing the egg was necessary if it was to break against the wall.

In the application of generalizations strategy, students generate hypotheses in the form of predictions, infer causal relationships, and establish a context through providing reasons (background conditions and presuppositions) for the predictions. The validity of the predictions is then challenged by the need to provide the informational and logical parameters that justify the predictions.

The chain of links connecting the prediction and the condition is critical, and the level of the prediction can be judged by the extent of the leap (the causal links) from a specific condition (Taba, Levine, and Elzey 1964). On the cognitive map for the demonstration lesson plan on page 223, the prediction that new students who look different from others will be made fun of is a lower-level prediction than the prediction that people will learn to accept those who are different from themselves. The first prediction entails a direct causal link to the focus situation, while the second prediction entails many conditions and events, a longer and more complex causal link.

The teacher as discussion leader will establish the parameters for the thinking levels of the students, the complexity of the relationships inferred, the validity of conclusions drawn, and the accuracy with which the generalization is affirmed or modified. In addition to understanding the critical nature of the causal links as previously explained, the discussion leader needs to follow carefully the steps of the strategy, remembering the sequence and purpose of each. The purpose of this section is to provide further information that will enable discussion leaders to successfully implement the application of generalizations strategy.

The discussion plan form should be referred to while leading the discussion. The plan, formulated and recorded carefully, should be used faithfully. Even experienced discussion leaders are more effective if they refer to their written plan.

Step 1—Predictions and Reasons

The purpose of Step 1 is to develop a list of predictions related to the focus topic or situation. The students should be stretching their minds and engaging in divergent thinking. Clarification should be asked for when necessary, but not to an extent that will interfere with the free flow of ideas. Variety is important—negative and positive aspects of the focus situation should be sought.

If students make several similar predictions, the teacher should ask, "What completely different things might occur?" or say, "We have quite a few, e.g., negative predictions. What *positive* events might you predict?"

Only a few predictions are needed to initiate the discussion, but they should sample at least three or four different dimensions of the situation. A variety of predictions is necessary if students are to perceive the relatedness of very different predictions.

After a list of predictions has been developed, the leader should select a few predictions that most closely relate to the content purpose of the discussion and ask for a variety of reasons that support these predictions. If time allows and the predictions seem relatively equal, support may be asked for all predictions. The focus of this part of the step is to explain or support predictions by verbalizing the causal link, the underlying generalization used for the predictive inference.

The most common error made at this step is neglecting to seek a variety (negative and positive) of predictions and a variety of support for selected predictions. Additionally, some people use "would" instead of "might" in the initial focus question, implying a reality base that should not exist. A problem that may confuse a novice occurs when students offer conditions rather than reasons in response to the support question. For example, "I predicted that no one would talk to the new family because they would be afraid their neighbors would get mad at them." This is not the *reason* the prediction was made; it is a necessary condition. In a similar situation the teacher can say, "I will be asking a different question in a minute, and I would like for you to remember your response until then. Right now I would like to know why you or anyone else might predict that no one would talk to the new people." This sequence is important, because conditions are more complex inferences than reasons, and the thinking processes should build on each other.

The role of the teacher at Step 1 of application of generalizations can be summarized as follows:

• To focus on a variety of predictions related to a specific situation or event
• To seek clarification as necessary,
• To record the predictions
• To seek a variety of support for selected predictions
• To ensure that reasons, not conditions, are given as support
• To limit the amount of time spent at this step

Step 2—Conditions and Reasons

The purpose of Step 2 is to identify the necessary conditions that make the selected predictions plausible. The conditions determine the limits of the prediction and the sufficient causes for its occurrence (no one will talk to a new family if everyone is insecure and concerned about their neighbor's opinion of them).

A condition is a particular type of inference, and as such it requires a particular type of support. The support should establish why the condition is necessary for the prediction to happen. The focusing questions should be similar to the following: "What else would have to happen or be true for . . . (to happen) or (fights to occur)?" "Why would that be necessary or (. . . it be necessary for the new kids not to be physically large)?"

If only a few predictions are selected at Step 1b for support, those predictions should be used for Step 2. If the leader sought support for all the predictions at Step 1b, those predictions with the best support should be used for Step 2.

At Step 2 some people experience a problem with the support question, which should be asked for each condition. The correct wording is "Why is that necessary?", *not* "Why do you feel that way?" or "Why do you say that?"

The teacher's role at Step 2 can be summarized as follows:

- To select those predictions that are most closely related to the content purpose and to seek necessary conditions for them
- To record the conditions accurately (may be abbreviated)
- To ask for support for all conditions offered

Step 3—Consequences (New Predictions), Reasons, Conditions, and Support

The purpose of Step 3 is to generate some long-term consequences of (one or several) previously inferred prediction(s). This step is an extension and recycling of the previous steps; the new predictions are built on the previous prediction(s) and conditions. Steps 3a and b are a recycling of steps 1a and b, and steps 3c and d are a recycling of steps 2a and b.

In Step 3a, the teacher should select as a basis for further predictions one or more predictions with long-term effects that relate to the content purpose of the discussion. Using only one prediction makes this step more manageable than using several. If a wide variety of consequences is sought, the end result of using one prediction is similar to that of extending two or three predictions at Step 3.

Steps 3c and d require that students infer conditions and support for selected consequences (new predictions). The condition and support questions are similar to those for steps 2a and b.

Step 3 can be repeated until the group has moved far enough away from the original predictions to make long-range (more abstract) predictions.

Students can be divided into small groups at Step 3, with each group being assigned a prediction and asked to brainstorm possible consequences. If experience and maturity levels warrant, small groups also might be able to continue with the other tasks of Step 3. Breaking into small groups is an excellent way to obtain a variety of responses and to encourage more students to participate. Students who seldom volunteer a response in a large group frequently will be comfortable contributing in the small-group setting.

Problems sometimes occur at Step 3 because of its complexity. Teachers can become confused and omit a part of the step or not ask the right question. Students, especially in the elementary grades, may not understand the focus question if "consequences" are asked for. When asking for consequences, the following is a clear question: "If all the things we said were necessary *did* happen, and . . . (prediction), what would happen *then?*" Notice that the question is not merely "What else would happen?" The cause–effect relationship and time factor are important here.

The teacher's role at Step 3 can be summarized as follows:

- To focus on the prediction(s) with the best possibilities for long-term effects (consequences)
- To record consequences (new predictions) accurately
- To seek support for the most relevant consequences
- To seek conditions and support for selected consequences
- To extend Step 3 until the consequences reflect long-term effects

Step 4—Drawing Conclusions

The purpose of Step 4 is for students to synthesize the ideas formulated in the preceding steps and to conclude what is the most likely effect or result of a specific event or situation. The cognitive task requires examining predictions, reasons, and conditions, synthesizing and evaluating what has been said, and reaching a conclusion.

The discussion leader should solicit responses from a variety of students, but the focus question should make clear the intent of a variety of respondents, but not necessarily of responses. That is, the question should be "Who else will tell us what they think is most likely to happen?"

The synthesis at Step 4 should be of inferences, reasons, and support. Occasionally, novice discussion leaders point to the chalkboard with everything from the discussion recorded there and ask, "What is the most likely thing to happen (e.g., when light-skinned people move into a community of dark-skinned people?)" Unfailingly, at least one student will respond with a prediction made at Step 1. To avoid this situation, erase the chalkboard, or roll up the butcher paper before asking the focus question.

The teacher's role at Step 4 can be summarized as follows:

- To ask a focus question that builds on the discussion and requires a conclusion
- To seek support for each conclusion
- To seek responses from a variety of students

Step 5—Modifying or Affirming a Generalization

The purpose of Step 5 is for students to evaluate the validity of a general statement in terms of a specific situation. The teacher may purposely provide a poor generalization, such as "All people are mean to others who look different from them," to give the students practice in detecting and correcting poorly founded general statements. Another option is to construct a value-laden generalization, such as "Dark-skinned people are intolerant of those who are different from them." Or the planning generalization may be used, or it may be changed slightly, to see how close the students can come to the "original" in their modifications. To have students validate an idea, provide a good generalization; to assess their critical thinking skills, offer a value-laden or poor one.

As at Step 4, the teacher should seek responses from a variety of students, but not necessarily a variety of responses. "Who else agrees or disagrees with this statement?" is one way to convey this intention.

Problems at Step 5 center primarily on the support question. It should not be asked in tandem with the focus question ("What changes, if any, would you make, and why?") and it should not be merely "Why?", but rather "Why would you (make that change/not change the statement)?"

The teacher's role at Step 5 can be summarized as follows:

- To provide a suitable general statement
- To seek support for each validation or modification
- To seek responses from many students

APPLICATIONS OF THE STRATEGY

The application of generalizations strategy can be used whenever the purpose is to predict consequences and explore necessary or attendant conditions. Usually a task of this type occurs at the end of a sequence or a sub-unit at a point when students already have developed the facts and the generalizations they need for application to the questions required by this task. However, this strategy also can be used at the beginning of a unit to provide an opportunity for students to hypothesize about a topic they will be studying. In essence, the students use what they already know, but expressed in a conditional form (if so-and-so, then so-and-so) to predict the consequences that might occur, and under what conditions.

As with the concept development and interpretation of data strategies, students can process one or several of the application of generalization steps in small groups or teams. The author suggests that if teachers want to use small groups for part of the strategy, steps 3 and 4 might be best. When students become very familiar with the process, they might be able to execute the entire strategy within small groups. However, sharing predictions, consequences, and conclusions is important to the thinking of the whole group.

When students have internalized the application of generalizations method of processing information, they can be encouraged to use it when they are organizing information to write. Scientific, expository, and creative writing lend themselves to hypothesizing, examining necessary attendant conditions, and drawing conclusions.

In searching for opportunities for students to apply generalizations, look for situations that lend themselves to setting up working hypotheses; that is, situations about which students can make predictions and check them against reality. For example, when the teacher knows that she or he is going to be absent from school in the near future, students can predict what will happen in the classroom during this absence. Making and exploring both positive and negative predictions provides a basis for checking the reality after the fact. Or students can predict what will happen in a story the teacher is reading to them, during science investigations, or with a current event such as a local or national election. As often as possible, select real events that can be checked—historical events, readings from different sources, or observable phenomena. Set up a situation, let the students hypothesize, and then guide them in checking whether or not their predictions were accurate. Some possible topics for application of generalization discussions are given on page 252.

Whether working in science, math, literature, or social studies, students eventually can check a working hypothesis against what actually happened, reexamine "incorrect" predictions, and search for other variables at work in the situation. This helps foster the idea of the tentativeness of knowledge. The more frequently students are sure something will turn out one way, find that it turned out another way, and uncover the reasons, the more thoughtful their future predictions will be. They will learn that since so many variables are at work in any situation, making an airtight prediction is practically impossible.

Fantasy situations are too far removed from reality to use as a basis for productive application of generalizations discussions. In choosing situations as a basis for predictions, examine them carefully for elements of fantasy. If necessary, change the situation to one that is realistic and reasonable. Simulations of realistic situations can be used successfully with the strategy, the key word being *realistic*.

As noted in the discussion of the content purpose of this strategy, two basic types of situations lend themselves to the application of generalizations, similar situations and changed variable situations.

Students' responses to the similar situation type of application tend to be more abstract than in changed variable applications, and they tend to make predictions giving more principles and explanations. With a similar situation, students tend to support their predictions without being asked; they reach back to the familiar situation and use it as a model in making predictions.

In the changed variable situation, only one variable is changed, and students seem to feel more comfortable making predictions. They also tend to build chains of consequences with this type of situation. For example, a group of students that had studied nomads was asked to predict what would happen if Bedouin nomads lost the market for their camels because oasis farmers were buying tractors. The prediction that the nomads would stay in one place led to predictions of needed housing and services, the development of cities, and a need for government. They set up a pattern, based on their experiences with communities, and, with the teacher's guidance, followed the pattern as they applied their generalizations.

Students need to learn early that the generalizations they make cannot be applied in every situation, but that this does not make them poor generalizations. By meeting many new and discrepant situations, students begin to reformulate their old generalizations and experience cognitive growth. They begin to think in terms of certain conditions being necessary for a prediction to be valid. They begin to ask themselves questions such as "When would this be true?" and "What would have to happen for this to be true?"

Encourage students to identify the variables in a situation so they will not expect to find a quick, easy way of applying knowledge. For example, an invention will cause change if the conditions are right, it does not violate tradition, and/or it is important to people. Students should learn to ask questions such as "What traditions will this violate?", "How many people might this affect?", or "What market, if any, exists for this product?" before making predictions.

If students are to understand systems, they need to deal with results of change within those systems. For that reason the question "If, as you predicted, X happened, what do you think might happen after that?" is critical to the strategy. This step emphasizes that change in one important dimension results in further change within the system.

During discussions, teachers may find they need to provide a model for the students. For example, if a class is discussing the loss of a market in a one-industry economy and the students are not able to make many predictions, the teacher might supply a model. The teacher could say, "Suppose that my pay used to be $50 for a day's work but now it has been reduced to $10." This brings the problem to the level of students who can think in tens more easily than in millions. They can make the transfer to the family's livelihood and then to communities and nations. Introducing a model by providing a concrete or familiar example will frequently trigger leaps in levels of thinking.

RELATIONSHIPS AMONG STRATEGIES

The cognitive tasks concept development, interpretation of data, and application of generalizations have been treated in this text as discrete tasks. However, they are interrelated, and a single discussion might have elements of all three in it. During an interpretation of data discussion a student or the teacher might say, "I wonder what would happen if . . .?" This line of thought may be pursued briefly, to establish a variety of relationships and encourage creative thinking.

Using the same content or data base for all three types of discussions, as in the demonstration lesson plans, illustrates the relationships among the three tasks. Teachers who are familiar with and comfortable using all the strategies find that in actual classroom practice a single discussion may involve one, two, or all of the cognitive tasks.

Finally, even when the primary focus of learning or a discussion is the cognitive tasks, human emotions may be considered. People do not experience changes in their way of life without having reactions and feelings; exploring these should be a part of the cognitive tasks. Whenever the class is discussing a situation in which people are involved, ask how people might feel about the situation, what it might mean to them, and how they might see the situation. Such questions validate the feelings and enhance cognitive growth. The door always should be left open to the affective domain and its possible application in a discussion using one or more of the cognitive tasks.

CHAPTER SUMMARY

The application of generalizations cognitive task requires students to apply previous knowledge (generalizations) through making and supporting predictions and inferring and supporting conditions and consequences. Further, in supporting conclusions and modification or verification of a provided general statement, students continue to apply previously known information. The strategy is useful whenever the goal is to provide opportunities to make and check hypotheses.

SAMPLE APPLICATION OF GENERALIZATION LESSON PLANS

DISCUSSION PLAN FORM

STRATEGY: Application of Generalizations

Lesson plan by Shirley Schiever

DISCUSSION PURPOSES

Content: To predict, on the basis of present knowledge, what students think will happen when they move to a new situation.

Process: To predict consequences, to support predictions with evidence or reasoning, to limit predictions by stating prior or attendant conditions, to draw warranted conclusions, and to suggest modifications and extensions of a given generalization.

Topic ___Starting middle school or junior high___

Level ___Elementary___

PREDISCUSSION PROCEDURES

Mention the apprehension most people feel before going to junior high school. Ask why students think they have these kinds of feelings.

MATERIALS

Butcher paper

Marker

BEHAVIORAL OBJECTIVES	FOCUSING QUESTIONS	TEACHER'S ROLE	SUPPORT PROCEDURES
STEP ONE—PREDICTIONS & REASONS a. Students will predict what will happen when they start junior high. b. Students will provide reasons for making selected predictions.	a. What are some things you think will happen when you start junior high school? b. Why might you predict that, e.g., you will get lost? Why else might . . . ?	1. Seek a variety of predictions. 2. Seek clarification as needed. 3. Record predictions. 4. Select predictions for which to seek reasons.	Seek variety of predictions—positive and negative, personal and general, short- and long-term. For each selected prediction relating to purpose, seek several reasons.
STEP TWO—CONDITIONS & SUPPORT a. Students will infer and state prior or attendant conditions necessary for predictions. b. Students will support their inferences with evidence or reasoning.	a. What else would have to be true for, e.g., you to make new friends? b. Why would that be necessary? a. What else . . . ? b. Why . . . ?	1. Record conditions. 2. Seek support for all conditions.	Select three to four predictions for which to get conditions and support. Seek three to four conditions (and support) for each selected prediction. Write conditions on butcher paper near each related prediction.

Form adapted from Institute for Staff Development 1971c, pp. 23 & 24.

BEHAVIORAL OBJECTIVES	FOCUSING QUESTIONS	TEACHER'S ROLE	SUPPORT PROCEDURES
STEP THREE—CONSEQUENCES, REASONS, CONDITIONS, SUPPORT (Recycle 1 & 2) a. Students will state possible consequences of (selected) predictions. b. Students will give reasons for selected consequences. c. Students will provide necessary or attendant conditions for consequences. d. Students will support conditions.	a. Assuming these conditions were true, and, e.g., you made new friends, what might happen then? b. Why might you predict, e.g., that you might feel grown up? Why else . . . ? c. What else would have to be true for this to happen? d. Why would this have to be true?	1. Record consequences. 2. Seek reasons for selected consequences. 3. Seek conditions and support.	Seek variety of reasons, consequences, and support for each selected prediction.
STEP FOUR—CONCLUSIONS & SUPPORT Students will state conclusions and reasons for conclusions.	a. From what we've been saying, what do you think is most likely to happen when you go to junior high school? Why is that most likely? b. Why do you think . . . ?	1. Seek support for each conclusion. 2. Seek conclusions from a variety of students.	
STEP FIVE—AFFIRMATION, MODIFICATION, OR EXTENSION OF GENERALIZATION a. Students will modify and extend given generalization. b. They will support the modifications and/or extensions.	a. Based on our discussion, how might you change this statement? b. Why do you think . . . ?	1. Seek support for each response. 2. Seek responses from a variety of students.	Write generalization on chalkboard: "New situations are bad."

Form adapted from Institute for Staff Development 1971c, pp. 24 & 25.

Copyright by Allyn and Bacon. Reproduction of this material is restricted to use with *A Comprehensive Approach to Teaching Thinking* by Shirley W. Schiever.

COGNITIVE MAP

STRATEGY: Application of Generalizations

Starting Jr. High		**Possible Long-term Consequences**
Focus Situation	Possible Immediate Consequences	

Join clubs	Feel grown up	Make new friends
Change classes	Have electives	Different teachers
Scared	Get lost	Miss lunch

Form adapted from Institute for Staff Development 1971c, p. 26.

DISCUSSION PLAN FORM

STRATEGY: Application of Generalizations

Lesson plan by Shirley Schiever

Topic __Cure for Cancer__

Level __Middle School, Junior High__

DISCUSSION PURPOSES

Content: To modify or extend the following generalization: Increased longevity brings benefits and new problems to society.

Process: To predict consequences of a circumstance, to support predictions with evidence or reasoning, to limit predictions by stating and supporting necessary prior or attendant conditions, and to draw warranted conclusions and suggest modifications or extensions of given generalizations.

PREDISCUSSION PROCEDURES

Mention medical breakthroughs in genetic engineering and treatment that may lead to cure for cancer.

MATERIALS

BEHAVIORAL OBJECTIVES	FOCUSING QUESTIONS	TEACHER'S ROLE	SUPPORT PROCEDURES
STEP ONE—PREDICTIONS & REASONS a. Students will predict what might happen if a cure for cancer were discovered. b. Students will give reasons that support selected predictions.	a. If a cure for cancer were discovered this year, what are some things that might happen? b. Why might you predict, e.g., there would be more people on Social Security?	1. Seek a variety of predictions. 2. Seek clarification as needed. 3. Record predictions. 4. Select predictions for which to seek reasons.	Seek reasons for predictions that relate to content purposes.
STEP TWO—CONDITIONS & SUPPORT a. Students will state prior or attendant conditions for predictions to occur. b. Students will state reasons conditions are needed.	a. What else would have to be true for, e.g., more people to be on Social Security? b. Why would that be necessary? Etc.	1. Record conditions. 2. Seek support for all conditions.	Select three or four predictions on which to focus. Ask for support for conditions immediately. Seek three to four conditions for each prediction.

Form adapted from Institute for Staff Development 1971c, pp. 23 & 24.

Copyright by Allyn and Bacon. Reproduction of this material is restricted to use with *A Comprehensive Approach to Teaching Thinking* by Shirley W. Schiever.

BEHAVIORAL OBJECTIVES	FOCUSING QUESTIONS	TEACHER'S ROLE	SUPPORT PROCEDURES
STEP THREE—CONSEQUENCES, REASONS, CONDITIONS, SUPPORT (Recycle 1 & 2) a. Students will state possible consequences of predictions. b. They will support predictions with reasons. c. They will state conditions for predictions. d. They will give support with reasons or evidence.	a. What else might you predict would happen if, e.g. more people are on Social Security? What else? Etc. b. What might lead you to predict that—? c. What else would have to happen or be true for —? d. Why would that be necessary?	1. Record consequences. 2. Seek reasons for selected consequences. 3. Seek conditions and support.	Seek several reasons and consequences for each original (selected) prediction. Seek several conditions for each selected consequence. Seek support for each condition.
STEP FOUR—CONCLUSIONS & SUPPORT a. Students will state a conclusion about what is likely to happen if cancer can be cured. b. They will support their conclusion with evidence or reasoning.	a. Thinking about our discussion, what do you think is most likely to happen if a cure is found for cancer? b. Why do you think that is most likely?	1. Seek support for each conclusion. 2. Seek conclusions from a variety of students.	
STEP FIVE—AFFIRMATION, MODIFICATION, OR EXTENSION OF GENERALIZATION a. Students will modify and expand a given generalization. b. They will support their modification/expansion.	a. Based on what we have said, how, if at all, might you change this statement? b. Why do you think . . . ?	1. Seek support for each response. 2. Seek responses from a variety of students.	Write on chalkboard: "Curing cancer would solve one of society's worst problems."

Form adapted from Institute for Staff Development 1971c, pp. 24 & 25.

COGNITIVE MAP
STRATEGY: Application of Generalizations

Focus Situation	Possible Immediate Consequences
Cure for Cancer	

Fewer sick people

More people on Social Security

Doctors have fewer patients

Increased life span

Fewer hospitals

Cancer Society abolished

Possible Long-term
Consequences

Form adapted from Institute for Staff Development 1971c, p. 26.

DISCUSSION PLAN FORM

STRATEGY: Application of Generalizations

Lesson plan by Shirley Schiever

Topic ___Aging of U.S. Population___

Level ___Secondary___

DISCUSSION PURPOSES

Content: To modify or extend the following generalization: The aging of the U.S. population will change many existing social and political institutions, values, and lifestyles.

Process: To predict consequences of a possible circumstance, to support predictions with evidence or reasoning, to limit predictions by stating and supporting necessary prior and attendant conditions, and to draw warranted conclusions and suggest modifications or extensions of given generalization.

PREDISCUSSION PROCEDURES

Give information: Experts have estimated that by the year 2030, 20% of the population of the U.S. will be 65 years of age or older.

MATERIALS

BEHAVIORAL OBJECTIVES	FOCUSING QUESTIONS	TEACHER'S ROLE	SUPPORT PROCEDURES
STEP ONE—PREDICTIONS & REASONS a. Students will predict what will happen if the population of elderly people is 20% of the total population. b. Students will give reasons that support selected predictions.	a. What do you predict will happen if 20% of the U.S. population is 65 or older? b. Why might you predict, e.g., Social Security would go bankrupt? Or what would lead you to predict . . . ? Why would you predict . . . ?	1. Seek a variety of predictions. 2. Seek clarification as needed. 3. Record predictions. 4. Select predictions for which to seek reasons.	Seek two or three reasons for predictions that relate to content purposes. Ask for predictions, then <u>go back</u> and get support.
STEP TWO—CONDITIONS & SUPPORT a. Students will state prior or attendant conditions for predictions to occur. b. Students will give reasons for conditions.	a. What else would need to happen or be true for, e.g., fewer teachers to be needed? b. Why would that be necessary? a. What other things . . . ? b. Why . . . ?	1. Record conditions. 2. Seek support for all conditions.	Select predictions with the most potential for long-range effects and that relate to the teaching generalization. Focus on three or four predictions. Ask for support question immediately. Seek three or four conditions for each prediction. Vary question stems. Listen carefully—be sure conditions aren't given as reasons and vice versa.

Form adapted from Institute for Staff Development 1971c, pp. 23 & 24.

BEHAVIORAL OBJECTIVES	FOCUSING QUESTIONS	TEACHER'S ROLE	SUPPORT PROCEDURES
STEP THREE—CONSEQUENCES, REASONS, CONDITIONS, SUPPORT (Recycle 1 & 2) a. Students will state short- and long-term consequences of predictions explored at Step 2. b. Students will provide reasons for predictions. c. Students will state necessary conditions for the consequences to occur. d. Students will support necessity of stated conditions.	a. Assuming that (condition) and (prediction), what might happen then? b. Why might, e.g., . . . ? c. What else would have to happen or be true for, e.g., more people to become doctors and nurses? d. Why would that be necessary?	1. Record consequences. 2. Seek reasons for selected consequences. 3. Seek conditions and support.	Seek several consequences for selected predictions before asking for reasons. Seek several reasons for selected consequences. Seek several conditions and support for each selected consequence.
STEP FOUR—CONCLUSIONS & SUPPORT a. Students will draw conclusions about the consequences of the aging of the U.S. population. b. Students will support these conclusions with evidence or reasoning.	a. Based on our discussion, what would be the most important consequence of the aging of the U.S. population? b. Why is that the most important?	1. Seek support for each conclusion. 2. Seek conclusions from a variety of students.	
STEP FIVE—AFFIRMATION, MODIFICATION, OR EXTENSION OF GENERALIZATION a. Students will modify or extend a given generalization. b. Students will support their modification or expansion.	a. Thinking about our discussion, how might you change this statement? b. Why do you think . . . ?	1. Seek support for each response. 2. Seek responses from a variety of students.	Write statement on board: "The aging of the U.S. population will change social and political institutions."

Form adapted from Institute for Staff Development 1971c, pp. 24 & 25.

COGNITIVE MAP

STRATEGY: Application of Generalizations

Generalization to be modified or validated: "The aging of a population will change social and political institutions."

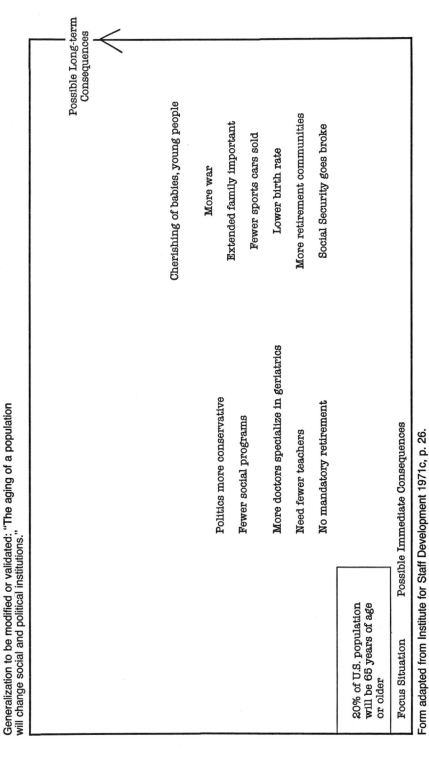

Focus Situation	Possible Immediate Consequences		Possible Long-term Consequences
20% of U.S. population will be 65 years of age or older	Politics more conservative	Cherishing of babies, young people	
	Fewer social programs	More war	
	More doctors specialize in geriatrics	Extended family important	
	Need fewer teachers	Fewer sports cars sold	
	No mandatory retirement	Lower birth rate	
		More retirement communities	
		Social Security goes broke	

Form adapted from Institute for Staff Development 1971c, p. 26.

SAMPLE TOPICS FOR APPLICATION OF
GENERALIZATION DISCUSSIONS

To Verify, Limit, or Extend a Generalization Related to	*Step 1 Focusing Question*
thoughtful decisions	What do you think would have happened if Bassanio had chosen the wrong casket?
enforcement of rules	What do you think would happen if the safety patrol at our school let their friends break school rules but made others obey them?
public services	What do you think would happen if (e.g., the electricity) in our city was unavailable for a week?
cultural change	What do you think would happen if the Mexican government launched a massive literacy campaign?
team play, taking turns	What do you suppose would happen if only one child of a team got the ball every time?
literature	What do you predict will happen next?
the role of rules in society	What happens when people break rules or laws?
tools and level of technology	Suppose 1000 years from now anthropologists were to uncover an intact house from our city. What could they tell about our society?
finite resources	What might happen if the world's supply of petroleum was depleted?
elements of weather	What would happen if air did not move?
environment	What might happen if the ozone layer was destroyed?
student/teacher relations	What do you think would happen in this room tomorrow if a substitute teacher was here instead of me?
effect of color	What do you think would happen if all white or light-colored food suddenly turned green?
climate and lifestyle	What predictions can you make about how people live if I tell you the climate where they live is ____?
interdependence	What would happen if all the . . . died suddenly?

13

Resolution of Conflict

The three strategies discussed previously—concept development, interpretation of data, and application of generalizations—deal with both the cognitive and affective domains. These strategies develop both domains by promoting a rational, logical approach to dealing with the world (cognitive) and also by providing an atmosphere in which students and their ideas are accepted without judgment (affective). The resolution of conflict strategy is more closely related to the affective domain than the others, since the data students work with deal with human behavior (feelings, actions, values). Questions based on the strategy elicit rational, thoughtful responses to this affective data. In this chapter a synthesis of existing information on the strategy is presented, and the information is clarified, expanded, and updated. (Unless otherwise noted, the information in this chapter is based primarily on three sources: Institute for Staff Development 1971d and n.d.; and Maker 1982b.)

Institute for Staff Development authors refer to two strategies: the "exploration of feelings" and the "resolution of conflict" strategies. While these terms describe the structure of the total approach, the author of this volume uses the name *resolution of conflict*, since this is the major emphasis of the strategy and the exploration of feelings is part of conflict resolution.

THE RESOLUTION OF CONFLICT TASK

The techniques used in conducting discussions based on conflict situations incorporate several of those in other strategies, as well as specific ones for this task. Elements specific to this strategy include making inferences about feelings, identifying and describing situations in discussion participants' own lives that are parallel to the one under consideration, and evaluating solutions to problems. In a resolution of conflict discussion, students are presented with a problem situation that includes a conflict between persons or groups, and the students are led through the following steps:

1. Recall data from the situation.
2. Infer (and support) the actions and feelings of people who are significant in the situation.
3. Propose and defend possible solutions to the problem.
4. Infer (and support) possible reactions to proposed solutions and subsequent consequences.
5. Relate the situation to similar experiences they have had or know of.
6. Describe the feelings of the people during these experiences.
7. Evaluate the way the situation was handled and explain the basis for their evaluation.
8. Consider possible alternatives that could have been chosen.
9. Generalize about how people usually deal with similar situations.

Purpose

We do not live in a world of pure cognition and rational thought processes. Momentous decisions usually are overlaid with cognition, but actually made on the basis of feelings, attitudes, or values (Trezise 1972). Students need to become aware of the emotional component of situations and to develop skills in dealing with this component. Through examining a presented situation and similar situations in their own lives, students learn to see such instances from a variety of perspectives and to evaluate alternative solutions and their consequences. As in the other strategies, the teacher as discussion leader guides the process so the consequences of illogical, irrational, or emotional thought and behavior become apparent to the students. The inductive approach allows individuals to discover for themselves the logical errors in some emotional arguments.

Among the most valuable human skills are those leading to conflict resolution. Human conflict is prevalent—inner, personal conflicts as well as conflicts between groups and individuals. Students need a method for and practice in resolving conflicts.

The resolution of conflict cognitive task provides students with practice using strategies that mature people use when involved in or mediating a conflict: listing relevant information, considering the feelings and points of view of those involved, examining a variety of proposed alternatives and their consequences, and evaluating solutions. By applying the same steps first to a presented situation and then to one or more experienced or known of by the students themselves, immediate transfer of the cognitive skills from one situation to another is accomplished. In the demonstration lesson plan in Figure 13–1, students explore a name-calling situation, then are asked to volunteer similar situations from their own experiences.

Providing the opportunity to make commitments and decisions helps students become more willing to make decisions, even in complex situations. Young people need to discover that no quick, easy, or perfect answers exist in conflict situations. Further, they need to realize that usually any solution will impose hardships on someone. The factors of human feelings, attitudes, and values complicate decision making, but are a part of life. Strategies to cope with complex decisions enable people to find workable solutions to problems in youth and adulthood.

Conceptualization of the Resolution of Conflict Task

As with all of the Hilda Taba Teaching Strategies, teachers need to conceptualize the resolution of conflict task before planning or leading a discussion based on the strategy. The purpose of the strategy is to teach students to apply logic and critical thinking to affective situations. As mentioned in connection with the other strategies, understanding the purpose of each step is critical to using the strategy effectively. Figure 13–2 is a symbolic representation of the strategy that may help novices to internalize it. The author suggests referring to this diagram while reading about the strategy, to assist in the formation of a mental image of the strategy's structure.

Rationale for Individual Steps

Step 1—Listing
The purpose of the first step is to identify, by listing, actions taken by key people in the conflict situation. Listing may serve to refresh the memories of some students, and it ensures that all are focusing on the same behaviors of the key people. Establishing a common base is necessary for the development of the discussion.

Step 2—Reasons for Actions and Feelings
The purpose of Step 2 is to help students see the complexity of human events and interactions. Mature judgment and moral development require the ability to take the perspective of other people. Step 2 of this strategy focuses students on the possible reasons for the behavior of both the "actor" and "other(s)" in the situation. Voicing and supporting a variety of possible reasons for behavior make the point that many explanations are possible and plausible for specific behaviors.

FIGURE 13–1 Demonstration Discussion Plan—Resolution of Conflict

STRATEGY: Resolution of Conflict
Lesson plan by Shirley Schiever

Topic ___Prejudice—Name Calling___
Level ___Demo—All___

DISCUSSION PURPOSES

Content: To propose and defend solutions to a conflict situation in which confrontation occurs over a derogatory name.

Process: To make inferences about the feelings of people involved in a conflict situation, to identify possible solutions and consequences, and to form generalizations about the ways people handle such situations.

PREDISCUSSION PROCEDURES

Arrange seating for discussion so all can see and hear each other.

MATERIALS

Tape, film, story, actual incident between students, or item from news media that tells of one or more people taunting a person or group with a derogatory name (nigger, spic, wop, faggot, sissy, etc.).

BEHAVIORAL OBJECTIVES	FOCUSING QUESTIONS	TEACHER'S ROLE	SUPPORT PROCEDURES
STEP ONE—DATA (Behaviors) a. Students will enumerate the actions of the (two to four people) involved in the situation.	a. What happened in the (story, film, etc.)? What did Nick do? What did Alicia do? What did their parents do?	1. Focus on behaviors of key people. 2. Record behaviors under "behaver's" name. 3. Limit data.	List actions by person. Solicit several actions for each of the main people involved.
STEP TWO—REASONS, FEELINGS, AND SUPPORT a. Students will state reasons for the behaviors of the "actor" and "others'" behavior. b. Students will state possible feelings of the "actor" and "others." c. Students will support their inferences about feelings with evidence or reasoning.	a. Why do you think, (e.g., Nick yelled, "Nigger!" to Alicia when she came out of her house)? b. How do you think Nick felt when he yelled "Nigger!"? c. Why do you think he felt mean? a. How do you think Alicia felt when Nick yelled at her? b. Why . . . ?	1. Seek variety of reasons for behaviors of key people. 2. Seek variety of feelings for each key person. 3. Seek support for feelings.	Seek a variety of reasons for selected actions of main participants in conflict (Nick, Alicia, both sets of parents). Seek support for each feeling inferred. Seek variety of feelings for each person.

Form adapted from Institute for Staff Development 1971d, p. 41.

(FIGURE 13–1—Continued)

BEHAVIORAL OBJECTIVES	FOCUSING QUESTIONS	TEACHER'S ROLE	SUPPORT PROCEDURES
STEP THREE—ALTERNATIVE SOLUTIONS (could do), CONSEQUENCES (reactions), SUPPORT a. Students will suggest several alternative actions for Nick and Alicia. b. Students will state possible consequences of alternative solutions. c. Students will support their inferred consequences with evidence or reasoning.	a. What are some things Alicia could do? b. How do you think (Nick) (her parents) would react if she did that? c. Why would (he) (they) react that way? a. What things could Nick do? b. How do you think . . . ? c. Why . . . ?	1. Seek a variety of possible solutions. 2. Record possible solutions. 3. Seek a variety of consequences for selected solutions. 4. Seek support for consequences.	Break class into small groups for this step. Have each group write alternative solutions and discuss consequences and reasons.
STEP FOUR—SELECTED SOLUTIONS (should do), SUPPORT, LONG-RANGE CONSEQUENCES, SUPPORT a. Students will state what they think is the best solution. b. Students will support their suggested solution. c. Students will predict consequences of solution. d. Students will support their predictions.	a. What do you think Alicia should do? b. Why should she . . . ? c. What do you think will happen eventually if she . . . ? d. Why do you think that will happen? c. What else . . . ? d. Why . . . ? a. Who else will tell us what Alicia should do?	1. Encourage each student to reach a conclusion. 2. Seek support for solutions, immediate, and delayed effects.	Seek responses from a variety of students.

Form adapted from Institute for Staff Development 1971d, p. 42.

(FIGURE 13–1—Continued)

BEHAVIORAL OBJECTIVES	FOCUSING QUESTIONS	TEACHER'S ROLE	SUPPORT PROCEDURES
STEP FIVE—DATA (similar situation) a. Students will recall the details of a similar situation.	a. What similar things have happened to you or someone you know, where someone calls an innocent person an ugly or hurtful name? What happened? What did (each person) do?	1. Seek situations similar to focus situation. 2. Seek actions of principal figures in situation.	If a student relates a personal experience, pursue steps 5–8 only with that person. If the situation happened to someone else, all can participate. Repeat cycle as time and interest allow.
STEP SIX—REASONS, FEELINGS, AND SUPPORT (similar situation) See Step 2a, b, and c.	a. Why do you think . . . ? b. How did you feel when . . . ? c. Why do you think you felt . . . ? b. How do you think the old man felt? c. Why . . . ?	1. Seek a variety of feelings and support.	Explore the feelings of both parties several times during the situation. Seek a variety of feelings for both parties. "How else might — have felt?" Seek support.
STEP SEVEN—EVALUATION OF SOLUTION AND SUPPORT a. Student will state reasons for selecting course of action taken. b. Student will evaluate course of action. c. Student will support evaluation of action.	a. What were your reasons for (doing what you did)? b. Thinking back now, how do you think you handled the situation? c. Why do you say, e.g., you were too mean to Linda?	1. If class participation is sought, make question general.	Vary question stems.

Form adapted from Institute for Staff Development 1971d, p. 43.

(FIGURE 13-1—Continued)

BEHAVIORAL OBJECTIVES	FOCUSING QUESTIONS	TEACHER'S ROLE	SUPPORT PROCEDURES
STEP EIGHT—ALTERNATIVE SOLUTIONS, CONSEQUENCES, SUPPORT a. Students will suggest ways situation could have been handled differently. b. Students will state consequences of handling situation. c. Students will support inferred consequences.	a. In what other ways could you have handled this situation? b. What do you think the consequences would have been if you had __? c. Why would that have happened?	1. Seek variety of alternatives and support. 2. Seek variety of consequences and support.	If situation does not involve participant personally, explore several alternatives. Follow one alternative, consequence, and support at a time, but seek a variety of consequences and support.
STEP NINE—GENERALIZATIONS & SUPPORT a. Students will state generalizations about people's responses to stereotypic and denigrating names. b. Students will support their generalization with evidence or reasoning.	a. Remembering our discussion about Nick and Alicia and what __, __, and __ told us, how do you think people usually handle a situation where someone calls them an unfair name? b. What from our discussion leads you to say that?	1. Seek support for general statements. 2. Seek participation by a variety of students.	Ask for a variety of students to respond. "Who else will tell us . . . ?"

Form adapted from Institute for Staff Development 1971d, p. 44.

(FIGURE 13–1–Continued)

RESOLUTION OF CONFLICT
COGNITIVE MAP

STEP 2	STEP 1	STEP 3a	STEP 3b AND 3c
Reasons and Feelings	Possible Data (Behaviors)	Possible Alternative Solutions	Possible Reactions, Consequences
angry upset jealous	Nick came into his yard stuck out his tongue called Alicia "Nigger"	Alicia talk to Nick Alicia call Nick "WOP"	Nick apologize Nick feel embarrassed Nick angry, hit Alicia They become enemies
hurt angry want to get even	Alicia played hopscotch didn't say hello to Nick, ignored him started crying, went into the house	Alicia tell her teacher Alicia be nice to Nick, try to make friends	Principal talk to Alicia and Nick Class discussion Nick feel ashamed They become friends
hurt angry sad	Alicia's mom hugged Alicia said she would call Nick's mom gave Alicia a cookie	Alicia ignore Nick	Alicia still feel hurt Nick won't learn anything Nobody in trouble

Form adapted from Institute for Staff Development 1971d, p. 45.

Copyright by Allyn and Bacon. Reproduction of this material is restricted to use with *A Comprehensive Approach to Teaching Thinking* by Shirley W. Schiever.

(FIGURE 13–1–Continued)

STEP 4a	STEP 4c		STEP 4e	STEP 5
Selected Solutions	→ *Consequences* →		→ *Long-Range Consequences*	*Sample Similar Situations*
Alicia talk to Nick, try to make friends	Become friends ─────── Nick becomes less prejudiced ─── Alicia learns how to handle name-calling		He feels better about himself He has more friends Alicia is strong, feels good about herself	Cecelia is overweight and her classmates call her "Fatty." Tom's older brother calls him "baby."
Alicia ignore Nick	He learns not to call names No one is in trouble			

STEP 9

Possible Generalizations

When people call names, everyone can end up feeling hurt.
Calling names hurts.
Calling names back doesn't solve the problem.

Form adapted from Institute for Staff Development 1971d, p. 45.

FIGURE 13–2 Graphic Representation—Resolution of Conflict, Steps 1–9

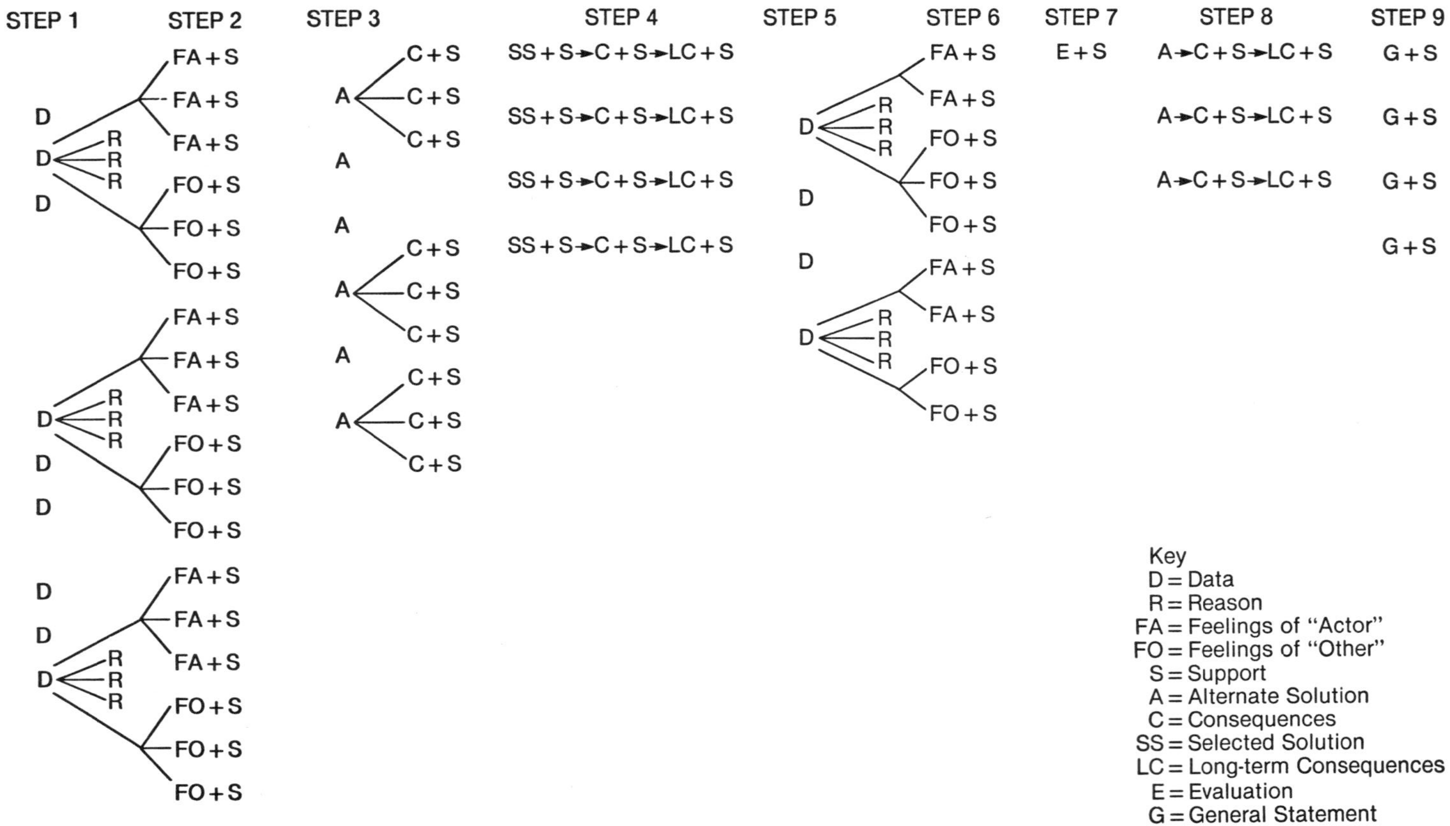
STEP 1
STEP 2
STEP 3
STEP 4
STEP 5
STEP 6
STEP 7
STEP 8
STEP 9
SS + S→C + S→LC + S
E + S
A→C + S→LC + S
G + S
Key
D = Data
R = Reason
FA = Feelings of "Actor"
FO = Feelings of "Other"
S = Support
A = Alternate Solution
C = Consequences
SS = Selected Solution
LC = Long-term Consequences
E = Evaluation
G = General Statement

Further, exploring the feelings of all persons involved illustrates that a variety of feelings are a legitimate and important aspect of human interactions.

Step 3—Alternative Solutions and Reactions

In exploring possible solutions and their consequences, students are developing a workable alternative to acting on the first idea that occurs to them or simply responding on an emotional level. Examining many alternatives offers the opportunity for choosing better ones. Further, the realization that in any situation at least a few options exist moves students toward mature emotional judgment and action.

The reactions of other people are an important part of evaluating alternative actions. Asking students to infer the reactions of various people and the reasons for these (inferred) reactions provides another chance for perspective taking.

Step 4—Selected Solutions, Support, and Long-Range Consequences

After students have explored consequences of alternative solutions, they can make an informed conclusion as to what is the *best* solution. Step 4 builds on previous steps, in having students assess solutions, take various factors into consideration, and select a preferred solution. However, since a solution does not end a problem with the involved person riding happily into the sunset, long-term consequences of the selected solutions must be explored. This reminds students that not only do problems have multiple causes, but that solutions have multiple effects. In this step, logic and rational thought are applied to the world of human emotions and behavior.

Steps 5 Through 8—Similar Situations

These steps are essentially a recycling of steps 1 through 4, so the purposes are the same, with one addition. When students are asked to relate situations with similar elements to the one just discussed and to apply the same cognitive strategies to the similar situations, they see that these processes are applicable to ordinary situations and everyday life. Thus, the additional purpose is to show the usefulness of the techniques for a variety of situations and people.

Step 9—Generalization and Support

The purpose of Step 9 is to require students to synthesize information from a variety of sources into a general statement about similar conflict situations. In finding the common ground or commonality among several incidents, some related by peers, students begin to codify human behavior. As they infer how and why people usually handle certain types of situations, they are internalizing realizations that come with emotional maturity: Actions occur for a variety of reasons and have a variety of feelings associated with them, multiple options of behavior exist, and solutions have consequences.

Overt and Covert Behaviors in Resolution of Conflict

Through overt responses and actions teachers are able to determine what covert processes (thinking) may be occurring. Both overt and covert behaviors must be kept in mind when planning a discussion that will facilitate cognitive and/or affective development. Figure 13–3 lists the purpose, overt and covert behaviors, and generic focusing questions for each step of the resolution of conflict strategy. This chart is designed as an aid in planning the discussion and formulating focusing questions.

PLANNING A RESOLUTION OF CONFLICT DISCUSSION

An effective resolution of conflict discussion requires careful planning. The teacher must choose the catalyst (story, film, current event) carefully to ensure attaining the objectives. Carefully thinking through possible responses and ways to probe or extend ideas is critical and should be done in conjunction with the development of a cognitive map and the completion of a discussion plan, which can be recorded on forms duplicated from Figure 13–4. Step-by-step instructions for planning a discussion follow.

Determining Discussion Purposes

The purposes of a resolution of conflict discussion are somewhat prescribed; the topic makes the discussion relevant to the curriculum and a defensible use of classroom time. The affective domain is important in and of itself, but many conflicts exist in or in relation to content areas, and these should be explored. History is full of human conflict, individual and group; literature abounds with accounts of conflict; and scientific and technological fields hold many examples of past and current conflict. The school and the student body offer a never ending source of conflict situations, some of which may be explored to enhance the affective development of the students. Instructional time is valuable and choices of what to teach

FIGURE 13–3 Over-Covert Behaviors—Resolution of Conflict (Focusing Situation)

STEP	1	2	3	4
Purpose of Step	*Develop List of Behaviors of Key People*	*Focus on Complexity of Human Behavior*	*Generate Possible Solutions & Reactions to These Solutions*	*Evaluate Solutions & Draw Conclusions*
OVERT Behavioral objectives	Enumerate specific, relevant data.	a. State inferences re actions. b. State inferences re possible feelings. c. State reasons supporting inferred feelings.	a. State alternative solutions. b. Suggest possible reactions to solutions. c. State reasons for inferences re reactions.	a. State preferred solution. b. Give reasons supporting conclusion. c. Suggest long-range consequences of preferred solution. d. Support consequences.
COVERT Thinking objectives	Recall. Differentiate relevant from irrelevant.	a. Infer possible reasons for actions. b. Infer possible feelings. c. Identify evidence or reasoning to support inferences.	a. Infer possible solutions. b. Infer possible reactions to solutions. c. Identify evidence or reasoning to support inferences re reactions.	a. Differentiate, evaluate, synthesize (conclude). b. Identify evidence to support conclusion. c. Infer possible effects & subsequent effects. d. Identify evidence or reasoning to support inferences re consequences.
FOCUSING QUESTION (General)	In the (story, film, etc.), what did __ do?	a. Why do you think __ acted as s/he did? b. How do you think s/he felt? c. Why do you think s/he was feeling that way?	a. What things could __ do? b. How do you think __ would react to that? c. Why do you think __ would react like that?	a. What do you think __ should do? b. Why do you think that would be best? c. What would be some consequences of __? d. Why do you say that would happen?

Adapted from Institute for Staff Development 1971d, p. 9.

(FIGURE 13–3–Continued)

Resolution of Conflict (Similar Situation)

STEP	5	6	7	8	9
Purpose of Step	Illustrate Similarities Between Situations	Take Perspective of Others	Evaluation of Solution	Recognize Existence of Alternative Solutions	Transfer Thinking to Other, Similar Situations; Broaden Perspective
OVERT Behavioral objectives	Describe situation similar to focus situation.	a. State possible reasons for behaviors in similar situation. b. State feelings of people. c. Support statements about feelings.	a. State reasons for action taken. b. State judgment of action taken. c. Cite reasons supporting judgment.	a. Suggest alternative actions. b. Suggest consequences of alternative actions. c. Provide reasons for inferred consequences.	a. Make general statement about specified type of situation. b. Cite evidence or reasoning to support statement.
COVERT Thinking objectives	Recall. Differentiate relevant from irrelevant.	a. Recall own feelings, infer feelings of others. b. Identify evidence or reasoning to support inferences.	a. Identify evidence or reasoning. b. Evaluate effectiveness of action. c. Identify evidence or reasoning to support evaluation.	a. Infer possible alternatives. b. Infer possible effects. c. Identify evidence or reasoning in support of inferences.	a. Generalize about type of situations discussed. b. Identify evidence to support general statement.
FOCUSING QUESTIONS (General)	What situations where —, have you or someone you know experienced? Describe what happened.	a. How did (you) feel? How do you think — felt? b. Why did you feel —? Why do you think — felt —?	a. What were your reasons for —? b. How effective do you think your action was? c. Why do you think your action was —?	a. How could you have handled the situation differently? b. What do you think the consequences of — would have been? c. Why do you think — would have happened?	a. Based on our discussion, what do you think people usually do in a situation where —? b. Why do you say that?

Adapted from Institute for Staff Development 1971d, p. 10.

FIGURE 13–4 Discussion Plan Form—Resolution of Conflict

STRATEGY: Resolution of Conflict

Topic _____
Level _____

DISCUSSION PURPOSES

PREDISCUSSION PROCEDURES

Content:

MATERIALS

Process:

BEHAVIORAL OBJECTIVES	FOCUSING QUESTIONS	TEACHER'S ROLE	SUPPORT PROCEDURES
STEP ONE—DATA (Behaviors)		1. Focus on behaviors of key people. 2. Record behaviors under "behaver's" name. 3. Limit data.	
STEP TWO—REASONS, FEELINGS, AND SUPPORT		1. Seek variety of reasons for behaviors of key people. 2. Seek variety of feelings for each key person. 3. Seek support for feelings.	

Form adapted from Institute for Staff Development 1971d, p. 41.

(FIGURE 13-4—Continued)

BEHAVIORAL OBJECTIVES	FOCUSING QUESTIONS	TEACHER'S ROLE	SUPPORT PROCEDURES
STEP THREE—ALTERNATIVE SOLUTIONS (could do), CONSEQUENCES (reactions), SUPPORT		1. Seek a variety of possible solutions. 2. Record possible solutions. 3. Seek a variety of consequences for selected solutions. 4. Seek support for consequences.	
STEP FOUR—SELECTED SOLUTIONS (should do), SUPPORT, LONG-RANGE CONSEQUENCES, SUPPORT		1. Encourage each student to reach a conclusion. 2. Seek support for solutions, immediate, and delayed effects.	

Form adapted from Institute for Staff Development 1971d, p. 42.

(FIGURE 13–4–Continued)

BEHAVIORAL OBJECTIVES	FOCUSING QUESTIONS	TEACHER'S ROLE	SUPPORT PROCEDURES
STEP FIVE—DATA (similar situation)		1. Seek situations similar to focus situation. 2. Seek actions of principal figures in situation.	
STEP SIX—REASONS, FEEL-INGS, AND SUPPORT (similar situation)		1. Seek a variety of feelings and support.	
STEP SEVEN—EVALUATION OF SOLUTION AND SUPPORT		1. If class participation is sought, make question general.	

Form adapted from Institute for Staff Development 1971d, p. 43.

(FIGURE 13–4–Continued)

BEHAVIORAL OBJECTIVES	FOCUSING QUESTIONS	TEACHER'S ROLE	SUPPORT PROCEDURES
STEP EIGHT—ALTERNATIVE SOLUTIONS, CONSEQUENCES, SUPPORT		1. Seek variety of alternatives and support. 2. Seek variety of consequences and support.	
STEP NINE—GENERALIZA- TIONS & SUPPORT		1. Seek support for general state- ments. 2. Seek participation by a variety of students.	

Form adapted from Institute for Staff Development 1971d, p. 44.
Copyright by Allyn and Bacon. Reproduction of this material is restricted to use with *A Comprehensive Approach to Teaching Thinking* by Shirley W. Schiever.

(FIGURE 13–4–Continued)

RESOLUTION OF CONFLICT
COGNITIVE MAP

STEP 2	STEP 1	STEP 3a	STEP 3b AND 3c
Reasons and Feelings	Possible Data (Behaviors)	Possible Alternative Solutions	Possible Reactions, Consequences

STEP 4a	STEP 4c	STEP 4e
Selected Solutions	Consequences	Long-Range Consequences

Form adapted from Institute for Staff Development 1971d, p. 45.

Copyright by Allyn and Bacon. Reproduction of this material is restricted to use with *A Comprehensive Approach to Teaching Thinking* by Shirley W. Schiever.

must be made daily; the affective domain must be recognized as a potent force and allotted time within the curriculum accordingly.

Discussions can center either on conflicts dealing with interpersonal situations (fights, arguments, wars) or intrapersonal situations (personal decisions). The content purpose of the discussion includes both the focus situation and similar situations, with major emphasis on similar situations.

The Institute for Staff Development authors state that having students form generalizations about the ways people deal with particular types of conflict situations is an optional purpose (and step) for resolution of conflict discussions. However, making generalizations is a developmental process necessary for complex thinking, and students should practice making general statements if they are to become proficient thinkers. Therefore, Step 9 should be included routinely in resolution of conflict discussions.

The following paragraphs detail the suggested steps for planning a resolution of conflict discussion.

Prediscussion Procedures and Materials

1. Decide what material and medium will provide the most effective catalyst for this discussion. On the planning form (page 267), note the prerequisite discussions or activities, and physical arrangements for the discussion. Students must have a frame of reference for taking in information, so that they can identify parallel situations and make value judgments about solutions. If using a historical or unfamiliar conflict situation, be sure to provide enough background information for them to construct a frame of reference.

2. The content purpose is stated in this way: "To propose and defend solutions to a conflict situation in which confrontation occurs (e.g., over derogatory name-calling)." Record the content purpose on the discussion plan form.

3. The process purpose is stated thusly: "To make inferences about the feelings of people involved in a conflict situation, to identify possible solutions and consequences, and to form generalizations about the ways people handle such situations." Record this purpose in the appropriate place on the form.

Behavioral Objectives, Focusing Questions, and Support Procedures

4. Refer to the chart on page 265 for the general behavioral objective for Step 1. Based on this general objective, write the specific objective for this step of your discussion, such as "Students will enumerate

the actions of Nick and Alicia after they see the film 'What's in a Name?'." Include in the objectives the specific people whose actions and feelings will be explored.

5. Based on the objective and using the general focusing question from the chart on page 265 as a guide, formulate the question for Step 1, such as "What happened (e.g., to Alicia) in the film?" Record the focusing question for Step 1 on the plan.

6. On the cognitive map (page 271), record possible data (responses to the focusing question) for each key character in the situation. If the possible responses to the focus question do not lead to accomplishing the step and discussion purposes, reformulate the question and repeat steps 4 through 6.

7. List support procedures for Step 1 on the planning form. These are reminders to ensure that this step of the discussion accomplishes its stated purpose.

8. Complete the plan, steps 2 through 4, using the overt/covert behavior chart, the plan form, and the cognitive map to record behavioral objectives, formulate focusing questions, and check responses for relation to the step and overall discussion purpose. Steps 5 through 9 do not require cognitive mapping. The sample lesson plans include these steps for the reader's information.

IMPLEMENTING THE STRATEGY

The resolution of conflict strategy has more steps than any of the other Hilda Taba Teaching Strategies, but even novice discussion leaders typically find it relatively easy and enjoyable to use. This may be due to the high degree of student interest in issues of conflict and the gratifying degree of growing self-awareness and self-disclosure observed in students. As with any teaching method, however, the success of these discussions depends on the teacher. The information in this section is included to help discussion leaders attain success, beginning with their first discussion.

Step 1—Data (Behaviors)

The behavioral objective, focusing question, and support procedures are like those for an interpretation of data discussion. The purpose is to develop a list containing a variety of data concerning what students read, saw, or heard in the situation.

If students are to make responsible decisions, they must have facts and the problem must be stated clearly. This is the function of

Step 1, and it may not be accomplished easily when using a real conflict situation or one that is very close to students. Some degree of objectivity is necessary if a factual base is to be established.

At Step 1, the data listed must be specific behaviors of the two or three key people in the focus conflict situation. As the data are listed, they should be placed under the name of the relevant person. If students do not volunteer actions of one or more of the key people, a question needs to be asked that will focus on this behavior, such as "What did Alicia's parents do?"

As with all discussions of this nature, record the student responses in their own words. If an inference is offered such as "Alicia's parents were trying to make a better life," ask what the parents *did* that led the student to believe they were trying to make a better life.

The purpose of listing the data at this step is to focus the group on the actions of the key people in the situation. This provides a common ground for the discussion.

The most common problems for beginners at this step are not focusing on specific behaviors of the key people and accepting inferences without clarification. Thinking of this step as listing data on actions may help alleviate these problems.

The teacher's role at Step 1 of resolution of conflict discussions includes the following:

- To focus students on the behaviors of the key people
- To record these behaviors under the name of the "behaver"
- To limit data (three to five behaviors per key person)

Step 2—Reasons, Feelings, and Support

This step of the discussion is based on the actions of the key figures, but asks students to infer reasons for these actions and the feelings of the "actor" as well as the feelings of "others" during the actions. A variety of feelings should be sought for each person during or regarding the selected action(s). This reinforces the realization that frequently an individual has mixed emotions about events and people in a conflict situation.

Sometimes novice discussion leaders forget to elicit a variety of feelings for both the actor and others at this step. A reminder in the support procedures column of the discussion plan may help one avoid this problem.

The teacher's role at Step 2 of resolution of conflict discussions includes the following:

- To focus on the reasons and feelings of key people
- To seek a variety of reasons and feelings

Steps 3 and 4—Possible and Recommended Solutions

Steps 3 and 4 both deal with solutions and consequences, although in different ways. At Step 3, the focus is on *possible* solutions and reactions of people to the solutions, while Step 4 elicits statements concerning what students think *should* be done, why, and the possible consequences, both short- and long-range.

The purpose of Step 3 is to focus on the variety of alternatives possible in conflict situations. Examining many alternatives offers the opportunity for choosing better ones. Examining reactions of others and the consequences of alternatives helps students learn to think through situations. In examining possible solutions and their consequences, students are developing a workable alternative to acting on the first idea that occurs to them or simply on an emotional level.

At Step 4, students should not vote on a "best" solution, nor should consensus be sought. The purpose of this step is to take students beyond the immediate situation to a preferred solution and its consequences. The emphasis is not on a variety of responses, but on having each participant think about what the best solution is and the short- and long-term effects of the solution. All students should make a conclusion and generalize effects (predict consequences) for themselves. If discussions involving real issues in the classroom or school result in differences of opinion as to resolution and consequences, one possibility is to try out each suggested solution and document what consequences follow each.

Forming small groups of students to perform the tasks at steps 3 and/or 4 is an effective procedure. A variety of possibilities exists: The whole group can suggest (and support) possible solutions and small groups can be formed to discuss (and support) individual views of the best solution; both steps can be accomplished within (the same) small groups; pairs of students can be assigned one or both tasks; or two different small-group configurations can be developed, one for each step.

When asking students to work in relatively autonomous groups, providing a structure, specific directions, and a list of tasks to be accomplished is critical. Including the plan for grouping and steps to be followed in the "Support Procedures" column of the lesson plan is part of good planning.

The author's experience indicates that discussion leaders have little trouble and make few errors at steps 3 and 4.

The teacher's role at Step 3 includes the following:

- To seek a variety of possible solutions
- To record (or see that each group's recorder lists) the possible solutions
- To seek a variety of consequences for selected solutions and support for these consequences

The teacher's role at Step 4 includes the following:

- To encourage each student to reach a conclusion (whether or not it is shared with the group)
- To seek support for the preferred solution, immediate and delayed effects of the solution, and support for the effects

Steps 5 Through 8—Similar Situation

The purpose of steps 5 through 8 is to demonstrate that the processes just engaged in are applicable to ordinary situations and everyday life conflicts. These steps essentially recycle steps 1 through 4, but the order is different since the event is past. At Step 7 the solution is evaluated, but no "best" solution is selected.

One of the keys to successful resolution of conflict discussions is a clear focus on what the conflict issue is. At Step 5 the teacher must understand and be able to state the objective of the step in precise terms. The focus question must be stated clearly and it should focus on the conflict issue. A question such as "Who has had, or knows someone who has had, an experience similar to this, when someone has to decide whether to be mean and hateful back to a person who hurts their feelings?" provides a focus on the situation of hurt feelings, the issue of type of response, and the decision.

The evaluation of the way students or someone they know handled a problem further develops the ability to make sound decisions. The questions "As you think about it now, how do you feel about the way you handled the situation?" and "What, if anything, would you do differently?" invite important deliberations about past decisions and/or actions. Such retrospection helps students apply logical thinking to emotional situations.

The teacher's role in steps 5 through 8 is to guide with sensitivity as students who volunteer explore similar situations. Judgments must be made on an individual basis whether or not to ask for class participation. If participation is asked, it can be asked in a way that depersonalizes the situation (e.g., "What other ways can people handle the pressure from peers to cheat?").

Usually steps 5 through 8 move quickly and are enjoyed by students. Ordinarily as soon as the focus question is asked at Step 5, several hands shoot up, volunteering a similar situation. Occasionally, however, students seem unable to think of one; therefore the wise teacher has a sample situation in mind, in case students need additional examples of the focus situation. These teacher-supplied samples should be used only as a last resort and in as brief a form as possible. The purpose of the samples is only to trigger students' recall of their experiences.

Steps 5 through 8 can be recycled as many times as student interest and time allow.

Step 9—Generalizations

The purpose of Step 9 is to require students to synthesize information from a variety of sources into a general statement about similar conflict situations. This offers students an opportunity to use the generalizing process and extend their own ideas to people in general. It also provides the teacher with an opportunity to evaluate students' increasing skill in generalizing.

As with Step 5 of interpretation of data, the focusing question occasionally presents a problem. However, most discussion leaders seem to be able to ask a question that leads students to make general statements, and few problems are experienced at this step.

The teacher's role at Step 9 includes the following behaviors:

- To word the focus question clearly so general statements are based on the discussion
- To seek support for the general statements
- To encourage participation by all students

General Tips on Implementation

When choosing a focus conflict for a discussion, choose a problem in which students have a vested interest. This heightens students' interest and facilitates the transfer of the skills and information to their everyday lives. When dealing with feelings, especially if an episode from the classroom or school surroundings is being used, students' perceptions of the facts may vary significantly. In such situations the teacher should attempt to obtain a clear statement of differences in perception of what occurred. One way to approach this is to list all the "facts" on butcher paper, which can be left in sight for the rest of the school day. The next day, or the following day, with the "old" set of facts not in evidence, the teacher again can ask the group to list the facts of the situation. The passing of time and cooling of passions may result in fewer contradictory statements of fact, and the teacher might feel that a discussion is possible. If the situation is too volatile to be discussed, a similar incident from a story, film, or TV program can be used as a focus situation. When students are emotionally involved with an issue, examining the reasons for behavior and feelings of various people is especially critical.

If students are to develop sensitivity to the idea that very different reactions to any situation are possible, they must have opportunities to look at situations from more than one point of view. This is why students should look at the feelings of not just the central, but several characters. Developing the understanding that different people react to the same situation in different ways requires that students look closely at a variety of reactions.

Resolution of conflict discussions require a safe environment for expressing and examining feelings. Teachers should cultivate relaxed and supportive approaches to provide this safety. A comfortable, supportive classroom environment enhances all learning, but such an environment is especially critical when issues related to emotions are being discussed. Students will have emotional reactions, and other students and the teacher must help support the person who is reacting. This supportive atmosphere must be developed through modeling as well as direct instruction and the disciplinary structure of the classroom.

Teachers who never ridicule a student nor allow students to ridicule each other are creating a safe environment where students may grow, mentally and emotionally. When the climate is such that students cannot afford to be honest, they tend to give an answer they think is acceptable to the teacher or to remain silent. If the teacher models judgmental reactions, students may become overly critical of the behavior of others. Should this occur, the teacher can move the discussion to the evaluation of one's own solutions.

The acceptance of all responses contributes to a safe classroom environment; even unusual or antisocial comments should be accepted (and recorded if appropriate to the step) at face value and the students encouraged to consider the consequences of such behaviors or feelings. Additionally, students must not be allowed to engage in excessive judging of their own or others' actions without progressing through the crucial steps of (a) exploring the criteria and values implicit in their judgment, (b) considering alternatives, and (c) considering consequences.

Questions alone will not ensure achieving discussion objectives; the selection of the focus situation is critical. In many cases, students have limited experience; the situation must allow them to get a sense of commonality of experience if they are to personalize it. This sense of commonality is the bridge between the familiar and the unfamiliar. For example, if the issue is respect for other people's property, the focus situation could be a story about a person picking something off of another's desk and accidentally breaking the object. Most students have had experience with this type of situation and can relate to it.

If students do not respond to a focus situation, reexamine the make-up of the class. Perhaps the situation is foreign to their experience, as a story about inner-city gang wars would be to students in an affluent suburb. When an episode does not seem to be meaningful to your students, examine it to determine whether it is a poorly chosen episode, or whether something is lacking in the experience of the students so they cannot relate to it. Select episodes that are not so far removed from the students' experience that they are unable to identify with them.

A sequence has been suggested for use in discussing human relations situations, but no one question sequence will meet all the needs of any discussion. As teachers lead discussions, they need to be constantly aware of their purpose and ask themselves, "Does this question really get at what I am trying to do?" Additionally, as students are guided through the sequence, teachers need to remember that responses and interpretations do not always have to be verbal— they can be written, or drawn, or role played, or expressed in any way students and teachers find comfortable and effective.

Writing lends itself easily to human relations activities. Both the teacher and students can learn a lot from responses written to focused, open-ended questions within a safe environment. Writing in response to open-ended questions gives students an opportunity to get a good look at their feelings and values. Some types of open-ended questions allow students to put themselves in the place of another person and write from that person's viewpoint. This also allows them an opportunity to identify with another person and to think about varying points of view.

Role playing is an effective way to explore and analyze human relations. Students can role play a variety of endings for a story or solutions to problems. Students who have difficulty seeing another person's point of view can be asked to role play someone else in a conflict situation. Role playing never should end the task, but always should be followed by debriefing, a guided discussion of the feelings and solutions dramatized.

If the discussion is related to a sensitive area of human relations, the teacher may wish to replace questions that relate to first-hand experience with questions that relate the incident to people the students have known or to episodes from books. This avoids confronting students with a situation in which they expose feelings they really do not wish to share. For instance, if a student is suffering the sting of a recent racial slur, discussing the inferred feelings and available alternatives of a character in a book is more comfortable than discussing the actual incident.

Evaluation

Evaluation of cognitive growth is part of the daily school routine. Evaluating students' progress in the affective realm is more difficult and not as commonly done. However, noting student interactions and reactions will provide information on affective development. Some benchmarks to expect include a reduction of hostility in the classroom, an opening up of little groups or cliques, and fewer isolates or outsiders. Watch for signs of social sensitivity and awareness. Students may begin choosing co-workers on the basis of the job to be done rather than on the basis of established friendships. Expect them to become more sensitive to the needs and reactions of people as they talk about human relations, about how they feel and how others feel or would react to a particular course of action.

As students have opportunities to discuss social situations from books, newspapers, the school, and the classroom, they will begin to ask for other points of view, to look at more than one editorial or cartoon, to wonder how somebody else might have seen an issue. Expect students to move away from egocentrism and ethnocentrism in the solution of problems; away from "I think she would like it because I do," or "Those customs are weird—we don't do it that way," to "She may not care for that, " and "Native Americans have customs that are different from ours."

APPLICATIONS OF THE RESOLUTION OF CONFLICT STRATEGY

Students deal constantly with conflict situations, both internal and external. They must make decisions about behavior, friends, family, and relationships as well as try to interact with others in socially acceptable ways. Observing recess in elementary schools or class-changing periods at middle, junior, and senior high schools brings to mind the number of conflicts students face daily. Providing a structure for dealing with these conflicts and practice in the skills of perspective taking and evaluation of alternatives enables students to be more effective and therefore feel better about themselves. Emotions can get in the way of thinking; students need skills to deal with affective issues and concerns so the way is cleared for completion of cognitive tasks.

Conflict resolution discussions should be related to the academic curriculum as well as to students' social interactions. Some possibilities are listed on page 300. Historical conflicts such as wars are obvious choices. Less obvious perhaps are the internal and external personal conflicts of well-known people; conflicts between groups of people such as Native American and early European settlers; and conflicts stemming from change, such as the labor union movement or current local, national, and global conflicts related to technology. When students consider the human side of issues, their learning becomes more personalized and meaningful.

As with all the strategies, some resolution of conflict tasks can be accomplished individually in writing, in cooperative learning groups, in teams, or through a combination of individual and small- and large-group work. The author believes that steps 3, 4, and 9 are the steps most suited to small-group and individual work. Sharing at least a portion of steps undertaken by small groups or individuals is critical for maximum benefit of the entire group.

CHAPTER SUMMARY

The resolution of conflict strategy, in which feelings, attitudes, and values are interpreted and explored, can be used with people of all ages. This strategy provides a way to apply rational cognition to emotions, a logical approach to the affective realm of feeling and behaving. Possible focus situations occur daily and also are found in content areas of the curriculum. Students who are able to interact in positive and meaningful ways with peers, family, and others will be happier, better-adjusted learners than those who do not have these skills.

SAMPLE DISCUSSION PLANS—RESOLUTION OF CONFLICT

DISCUSSION PLAN
STRATEGY: Resolution of Conflict
Institute for Staff Development 1971d
DISCUSSION PURPOSES

Content: To propose and defend possible solutions to a conflict situation in which one has to decide whether to live up to his responsibilities or please someone else he cares about.

Process: To make inferences about the feelings of people involved in a conflict situation, to identify possible solutions and consequences in dealing with a situation, and form generalizations about the ways people handle such conflict situations.

Topic   Living Up to One's Responsibility
Level   Elementary
PREDISCUSSION PROCEDURES

Read the first two chapters of Old Yeller to the students.
Reminder—we're talking about feelings; respect each other's feelings.

MATERIALS
Gipson, Fred. Old Yeller.

BEHAVIORAL OBJECTIVES	FOCUSING QUESTIONS	TEACHER'S ROLE	SUPPORT PROCEDURES
STEP ONE—DATA (Behaviors) Students will relate data from the first two chapters of Old Yeller with special emphasis on the behaviors of the key characters.	What did Travis do when he found the dog? What did little Arliss do? What did their mother do?	1. Focus on behaviors of key people. 2. Record behaviors under "behavior's" name. 3. Limit data.	Focus on behavior of Travis, Arliss, and their mother.
STEP TWO—REASONS, FEELINGS, AND SUPPORT a. Students will state reasons for behaviors of Travis, Arliss, and mother. b. Students will state inferred feelings of key characters. c. Students will support their inferences with evidence or reasoning.	a. Why do you think Travis kicked the dog? Why else . . . ? b. How do you think Travis felt when he kicked the dog? c. Why would he be feeling, e.g., angry? a. Why do you think Arliss was . . . ? Etc.	1. Seek variety of reasons for behaviors of key people. 2. Seek variety of feelings for each key person. 3. Seek support for feelings.	

Form adapted from Institute for Staff Development, 1971d, p. 41.

BEHAVIORAL OBJECTIVES	FOCUSING QUESTIONS	TEACHER'S ROLE	SUPPORT PROCEDURES
STEP THREE—ALTERNATIVE SOLUTIONS (could do), CONSEQUENCES (reactions), SUPPORT a. Students will propose alternative solutions to Travis's conflict. b. Students will state inferences about reactions to each solution. c. Students will support their statements with evidence or reasoning.	a. What are some of the things that Travis could do? b. What may happen if he chooses, e.g., to try to sell the dog? c. Why do you think it may, e.g., make Arliss run away? (What may his mother do? What effect may this have on Arliss? Why would it have this effect?)	1. Seek a variety of possible solutions. 2. Record possible solutions. 3. Seek a variety of consequences for selected solutions. 4. Seek support for consequences.	Explore several alternative solutions. Ask what consequences any proposed course of action would have on all those involved—what may be their reactions to any chosen alternative? Each time inferences are made, have student give reasons, possibly referring to data of story for support.
STEP FOUR—SELECTED SOLUTIONS (should do), SUPPORT, LONG-RANGE CONSEQUENCES, SUPPORT a. Students will state preferred solution to the conflict. b. Students will give reasons for selecting a solution. c. Students will state inferred long-range consequences of selected solutions. d. Students will support their inferences about consequences.	a. What do you think Travis should do? b. What makes you think that, e.g., he should build a pen for the dog? c. If he does do that, what do you think will happen? d. Why do you think that, e.g., he will grow to like the dog? a. What does someone else think Travis should do? b. Why should . . . ? c. If he does . . . ? d. Why do you think . . . ?	1. Encourage each student to reach a conclusion. 2. Seek support for solutions, immediate, and delayed effects.	Since there is no one best solution when a group is thinking, try to get the students to respond with different ideas. Get reasons why they think as they do. Seek a variety of consequences and ask for the reasons and necessary conditions for them to occur.

Adapted from Institute for Staff Development 1971d, p. 42.

BEHAVIORAL OBJECTIVES	FOCUSING QUESTIONS	TEACHER'S ROLE	SUPPORT PROCEDURES
STEP FIVE—DATA (similar situation) Students will relate details of similar situations in which someone had tried to decide whether to face his/her responsibilities or do something to please someone else.	What other situations do you know of, where someone had to decide between something s/he thought was important and pleasing someone else? What happened? What did — do?	1. Seek situations similar to focus situation. 2. Seek actions of principal figures in situation.	Be sure that the students clearly understand wherein the conflict lies before you ask them to recall a similar situation. If they have difficulty, use one of the sample situations on the cognitive map as an additional stimulus. Recycle steps 5–8 several times.
STEP SIX—FEELINGS AND SUPPORT (similar situation) a. Students will state feelings they or those involved had in the similar situations. b. Students will give reasons for their statements.	a. How did you feel, e.g., when your brother asked you? b. How do you think he felt? c. Why do you think he felt, e.g., excited?	1. Seek a variety of feelings and support.	When exploring feelings, be sure to consider the feelings of all concerned. Students also should be encouraged to consider the variety of feelings people have in conflict situations.
STEP SEVEN—EVALUATION OF SOLUTION AND SUPPORT a. Students will state reasons for their actions in the situation. b. Students will evaluate their solution to the situation. c. Students will give reasons for their evaluation.	a. What were your reasons for, e.g., saying no? b. When you think about it now, how well do you think you managed the situation? c. Why do you think that, e.g., it was a good lesson for him to learn?	1. If class participation is sought, make question general.	over the way the conflict was resolved. If it is a student's own experience, don't allow the others to judge the resolution.

Form adapted from Institute for Staff Development 1971d, p. 43.

BEHAVIORAL OBJECTIVES	FOCUSING QUESTIONS	TEACHER'S ROLE	SUPPORT PROCEDURES
STEP EIGHT—ALTERNATIVE SOLUTIONS, CONSEQUENCES, SUPPORT a. Students will propose alternative solutions to similar situations. b. Students will predict possible outcomes of these alternatives. c. Students will support suggested alternatives and predictions with evidence or reasoning.	a. What are some other things you might have done instead? b. If you had, e.g., let him play for 15 minutes, what might have happened? or How would things have worked out differently if you had done that? c. Why do you think, e.g., your parents would have been disappointed? a. What other things might — have done? Etc.	1. Seek variety of alternatives and support. 2. Seek variety of consequences and support.	Allow for a variety of solutions, but always with reference to the consequences of the action to keep solutions in the real world. Encourage other students to suggest alternative solutions and consequences. Recycle as time allows.
STEP NINE—GENERALIZATIONS & SUPPORT a. Students will make general statements about how people solve similar problems. b. Students will support their general statements with evidence from the discussion.	a. Thinking about our discussion of Travis's situation and other, similar ones, what do you think people usually do when they have to solve a problem like this? b. Why do you think that?	1. Seek support for general statements. 2. Seek participation by a variety of students.	

Form adapted from Institute for Staff Development 1971d, p. 44.

RESOLUTION OF CONFLICT
COGNITIVE MAP

STEP 2 Reasons and Feelings	STEP 1 Possible Data (Behaviors)	STEP 3a Possible Alternative Solutions	STEP 3b AND 3c Possible Reactions, Consequences
angry upset hungry	**Travis** kicked at dog says dog is smart but doesn't want him did Papa's chores	kill the dog poison the dog let them keep the dog	Arliss would never forgive him his mother would be hurt Arliss might behave better mother would be happy Arliss would love him more he might get to like the dog
angry upset loves dog lonely	**Little Arliss** petted the dog hit Travis with stick hugged the dog	sell the dog	father may come home & buy Travis a dog too
upset frustrated	**Mama** took stick away from Arliss asked Travis to go hunting asked Travis to think	build a dog pen & train the dog	Arliss happy & help take care of the dog father proud of him
	Dog ate the meat fell over and howled		

Form adapted from Institute for Staff Development 1971d, p. 45.
Copyright by Allyn and Bacon. Reproduction of this material is restricted to use with *A Comprehensive Approach to Teaching Thinking* by Shirley W. Schiever.

STEP 4a	STEP 4c	STEP 4e	STEP 5
Selected Solutions	Consequences	Long-Range Consequences	Sample Similar Situations
build a pen and train the dog		grow to love the dog	1. You are responsible for walking your brother (or sister) home from school. Your brother asks if he can stop and play for a while with some new friends he has made.
		dog escapes and does more damage → get rid of dog	
		father brings home a female dog and they have puppies	
kill the dog .		Arliss breaks something Travis likes	2. You have made a deal with your parents to clean the garage on Saturday to pay for the movie you wanted to see. On Saturday, your best friend asks you to help him select a new bike his dad is buying him.
		Travis would be sorry later → try to get another dog → Arliss kills the new dog	
		father and mother angry for killing something	
		father and mother proud he made a decision → get him another dog	

SYNOPSIS: OLD YELLER

This is the story of a farm family in the 1860s; father, mother, Travis, a young teen-ager, and 5-year-old Arliss. When the father has to be away from the farm for a few months, he leaves Travis as the "man on the place." Travis takes his responsibility seriously and when the big, ugly, yellow dog shows up one night, steals their meat and swims in their drinking water, he wants to drive him off or kill him. Unfortunately, Arliss has taken to the dog and his mother leaves the decision to Travis.

STEP 9

Possible Generalizations

Sometimes people can do both if they talk about the problem to the person whom they don't want to hurt.

It's better to do what you're supposed to, even if it hurts someone.

Form adapted from Institute for Self Development 1971d, p. 45.

DISCUSSION PLAN
STRATEGY: Resolution of Conflict
Institute for Staff Development 1971d

Topic __Breaking a Rule__
Level __Middle School, Junior High__

DISCUSSION PURPOSES

Content: To propose and defend solutions to a conflict situation in which a confrontation occurs over the breaking of a rule.

Process: To make inferences about the feelings of people involved in a conflict situation, to identify possible solutions and consequences in dealing with a situation, and to form generalizations about the ways people handle such conflict situations.

PREDISCUSSION PROCEDURES

Arrange the group so that all can hear the tape and each other.
Indicate that they will be listening to an episode between a mother and daughter in which the daughter didn't come in on time.

MATERIALS

Tape (or film) of mother/daughter conflict.

BEHAVIORAL OBJECTIVES	FOCUSING QUESTIONS	TEACHER'S ROLE	SUPPORT PROCEDURES
STEP ONE—DATA (Behaviors) Participants will enumerate particular statements made by the mother and the daughter.	a. What did you hear being said on the tape? b. What did you hear the mother saying? c. What did you hear the daughter saying?	1. Focus on behaviors of key people. 2. Record behaviors under "behaver's" name. 3. Limit data.	Ask for clarification if someone says something like "the daughter came in late" by asking, e.g., What was said that led you to say that? If people make inferences, ask for specific data by saying, "What did you hear being said?" Seek a variety of items for both mother and daughter, so that all elements in the episode come out.
STEP TWO—REASONS, FEELINGS, AND SUPPORT a. Participants will state inferences regarding the reasons the mother and daughter acted as they did. b. Participants will infer and state the feelings of the mother and daughter. c. Participants will provide evidence or reasoning to support their inferences.	a. Why do you think the mother, e.g., used the tone of voice she did? a. Why do you think the daughter, e.g., said "You got anything to eat around here?" b. What do you think the daughter's feelings were, e.g., while talking to her mother? c. What would make you think, e.g., she felt resigned?	1. Seek variety of reasons for behaviors of key people. 2. Seek variety of feelings for each key person. 3. Seek support for feelings.	

Form adapted from Institute for Staff Development 1971d, p. 41.

BEHAVIORAL OBJECTIVES	FOCUSING QUESTIONS	TEACHER'S ROLE	SUPPORT PROCEDURES
STEP THREE—ALTERNATIVE SOLUTIONS (could do), CONSEQUENCES (reactions), SUPPORT a. Participants will suggest what they think are some things the mother could do and/or the daughter could do. b. Participants will indicate what they think the consequences would be for each solution in terms of 1. the other's reaction 2. other consequences c. Participants will offer reasons to support their inferences.	a. What are some things the mother could do? Note: This could focus either on alternative ways of dealing from the beginning or at the end of the episode. b. How do you think the daughter would react, e.g., if the mother called a family conference? c. Why do you think the daughter, e.g., would be belligerent? a. What are some possible ways the daughter could deal with the situation? Etc.	1. Seek a variety of possible solutions. 2. Record possible solutions. 3. Seek a variety of consequences for selected solutions. 4. Seek support for consequences.	The group could be broken up into teams of five or six to develop possible solutions. Assign the teams, locations, and recorder first, and then ask the focusing question. After 5 minutes, have the recorder for each team report out one of their ideas to be recorded on the board or butcher paper. Be sure each team has at least one opportunity to report, but ask that it be a different solution than ones already given.
STEP FOUR—SELECTED SOLUTIONS (should do), SUPPORT, LONG-RANGE CONSEQUENCES, SUPPORT a. Participants will conclude as to the best solution. b. Participants will support their conclusions with evidence or reasoning. c. Participants will predict consequences of their solution. d. Participants will support their predictions with evidence or reasoning.	a. Looking over the possible solutions we have listed, which do you think is the best thing, e.g., the mother could do? b. Why would, e.g., restricting the daughter be the most appropriate? c. What do you think would be some long-term effects, e.g., of the daughter offering to help out more around the house? d. What is your reasoning behind your idea that, e.g., the mother would gain a new perspective of her daughter?	1. Encourage each student to reach a conclusion. 2. Seek support for solutions, immediate, and delayed effects.	The group could work in teams again to select what they think are the best solutions and why. As the teams report, tally their selections and ask for their reasons. Let the teams that selected the same solution develop consequences and reasons. Select one "best" solution at a time and explore the consequences for it. Another alternative would be to have some of the teams deal with the consequences of "best solutions" for the mother and the rest deal with those related to the daughter.

Form adapted from Institute for Staff Development 1971d, p. 42.

BEHAVIORAL OBJECTIVES	FOCUSING QUESTIONS	TEACHER'S ROLE	SUPPORT PROCEDURES
STEP FIVE—DATA (similar situation) Participants will relate similar situations they know about in which there was a confrontation over a broken rule.	Thinking over this incident, what are some similar situations you have experienced or know about in which a confrontation occurs over a broken rule? What happened? What did you (or the other person) do?	1. Seek situations similar to focus situation. 2. Seek actions of principal figures in situation.	If a person is relating a situation in which s/he is personally involved, steps 5–8 should be pursued with only that person. If the incident happened to someone else, all can participate. Repeat cycle 5–8 several times.
STEP SIX—REASONS, FEELINGS, AND SUPPORT (similar situation) a. Participants will infer and/or remember the feelings of the people in the situation. b. Participants will support their statements about feelings.	a. How do you think your mother felt when, e.g., she found out you had not been at your girlfriend's house as you had told her? b. Why do you think she was, e.g., both hurt and angry at the same time?	1. Seek a variety of feelings and support.	Explore the feelings of both parties at different times during the situation. Seek a variety of feelings for both by asking, e.g., How else could the (mother) (daughter) have felt?
STEP SEVEN—EVALUATION OF SOLUTION AND SUPPORT a. Participants will state the reasons for selecting the course of action taken. b. Participants will state to what extent they think the course was effective.	a. What were your reasons for doing what you did? b. Thinking back on the situation now, how do you feel about the way you handled it? c. Why do you think, e.g., you were probably too lenient?	1. If class participation is sought, make question general.	Vary the focusing question at part b. by asking it in such ways as: What is your opinion of the way you (or the person involved) handled the situation? What do you think of the way the problem was resolved?

Form adapted from Institute for Staff Development 1971d, p. 43.

BEHAVIORAL OBJECTIVES	FOCUSING QUESTIONS	TEACHER'S ROLE	SUPPORT PROCEDURES
STEP EIGHT—ALTERNATIVE SOLUTIONS, CONSEQUENCES, SUPPORT a. Participants will suggest ways the situation could have been handled differently. b. Participants will indicate what they think the consequences of handling the situation differently would have been. c. Participants will state reasons why they think those consequences would result.	a. In what ways do you think, e.g., you might have handled it differently? b. What do you think the consequences would have been of, e.g., restricting your activities for a month? c. Why do you think, e.g., you would have thought twice about doing it again?	1. Seek variety of alternatives and support. 2. Seek variety of consequences and support.	If the situation does not personally involve the participant, explore several alternatives. Follow through on one alternative, consequences, and support at a time, but ask for a variety of ideas in terms of consequences and support.
STEP NINE—GENERALIZATIONS & SUPPORT a. Participants will form generalizations about the ways people handle situations in which a rule has been broken. b. Participants will provide evidence based on the discussion and their experience to support their general statements.	a. Thinking back over the whole discussion and the different situations we've explored, what could you say generally about the way people deal with situations in which a rule has been broken? b. What did we say that would lead you to say, e.g., they generally act on impulse and anger rather than on rational consideration of an appropriate solution?	1. Seek support for general statements. 2. Seek participation by a variety of students.	Allow time for people to think about the question and write down a statement. Then ask for students to share their ideas orally.

Form adapted from Institute for Staff Development 1971d, p. 44.

RESOLUTION OF CONFLICT
COGNITIVE MAP

STEP 2 *Reasons and Feelings*	STEP 1 *Possible Data (Behaviors)*	STEP 3a *Possible Alternative Solutions*	STEP 3b AND 3c *Possible Reactions, Consequences*
angry frustrated persecuted anxious	MOTHER going to mess up my kitchen what time did you get in—had a deadline	MOTHER restrict her let father handle the situation	daughter angry daughter accepts father annoyed daughter confused mother relieved
annoyed irritated resigned overwhelmed	your friends—why does Carol wear so much makeup	call a family council on rules	daughter skeptical daughter pleased daughter irritated
	seems like it's the old story	see a psychiatrist or minister	
	spent five hours cleaning up we're always arguing	have a long talk with daughter to work out a mutually agreeable arrangement	daughter skeptical at first daughter unwilling daughter relieved and willing
guilty "here we go again" frustrated annoyed	DAUGHTER got anything to eat	DAUGHTER apologize and offer to help out	mother accepts and relaxes
	I called	do nothing	mother skeptical
self-confident belligerent	wanted to get some food	ask for a conference with mother and father to work out new rules	mother dictatorial mother pleased and willing
	don't have to argue, I'm ok, I can take care of myself		

Form adapted from Institute for Staff Development 1971d, p. 45.

STEP 4a	STEP 4c	STEP 4e	STEP 5
Selected Solutions ———→	Consequences ———→	Long-Range Consequences ———→	Sample Similar Situations
MOTHER restrict daughter		cheats on restriction becomes less communicative obeys the rule seeks help from father	1. daughter said she was spending the night at friend's house, went someplace else and mother found out
long talk with daughter		ends up in worsened relationship both become more understanding of other's point of view establish new rules	2. coach finds out some of his star players are breaking training rules
			3. class president skips school to attend demonstration and gets arrested
DAUGHTER apologize and offer to help		mutual agreement on new rules same old story more privileges	4. principal finds out one of his "better" teachers is leaving his class unattended to go to the teachers' lounge

STEP 9

Possible Generalizations

Most people try to be reasonable when a rule has been broken.

Most parents will listen to reasons when a rule is broken.

DISCUSSION PLAN
STRATEGY: Resolution of Conflict
Lesson plan by Fran Peterman
DISCUSSION PURPOSES

Topic   Value Conflict
Level   Secondary

Content: To propose and defend various approaches to solving a conflict in which people's values prevent them from appreciating each other's point of view.

Process: To make inferences about the feelings of people involved in a conflict situation, to identify possible solutions and consequences in dealing with a situation, and to form generalizations about the ways people handle such conflicts.

PREDISCUSSION PROCEDURES

Arrange students in semicircle. Direct students to listen carefully to taped discussion between student and teacher regarding the student's request to go on a field trip when the teacher has planned an important culminating activity to wind up and review a unit.

MATERIALS
Tape of discussion.

BEHAVIORAL OBJECTIVES	FOCUSING QUESTIONS	TEACHER'S ROLE	SUPPORT PROCEDURES
STEP ONE—DATA (Behaviors) Students will enumerate details of what they heard on the taped discussion, with emphasis on behaviors of the teacher and the student.	What did the teacher say/do in the tape we just heard? What did the student say/do?	1. Focus on behaviors of key people. 2. Record behaviors under "behavers" name. 3. Limit data.	Seek a variety of responses from many participants.
STEP TWO—REASONS, FEELINGS, AND SUPPORT a. Students will state inferences as to the reasons for actions of the teacher and student. b. Students will state inferred feelings of both parties. c. Students will support their inferences.	a. Why do you think, e.g., the teacher is having a hard time making up her mind? Why, e.g., was the student angry? b. How do you think, e.g., the teacher felt when the student asked her to sign the permission form? c. Why do you think she felt, e.g., outraged?	1. Seek variety of reasons for behaviors of key people. 2. Seek variety of feelings for each key person. 3. Seek support for feelings.	Encourage a variety of reasons. What else might she have felt? What makes you think . . . ? What are some reasons you think . . . ?

Form adapted from Institute for Staff Development 1971d, p. 41.

BEHAVIORAL OBJECTIVES	FOCUSING QUESTIONS	TEACHER'S ROLE	SUPPORT PROCEDURES
STEP THREE—ALTERNATIVE SOLUTIONS (could do), CONSEQUENCES (reactions), SUPPORT a. Students will state actions the student and/or teacher could take to resolve the conflict. b. Students will predict possible reactions to their suggested solutions. c. Students will support their inferences with evidence or reasoning.	a. What could the teacher do to resolve the problem she is having with her student? b. If the teacher —, how might the student react? c. Why do you think the teacher would —? a. What do you think the student could do to resolve the conflict? b. If the student . . ., how might the teacher react? c. Why do you think the teacher would . . . ?	1. Seek a variety of possible solutions. 2. Record possible solutions. 3. Seek a variety of consequences for selected solutions. 4. Seek support for consequences.	Elicit a variety of responses. What does someone else think, e.g., the teacher could do? Seek alternative actions for both the teacher and the student.
STEP FOUR—SELECTED SOLUTIONS (should do), SUPPORT, LONG-RANGE CONSEQUENCES, SUPPORT a. Students will state what should be done to resolve the conflict. b. Students will state reasons for selecting solutions. c. Students will make inferences about what might happen if certain actions are taken to resolve the conflict. d. Students will state reasons to support possible consequences.	a. What do you think the student/teacher should do? b. Why do you think — should —? c. What do you think would happen if . . . ? d. Why do you think . . . ?	1. Encourage each student to reach a conclusion. 2. Seek support for solutions, immediate, and delayed effects.	Seek a variety of responses. What does someone else think . . . ? What else should — do if . . . ? Alternate questions (i.e., about teacher/student).

Form adapted from Institute for Staff Development 1971d, p. 42.

BEHAVIORAL OBJECTIVES	FOCUSING QUESTIONS	TEACHER'S ROLE	SUPPORT PROCEDURES
STEP FIVE—DATA (similar situation) Students will recall similar situations in which people's different values prohibited their understanding each other's point of view.	What situations like this do you know of, where people are in conflict because they hold differing values? What happened? What did — do? Etc.	1. Seek situations similar to focus situation. 2. Seek actions of principal figures in situation.	Encourage participation. What similar situations have others of you encountered?
STEP SIX—FEELINGS AND SUPPORT (similar situation) a. Students will state how they and the other people felt in the situations they describe. b. Students will state evidence or reasoning to support their statements about feelings.	a. How did you feel when . . . ? b. Why did you feel __? a. How do you think __ felt when __? b. Why would s/he feel that way?	1. Seek a variety of feelings and support.	Encourage positive, mutual respect and support. Extend students' awareness and vocabulary for expressing feelings. What's another word for . . . ?
STEP SEVEN—EVALUATION OF SOLUTION AND SUPPORT a. Students will state reasons for their actions. b. Students will evaluate the effectiveness of their actions. c. Students will state reasons for their evaluations.	a. Why did you __? b. Looking at the situation now, how well do you feel you handled the situation? c. Why do you say __?	1. If class participation is sought, make question general.	Vary the question stems.

Form adapted from Institute for Staff Development 1971d, p. 43.

BEHAVIORAL OBJECTIVES	FOCUSING QUESTIONS	TEACHER'S ROLE	SUPPORT PROCEDURES
STEP EIGHT—ALTERNATIVE SOLUTIONS, CONSEQUENCES, SUPPORT a. Students will state other actions that could have been taken. b. Students will predict consequences of alternative actions. c. Students will state reasons for their predicted consequences.	a. In looking back at the situation you just described, how might you have handled the situation differently? b. How would things have worked out differently if . . . ? c. Why do you think . . . might have happened? Why do you think . . . ?	1. Seek variety of alternatives and support. 2. Seek variety of consequences and support.	Encourage students to examine each other's situations. What else might — have done? What might have been the consequences of . . . ? Why? What else might have happened if . . . ? Use a variety of questions. Encourage a variety of responses. What different things might — have done?
STEP NINE—GENERALIZATIONS & SUPPORT a. Students will make general statements about how people deal with conflicts that arise because of differing values. b. Students will state evidence or reasoning to support their general statements.	a. Thinking of our discussion, what do you think people usually do when they face a conflict of values? b. Why do you think —?	1. Seek support for general statements. 2. Seek participation by a variety of students.	

Form adapted from Institute for Staff Development 1971d, p. 44.

RESOLUTION OF CONFLICT
COGNITIVE MAP

STEP 2 Reasons and Feelings	STEP 1 Possible Data (Behaviors)	STEP 3a Possible Alternative Solutions	STEP 3b AND 3c Possible Reactions, Consequences
FEELINGS hopeful about trip scared of reaction excited about possibility patient with request indecision about decision unhappy about request disappointed that student won't be there anxious to go disappointed in teacher's response willing to do more angry frustrated helpless **REASONS** teacher thinks review is important student wants to be out of class student loves field trips teacher dislikes co-curricular activities that compete with class time	student greets teacher student hands teacher permission form teacher reads form teacher hedges teacher says she has important plans student begs permission teacher says she can't allow her to miss class student promises to complete make-up work student explains she'll get notes from classmates teacher says the activity provides essential review student explains why she wants to go teacher says no student grabs paper teacher calls out, "Let's discuss this" student says, "You witch"	**COULD DO** student tape lecture teacher videotape lecture student explain the content, reasons for trip teacher explain her feelings student say how much she enjoys teacher's class and regrets missing it student could have parent discuss issue with teacher	If the teacher videotaped the lesson, the student would miss very little. If the student explained her feelings about the class, the teacher might be more willing to go along. If the teacher explained her feelings, the student might do the same and reach a compromise.

Form adapted from Institute for Staff Development 1971d, p. 45.

STEP 4a	STEP 4c	STEP 4e	STEP 5
Selected Solutions ———	——→ Consequences ———	——→ Long-Range Consequences ———	Sample Similar Situations
explain feelings		develop mutual respect and understanding	1. Supervising teacher doesn't like a chosen discussion topic.
videotape lesson		better grade and understanding of why teacher didn't want her to miss class	2. Parents won't support your decision to marry young.
			3. Professor rejects your research topic.
			4. Boyfriend doesn't want you to go to the Carni Gras with other male friends.

STEP 9

Possible Generalizations

People usually

1. try to make decisions that are fair
2. will listen to an explanation of differing viewpoints
3. will accept negotiation or compromises

Form adapted from Institute for Staff Development 1971d, p. 45.

SAMPLE TOPICS FOR RESOLUTION OF CONFLICT DISCUSSIONS

A Conflict Issue Related to	*Sample Step 5 Focusing Question*
the use of force	What similar situations do you know about, in which you or someone you know had to decide whether to use force to solve a problem?
unintentional harm to another	What things have happened to you or someone you know, when you accidentally caused someone else to lose something that was important to them?
telling on another	What other situations like this do you know about, where a person had to decide whether or not to tell on someone else?
a person with talents who is a trouble-maker	In what other situations have you or someone you know been involved, in which you needed the talents of a person who causes trouble?
varying versions of events	In what other situations has this happened, when you or someone you know disagree about what has happened and no one seems to know for sure?
responsibilities	When has something like this happened to you or someone you know, in which someone is tempted to neglect their responsibility to have fun?
dealing with insults	What similar situations have you or someone you know experienced, in which someone has embarrassed or insulted you in public?
personal choice	What situations such as this have you or someone you know experienced, in which a young person and his or her parents disagree about appropriate clothing or behavior?
civil disobedience	What other situations have you been in or know about, in which someone has to decide whether or not to do something wrong or illegal for a good cause?
racial prejudice	What similar situation has happened to you or someone you know, in which a person has to decide whether or not to back out of a commitment because of someone else's prejudice?

Conclusion

Living, breathing, eating, and sleeping with thinking components and competencies, curriculum considerations, and teaching strategies for nearly two years may cause unpredictable and perhaps bizarre behavior. As the light began to appear at the end of the tunnel, a nearly overpowering urge engulfed the author. The temptation was to abandon the word processor and to scrawl "THE END" in red marker on the final manuscript page. Never before had the satisfaction, finality, and sense of closure created by a bold notice of "the end" been so eagerly sought.

As the rush of elation at the idea of actually completing this work and the impulse to grab the red marker subsided, thoughtful consideration was possible and even welcome. In retrospect, the completion of this manuscript is more a beginning than an end. The concepts, principles, conclusions, and generalizations presented here are not "finished," nor will they ever be. As the Spiral Model is applied in various settings and reactions and experiences are noted, the model will grow and change. This growth will result in a finer, more clearly defined model, and perhaps in a slightly clearer look at the wonders of human thought.

May the reader accept what is offered here in the spirit it is given. Take and use those elements that make sense or are intriguing; think about, modify, and/or analyze those that are not. If this book acts as a catalyst for reflective thought, analytical scrutiny, and/or joyous intellectual pursuit, it has accomplished its purpose.

References

AHN, C. 1973. *Project ACT (A project to advance critical thinking). Project termination report.* Washington, DC: Office of Education (DHEW). (ERIC Document Reproduction Service No. ED 086 945.)

AUSUBEL, D. P. 1966. Meaningful reception learning and the acquisition of concepts. In H. J. Klausmeier and C. W. Harris (Eds.), *Analyses of concept learning* (pp. 157–175). New York: Academic Press.

BARNES, C. A. 1988, February. (Letter to the editor.) *The Teaching Profession,* Vol. 2, No. 2.

BATSON, A. D. 1981. *Questioning: A reading/thinking foundation for the gifted.* Paper presented at the Annual Meeting of the Southwest Regional Conference of the International Reading Association, San Antonio, TX, January 29–31, 1981. (ERIC Document Reproduction Service No. ED 201 999.)

BEYER, B. K. 1987. *Practical strategies for the teaching of thinking.* Boston: Allyn and Bacon.

BLOOM, B. S. (Ed.). 1956. *Taxonomy of educational objectives: Handbook I: Cognitive domain.* New York: McKay.

BODNAR, J. 1980. *Discussion evaluation procedures.* Unpublished paper.

BRANSFORD, J., R. SHERWOOD, N. VYE, and J. RIESER. 1986. Teaching thinking and problem solving: Research foundations. *American Psychologist,* 41, 10, 1078–1089.

BRUNER, J. S. 1960. *The process of education.* Cambridge, MA: Harvard University Press.

BRUNER, J. S., J. J. GOODNOW, and G. A. AUSTIN. 1956. *A study of thinking.* New York: Wiley.

CARIN, A. A., and R. B. SUND. 1971. *Developing questioning techniques.* Columbus, OH: Merrill.

CARIN, A., and R. B. SUND. 1978. *Creative questioning and sensitive listening techniques.* Columbus, OH: Merrill.

CHAUDHARI, U. S. 1975. Questioning and creative thinking: A research perspective. *Journal of Creative Behavior,* 9, 1, 30–34.

COLLINS, A., and J. S. BROWN. In press. Cognitive apprenticeship: Teaching students the craft of reading, writing, and mathematics. In L. B. Resnick (Ed.), *Cognition and instruction: Issues and agendas.* Hillsdale, NJ: Erlbaum.

CORNBLETH, C. 1977. Using questions in social studies. *How to do it notebook series 2.* Arlington, VA: National Council for the Social Studies.

COSTA, A. L. 1985a. Teacher behaviors that enable student thinking. In A. L. Costa (Ed.), *Developing minds: A resource book for teaching thinking* (pp. 125–137). Alexandria, VA: Association for Supervision and Curriculum Development.

COSTA, A. L. (Ed.). 1985b. *Developing minds: A resource book for teaching thinking.* Alexandria, VA: Association for Supervision and Curriculum Development.

COSTA, A. L., R. HANSON, H. F. SILVER, and R. W. STRONG. 1985. Building a repertoire of strategies. In A. L. Costa (Ed.), *Developing minds: A resource book for teaching thinking* (pp. 141–143). Alexandria, VA: Association for Supervision and Curriculum Development.

COSTA, A. L., and B. PRESSEISEN. 1985. A glossary of thinking skills. In A. L. Costa (Ed.), *Developing minds: A resource book for teaching thinking* (pp. 309–313). Alexandria, VA: Association for Supervision and Curriculum Development.

COX, P. L. 1983. Complementary roles in successful change. *Educational Leadership, 41,* 3, 10–13.

DETTMER, P. 1986. Gifted program inservice and staff development: Pragmatics and possibilities. *Gifted Child Quarterly, 30,* 3, 99–102.

DILLON, J. T. 1982. The multi-disciplinary study of questioning. *Journal of Educational Psychology, 74,* 2, 147–165.

DILLON, J. T. 1988. *Questioning and teaching.* Columbia University, NY: Teachers College Press.

ENNIS, R.H. 1962. A concept of critical thinking. *Harvard Educational Review, 32,* 1, 81–111.

ENNIS, R.H. 1985a. A logical basis for measuring critical thinking skills. *Educational Leadership, 43,* 2, 44–48.

ENNIS, R. H. 1985b. Goals for a critical thinking curriculum. In A. L. Costa (Ed.), *Developing minds: A resource book for teaching thinking* (pp. 54–57). Alexandria, VA: Association for Supervision and Curriculum Development.

FELDHUSEN, J. F., and D. J. TREFFINGER. 1980. *Creative thinking and problem solving in gifted education.* Dubuque, IA: Kendall/Hunt.

FENSTERMACHER, G. D., and D. C. BERLINER. 1983. *A conceptual framework for the analysis of staff development.* Santa Monica, CA: Rand Corporation.

GAGNÉ, R. M. 1966. The learning of principles. In H. J. Klausmeier and C. W. Harris (Eds.), *Analyses of concept learning* (pp. 81–95). New York: Academic Press.

GALLAGHER, J. J., M. J. ASCHNER, and W. JENNÉ. 1967. *Productive thinking of gifted children in classroom interaction.* Washington, DC: Council for Exceptional Children.

GALLOWAY, C. M., and M. C. SELTZER. 1980. Exchange and mutuality: Growth conditions for teacher development. *Theory into Practice, 19,* 4, 262–265.

GETZELS, J. W. 1975. Problem-finding and the inventiveness of solutions. *Journal of Creative Behavior, 9,* 1, 12–18.

GETZELS, J. W., and M. CSIKSZENTMIHALYI. 1967. Scientific creativity. *Science Journal, 3,* 9, 80–84.

GLASER, R. 1984. Education and thinking. The role of knowledge. *American Psychologist, 39,* 2, 93–104.

GOODLAD, J. I. 1984. *A place called school.* New York: McGraw-Hill.

GORDON, W. J. 1961. *Synectics.* Cambridge, MA: Synectics, Inc.

GUILFORD, J. P. 1967. *The nature of human intelligence.* New York: McGraw-Hill.

HALPERN, D. F. 1984. *Thought and knowledge: An introduction to critical thinking.* Hillsdale, NJ: Erlbaum.

HANNINEN, G. E. 1983. *The Hilda Taba teaching strategies and creativity.* Unpublished paper, University of Arizona, Division of Special Education and Rehabilitation, Tucson, AZ.

HANNINEN, G. E. 1989. *The effects of the Hilda Taba teaching strategies on critical and creative thinking.* Doctoral dissertation, University of Idaho.

HEIMAN, M. and J. SLOMIANKO. 1986. *Critical thinking skills.* Washington, DC: National Education Association.

HUBERMAN, A. M. 1983. School improvement strategies that work: Some scenarios. *Educational Leadership, 41,* 3, 23–27.

HUNKINS, F. P. 1968. The influence of analysis and evaluation questions on achievement in social studies. *Educational Leadership Research Supplement, 1,* 1, 326–332.

HUNKINS, F. P. 1989. *Teacher thinking through effective questioning.* Boston: Christopher-Gordon.

HUNKINS, F. P. 1976. *Involving students in questioning.* Boston: Allyn and Bacon.

HYRAM, G. H. 1957. An experiment in developing critical thinking in children. *Journal of Experimental Education, 26,* 2, 125–132.

INSTITUTE FOR STAFF DEVELOPMENT. n.d. *Hilda Taba teaching strategies program leaders manual.* Miami, FL: Institute for Staff Development.

INSTITUTE FOR STAFF DEVELOPMENT. 1971a. *Hilda Taba teaching strategies program: Unit 1.* Miami, FL: Institute for Staff Development.

INSTITUTE FOR STAFF DEVELOPMENT. 1971b. *Hilda Taba teaching strategies program: Unit 2.* Miami, FL: Institute for Staff Development.

INSTITUTE FOR STAFF DEVELOPMENT. 1971c. *Hilda Taba teaching strategies program: Unit 3.* Miami, FL: Institute for Staff Development.

INSTITUTE FOR STAFF DEVELOPMENT. 1971d. *Hilda Taba teaching strategies program: Unit 4.* Miami, FL: Institute for Staff Development.

ISHAM, M. M. 1982. Hilda Taba, 1904–1967: Pioneer in social studies curriculum and teaching. *Journal of Thought, 17,* 3, 108–124.

JOYCE, B., and B. SHOWERS. 1980. Improving inservice training: The message of research. *Educational Leadership, 37,* 5, 379–385.

JOYCE, B., and B. SHOWERS. 1982. The coaching of teaching. *Educational Leadership, 49,* 1, 4–10.

KATZ, S. E. 1976. *The effect of each of four instructional treatments on the learning of principles by children.* Madison, WI: University of Wisconsin, Wisconsin Research and Development Center for Cognitive Learning.

KLAUSMEIER, H. J. 1980. *Learning and teaching concepts.* New York: Academic Press.

KLAUSMEIER, H. J. 1985. *Educational psychology* (5th ed.). New York: Harper & Row.

KLAUSMEIER, H. J., E. S. GHATALA, and D. A. FRAYER. 1974. *Conceptual learning and development: A cognitive view.* New York: Academic Press.

KOHLBERG, L. 1971. Stages of moral development as the basis for moral education. In C. M. Beck, B. S. Crittenden, and E. V. Sullivan (Eds.), *Moral education: Interdisciplinary approaches* (pp. 23–92). New York: Newman Press.

KRATHWOHL, D. R., B. S. BLOOM, and B. B. MASIA. 1964. *Taxonomy of educational objectives. Handbook II: Affective domain.* New York: McKay.

LOUCKS, S. F. 1983. At last: Some good news from a study of school improvement. *Educational Leadership, 41,* 3, 4–5.

LOUCKS, S. F., and D. A. ZACCHEI. 1983. Applying our findings to today's innovations. *Educational Leadership, 41,* 3, 28–31.

MACKIE, J. L. 1980. *The cement of the universe: A study of causation.* New York: Oxford University Press.

MAKER, C. J. 1982a. *Curriculum development for the gifted.* Rockville, MD: Aspen Systems Corporation.

MAKER, C. J. 1982b. *Teaching models in education of the gifted.* Rockville, MD: Aspen Systems Corporation.

MAKER, C. J. 1986. *Frames of discovery: A process approach to identifying talent in special populations.* Unpublished paper, University of Arizona, Division of Special Education and Rehabilitation, Tucson, AZ.

MANSON, G., and A. A. CLEGG, JR. 1970. Classroom questions: Keys to children's thinking? *Peabody Journal of Education, 47,* 5, 302–307.

MARZANO, R. J., R. S. BRANDT, C. S. HUGHES, B. F. JONES, B. Z. PRESSEISEN, S. C. RANKIN, and C. SUHOR. 1988. *Dimensions of thinking: A framework for curriculum and instruction.* Alexandria, VA: Association for Supervision and Curriculum Development.

MCCARTHY, B. 1986. *The 4MAT system.* Barrington, IL: EXCEL, Inc.

MCCARTHY, B., and S. LEFLAR. 1983. *4MAT in action.* Barrington, IL: EXCEL, Inc.

MCCARTHY, B., S. LEFLAR, and M. MCNAMARA. 1987. *The 4MAT workbook: Guided practice in 4MAT lesson and unit planning.* Barrington, IL: EXCEL, Inc.

MCCARTHY, B., B. SAMPLE, and B. HAMMOND. 1985. *4MAT and science: Towards wholeness in science education.* Barrington, IL: EXCEL, Inc.

MCKENZIE, G. R. 1972. Some effects of frequent quizzes on inferential thinking. *American Educational Research Journal, 9,* 2, 231–240.

NARDI, A. H., and C. E. WALES. 1985. Teaching decision-making with guided design. In A. L. Costa (Ed.), *Developing minds: A resource book for teaching thinking* (pp. 220–223). Alexandria, VA: Association for Supervision and Curriculum Development.

NOLLER, R. B., S. J. PARNES, and A. M. BIONDI. 1976. *Creative action book.* New York: Scribner.

NORRIS, S. P., and L. M. PHILLIPS. 1987. Explanations of reading comprehension: Schema theory and critical thinking theory. *Teachers College Record, 89,* 2, 281–306.

PARNES, S. J. 1981. CPSI: The general system. In W. B. Barbe and J. S. Renzulli (Eds.), *Psychology and education of the gifted* (pp. 304–314). New York: Irvington.

PAUL, R. W. 1986. *Critical thinking and the critical person.* ERIC Document Reproduction Service No. ED 273 511.

PERKINS, D. N. 1985. What creative thinking is. In A. L. Costa (Ed.), *Developing minds: A resource book for teaching thinking* (pp. 58–61). Alexandria, VA: Association for Supervision and Curriculum Development.

PIAGET, J. 1977. *The essential Piaget.* New York: Basic Books.

PRESSEISEN, B. Z. 1985a. *Thinking skills throughout the curriculum: A conceptual design.* Philadelphia: Research for Better Schools.

PRESSEISEN, B. Z. 1985b. Thinking skills: Meanings and models. In A. L. Costa (Ed.), *Developing minds: A resource book for teaching thinking* (pp. 43–48). Alexandria, VA: Association for Supervision and Curriculum Development.

PRESSEISEN, B. Z. 1986. *Thinking skills: Research and practice*. Washington, DC: National Education Association.

RAMPAUL, W. E. 1976. *The relationship between conceptual learning and development, concept achievement, educational achievement, and selected cognitive abilities*. Madison, WI: University of Wisconsin, Wisconsin Research and Development Center for Cognitive Learning.

REDFIELD, D. L., and E. W. ROUSSEAU. 1981. A meta-analysis of experimental research on teacher questioning behavior. *Review of Educational Research, 51*, 2, 237–245.

ROWE, H. 1985. *Problem solving and intelligence*. Hillsdale, NJ: Erlbaum.

ROWE, M. B. 1974a. Wait-time and rewards as instructional variables, their influence on language, logic, and fate control: Part I—Wait-time. *Journal of Research in Science Teaching, 11*, 2, 81–94.

ROWE, M. B. 1974b. Relation of wait-time and rewards to the development of language, logic, and fate control: Part II—Rewards. *Journal of Research in Science Teaching, 11*, 4, 291–308.

RUMELHART, D. E., and A. ORTONY. 1977. The representation of knowledge in memory. In R. C. Anderson, R. J. Spiro, and W. E. Montague (Eds.), *Schooling and the acquisition of knowledge* (pp. 99–135). Hillsdale, NJ: Erlbaum.

SCHIEVER, S. W. In preparation. Differentiating the learning environment for gifted students. In C. J. Maker (Ed.), *Critical issues in gifted education. Volume III: Educating gifted students in the regular classroom*. Austin, TX: Pro-Ed Publishers.

SCHIEVER, S. W. 1986. *The effect of two teaching/learning models on the higher cognitive processes of students in classes for the gifted*. Doctoral dissertation, University of Arizona.

SEIGER-EHRENBERG, S. 1985. BASICS. In A. L. Costa (Ed.), *Developing minds: A resource book for teaching thinking* (pp. 241–243). Alexandria, VA: Association for Supervision and Curriculum Development.

SIEGLER, R. S., and D. D. RICHARDS. 1982. The development of intelligence. In R. J. Sternberg (Ed.), *Handbook of human intelligence* (pp. 897–971). Cambridge, England: Cambridge University Press.

STERNBERG, R. 1985a. Teaching critical thinking, part 1: Are we making critical mistakes? *Phi Delta Kappan, 67*, 3, 194–198.

STERNBERG, R. 1985b. Teaching critical thinking, part 2: Possible solutions. *Phi Delta Kappan, 67*, 4, 277–280.

STERNBERG, R. J. 1986. *Critical thinking: Its nature, measurement, and improvement*. Washington, DC: National Institute of Education. (ERIC Document Reproduction Service No. ED 272 882.)

TABA, H. 1962. *Curriculum development theory and practice*. New York: Harcourt Brace Jovanovich.

TABA, H. 1966. *Teaching strategies and cognitive functioning in elementary school children*. Cooperative Research Project No. 2404. San Francisco: San Francisco State College.

TABA, H. 1975. Learning by discovery: Psychological and educational rationale. In W. B. Barbe and J. R. Renzulli (Eds.), *Psychology and education of the gifted* (pp. 346–354). New York: Irvington.

TABA, H., M. C. DURKIN, J. R. FRAENKEL, and A. H. MCNAUGHTON. 1971. *A teacher's handbook to elementary social studies*. Reading, MA: Addison-Wesley.

TABA, H., S. LEVINE, and F. F. ELZEY. 1964. *Thinking in elementary school children.* U.S. Office of Education Cooperative Research Project, No. 1574. San Francisco: San Francisco State College. (ERIC Document Reproduction Service No. ED 003 285.)

TAYLOR, C. W. 1986. Cultivating simultaneous growth in both multiple creative talents and knowledge. In J. S. Renzulli (Ed.), *Systems and models for developing programs for the gifted and talented* (pp. 306–351). Mansfield Center, CT: Creative Learning Press.

TRABASSO, T. 1986. *The achievement of global coherence through local causal inferences in narrative comprehension and production.* Paper read at the 11th Annual Boston University Conference on Language Development, Boston. (ERIC Document Reproduction Service No. ED 299 573.)

TRABASSO, T., and L. L. SPERRY. 1985. Causal relatedness and importance of story events. *Journal of Memory and Language, 24,* 5, 595–611.

TRABASSO, T., and P. VAN DEN BROEK. 1985. Causal thinking and the representation of narrative events. *Journal of Memory and Language, 24,* 5, 612–630.

TREZISE, R. L. 1972. The Hilda Taba teaching strategies in English and reading classes. *English Journal, 61,* 4, 577–580, 593.

UNITED STATES DEPARTMENT OF EDUCATION. 1986. *What works: Research about teaching and learning.* Washington, DC: U.S. Department of Education.

WALLEN, N. E., M. C. DURKIN, J. R. FRAENKEL, A. J. MCNAUGHTON, and E. I. SAWIN. 1969. *The Taba Curriculum Development Project in Social Studies.* Menlo Park, CA: Addison-Wesley.

WATTS, G. H., and R. C. ANDERSON. 1971. Effects of three types of inserted questions on learning from prose. *Journal of Educational Psychology, 62,* 5, 387–394.

WHITEHEAD, A. N. 1929. *The aims of education.* New York: Macmillan.

WILLIAMS, F. E. 1986. The cognitive-affective interaction model for enriching gifted programs. In J. S. Renzulli (Ed.), *Systems and models for developing programs for the gifted and talented* (pp. 461–484). Mansfield Center, CT: Creative Learning Press.

WILSON, M. 1988. Critical thinking: Repackaging or revolution? *Language Arts, 65,* 6, 543–551.

WINOCUR, S. L. 1985. Developing lesson plans with cognitive objectives. In A. L. Costa (Ed.), *Developing minds: A resource book for teaching thinking* (pp. 87–93). Alexandria, VA: Association for Supervision and Curriculum Development.

INDEX